CHECHNYA:
THE INSIDE STORY

FROM INDEPENDENCE TO WAR

Mairbek Vatchagaev

Published by Open Books

Copyright © 2019 by Mairbek Vatchagaev

Interior design by Siva Ram Maganti

Cover images © M-SUR shutterstock.com/g/M-SUR

ISBN-13: 978-1948598170

This book is dedicated to the memory of Ms. Maria Bennigsen-Broxup

Contents

Acknowledgments

I would like to thank my friend Glen Howard for his assistance in publishing this book. I also express my sincere gratitude to Fanny Bryan for her huge contribution in translation and to Frederic Cople Jaher for his valuable guidelines. I am also grateful to Hussein Iskhanov for sharing his memories, describing the details of those events.

This book would not have been possible without the support of The Smith Richardson Foundation.

Introduction

Historical Note

Situated on the northern slope of the Greater Caucasus mountain range, the Republic of Chechnya is merely 15,600 square kilometers. Two bloody wars brought it to world attention at the end of the twentieth century. Its inhabitants, the Chechens, are one of the oldest indigenous peoples of the Caucasus.

Chechens call themselves Nokhchi. Ancient Armenian sources describe them as Nakhchimatians. Georgian sources give them various names: Tsanars, Durdzuks, and Kistins. Dating back to the sixteenth century, Russian documents identify them as Chechens, borrowing the name from Chechenya's neighbors, who mostly use a variation of that term: the Kabardians call them Shashans; Ossetians call them Tsatsans; Lezghins – Chachanler, Avars and Dargins – Chachans.

Twenty-two years have passed since the first Chechen war began in November 1994. It ended in August 1996 with the signing of an armistice agreement between the Chechens and Russians.

Coming a decade after the Soviet defeat in Afghanistan, the Chechen war dealt another devastating blow to the myth of the invincible Soviet army. The world watched as a handful of Chechens, united by their desire for independence, routed the Russian army. Chechens had hoped they would find support in the West, especially in view of the Russian army atrocities. To understand why assistance was not forthcoming, it is necessary to reexamine events from the perspectives of the combatants, participants, and observers.

The literature about the war shows a huge disparity between Russian and Chechen sources. Journalism, scholarship, memoirs, or fiction authored by Russians, or reflecting their views, number in the thousands, whereas Chechens have scarcely written two dozen accounts. The disparity *stems primarily from the fact that for Chechens the war has not yet ended; therefore, few consider themselves morally and emotionally ready to write about it. The gap is partly filled by reports of a few eyewitness journalists published in the West.*

Any narrative of events in Chechnya following the collapse of the Soviet Union in 1991 should help dispel the mystery of what took place on the Chechen side. This memoir presents what I have witnessed. Since I was involved on one side of the conflict, I may be accused of promoting the Chechen vision. It would be difficult to pretend not to be a Chechen, in particular as I defend my ethnic and national identity. I want to describe what I saw and how I got involved in these processes. I want to offer one Chechen's opinion of how the conflict with Russia evolved, of how one had to make difficult decisions, at times changing his whole view of life, at this crucial moment in the history of his people. It is the story of a Chechen who, in search of the history of his people, became a participant in the story. Whether it was a random choice or predetermined by a Chechen mentality is for you to judge.

Chapter 1

PRELUDE

What Is a Homeland?

After my exile to France, a friend asked me what "homeland" means to me; with what, or with whom do I associate the concept. I responded that it was with my village cemetery. My friend's eyes showed incomprehension, even shock. But for me my village cemetery is the story of my family, my village, and my people. According to tradition, a Chechen must know at least seven generations of ancestors on his father's side. In the cemetery of my village of Avtury in the Shali district, I always visited the tomb of the founder of my name, Vachg haji.

Historical Note

My great-great-grandfather, Vachg-haji, according to village history, was its richest inhabitant of the mid-nineteenth century. He was the one Chechen that Imam Shamil allowed to smoke, despite a strict ban on smoking. The bestowal of this favor demonstrated how Chechens ignored restrictions imposed by the formidable imam and how Shamil made exceptions for Chechens.

Shamil had introduced the Sharia and strictly enforced his understanding of it, including prohibition of smoking and drinking. In the 1850s, he visited Avtury, and every morning he was informed that a Russian sniper had killed one of the Chechens standing guard at night at the entrance to the village. One day the shootings stopped. Wanting to know how such a fine shot had been eliminated, Shamil summoned the man thought to be responsible, Vachg-haji. However, his attempts to learn details ran into my ancestor's reluctance to talk. Only after Shamil gave his word not to

1

get angry, did Vachg-haji explain that despite the prohibition, he was smoking and that the shooter used the glow of his cigarette to direct his fire. Several cigarettes later, my great-great-grandfather was able to locate the sniper and successfully return the gunfire. The Russian never fired again no matter how many cigarettes he lit. Laughing, Shamil publicly proclaimed that Vachg-haji was allowed to smoke, but he asked him to quit as a favor. Touched by this gesture, my ancestor never smoked again. He fought the Russians with Imam Shamil and forced them to reckon with him after their conquest of Chechnya in 1859. He never served the Russian establishment, although his authority and position would have made him a welcome ally. He made the Hajj to Mecca seven times and died at the age of a hundred, which was a record in that period of war.

I visit the cemetery and see my village history in the names of the dead. Also in that cemetery is the tomb of my grandfather Maaz who hid for eleven years to avoid arrest in Soviet times. There also is my grandfather's brother, Abbas, who during the period of militant atheism secretly taught Islamic theology to children in his vegetable garden, an act that could have landed him in jail. Here are the graves of my father and my older brother, Aslanbek; the grave of the father of a famous Sufi sheikh, Bamat-Giri Mitaev; and that of Akhmad Avturi, legendary in Chechnya for his courage and courteous treatment of the enemy. The cemetery is my history, a manifestation of my country's past. If I were to return after fourteen years, however, I would not recognize my rural cemetery. The last two wars have tripled its size: three times as many people died in the two recent Russian-Chechen wars than in the wars of the previous four centuries!

The First Step into Adulthood

After graduating from high school at the age of sixteen, I enrolled in the history department of the Chechen-Ingush State University in Grozny. It was 1982, the last year of the communist era of Leonid Brezhnev. I believe my generation was lucky. We grew up during the "building of socialism" and also witnessed its disintegration and the birth of new countries from the ashes of the Soviet Union.

In the 1980s the history department was one of the most prestigious at the university, and competition was fierce for a very few places in it. Most students, however, were not admitted on their qualifications, but because they were the children of members of the Communist Party or the government. Those, like myself, accepted on merit, represented no more than a fifth of the total aspirants. Different social groups distrusted one another, and the resulting atmosphere was not conducive to study. That was my first disappointment in the department.

My second disillusionment was that in a history department of a Chechen university, Chechen history was not taught. Courses were offered in the history of Latin America, China, Europe, India, Japan, the United States, and, naturally, Russia. If we came to a topic touching upon Chechnya, our teachers changed the subject and ended discussion.

I soon realized very little had been written on Chechnya. At universities in neighboring republics, students were taught courses in the history of their people and were free to choose any subject or period of that history. When we were offered essay topics on Chechnya in our Russian classes, we were instructed to explain how Chechens had welcomed the Russian army that came to colonize their homeland in the second half of the eighteenth century. Imam Shamil or other Chechen heroes, who for many decades fought the era's most powerful army, were taboo. We were taught that Chechens welcomed the Soviet regime, which had eliminated most of the intellectual class and killed or exiled to Siberia tens of thousands of people, simply because they could read. But we never heard how Chechens defended their country against the White Army of General Denikin during the Russian Civil War, or against the Bolsheviks in 1919 and 1920.

It seemed as if Chechens were blamed for their very existence. It was humiliating and degrading, and we increasingly felt contempt instead of devotion to the Soviet Union. It is important to point out that we did not hate a country that could not hide its hatred and fear of us. It became difficult for us Chechens to consider the Soviet Union as our own country. We were guilty before Soviet power and had to bear the cross of repentance. Although we were not alone in disliking the Soviet regime, we were the only ones to reject it as a legitimate power.

Alexander Vlasov, First Secretary of the Chechen-Ingush Autonomous Republic, made one of the best assessments of Chechnya during the Soviet era. In a 1982 meeting in preparation for the sixtieth anniversary of Soviet power in the republic, he affirmed that "sixty years after the establishment of the Soviet regime in Chechnya we have to admit that the authority of the Communist Party is limited exclusively to the borders of the city of Grozny. Beyond, power is held by Sufi sheikhs and their disciples (or *murids)*."

Russian Grozny

My next disenchantment was the city of Grozny. Studying at its university and spending most of my time there, I became aware that the townspeople, most of them Russians, did not like Chechens. Had I been told before entering the university that strong nationalist views were to be found in Grozny, I would not have believed it.

Happily and noisily discussing our admission to the university, our group of five Chechens took a tram in Grozny. To our surprise, several elderly Russian women started screaming and commanding us to stop talking gibberish and to switch to Russian! Our response that we were at home and had the right to speak in a language that was enshrined in the constitution only caused a new outburst. The tram stopped between two stations, and we were given the choice of getting off or being taken to the police. We got off the tram. Two of us, residents of a village near Grozny and well acquainted with the mood in the city, tried to explain to the rest of us that what had happened was a common occurrence. We, however, recoiled from accepting that Chechens, subjects of the Russian Federation, were denied the right to speak their own language in public transport. This was my first encounter with the multinational city of Grozny. Later, I learned from Chechen elders that in 1957 the Russian population of Grozny rioted after learning of the Communist Party's decision to allow Chechens to return to their historical homeland after thirteen years of deportation.

Historical Note

When they first came into contact, relationships between Chechens and Russians were neighborly, engaging in trade and forming bonds of kinship. The first recorded contact between Chechens and Russians dates back to the twelfth century, when Yury Bogolyubsky, after the murder of his father, Grand Prince Andrei Bogolyubsky of Vladimir-Suzdal, fled to the Alan Kingdom of Magas, where according to some sources he found protection among the Chechens of the capital. Academic opinion places that capital on the river Sunzha, presumably near the present-day village of Alkhan-Kala, eighteen kilometers from Grozny. It was not chance that brought the fugitive prince to the kingdom. Yury Bogolyubsky's marriage to the Georgian Queen Tamar was negotiated there in 1185. Queen Tamar's numerous Chechen and Ossetian relatives had suggested the marriage, expecting the prince to regain his father's throne.

As serfdom deepened in Russia, Chechens welcomed peasants fleeing to the Caucasus in search of freedom, and allowed them settle in the valley of the river Terek. Before long, the lives of the new immigrants (later known as Cossacks) became closely intertwined with those of their Chechen neighbors. They imitated Chechen lifestyle and customs; the cherkeska, the Cossacks' traditional dress, for example, was copied from the Chechen highlander garb. Complementing each other, Chechens and settlers enriched each others' cultures and promoted inter-ethnic amity.

In the early sixteenth century, the Caucasus became entangled in the hostility between the Ottoman Empire and the Tsardom of Muscovy. These powers influenced the politics of Chechens and other peoples of the Caucasus until at least the middle of the eighteenth century.

For Chechens, the rise of the centralized Tsardom of Muscovy and its expansion to the south meant instability and sporadic wars. The first casualty of the changing political situation was the friendly relations between Chechens and Cossacks. Muscovy, looking upon Cossacks living along the Terek as a potential base for the sustainable presence of Muscovy in the region, made efforts to win them to its side. Since then Chechens and Cossacks have been in frequent conflict.

My First Riot in the Period of Perestroika

My call to serve in the Soviet army came in June 1984, interrupting my university studies. If my student years taught me a great deal, not only of history but also of life, my year and a half in the army seemed to have taught me nothing since it had not improved much from its imperial predecessor.

After returning home from the army, I was allowed to continue my junior year in September 1986. It was the beginning of Perestroika, and there was an atmosphere of freedom that radically changed our lives. Gone were the days when we could only discuss issues with trusted friends and only in secret. The student body demanded changes in the curriculum. Transformation, however, was difficult, since the teaching staff had been accustomed to obeying Party guidelines.

At a meeting of the Komsomol (Communist youth organization), I was elected a delegate instead of the department's candidate. The department and university administration had not anticipated my nomination since I had not applied for the position and my candidacy had not been discussed among the students. Only the unexpected vote of the seniors gave me the victory.

My new position demanded some action. One subject feared like the plague by all faculty members was the Chechen deportation. The very mention of deportation could lead to serious consequences, including expulsion from the university. Perestroika, however, enabled us not only to talk freely among ourselves about pressing social issues, but also to raise questions never before heard within the university's walls. Inspired by the new policy of openness, we asked our professor of scientific communism to explain why in 1944 the Communist Party had deported the entire ethnic group to the steppes of Central Asia and Kazakhstan and to the camps of Siberia. Our professor, dedicated to the glorification of the Communist Party, claimed that Chechens were to blame, implying that Chechens, including old men, women, and small children, were the offenders. The entire people, he argued, had collaborated with the Germans during WWII and for that reason had been banished. Brainwashed with that kind of propaganda, university professors, like ordinary people, never questioned the Party's decision.

The whole country believed that Chechens had collaborated with the Germans and therefore Stalin had deported them. Even if Chechens had shown a desire to cooperate with the Germans, they could not have done so. The Germans never made it as far as Chechnya; so Chechens could not have collaborated with people they had never seen! But such details were of little importance in the post-war Soviet Union. Chechens had been cast as villains, as enemies of the people, struggling against Soviet power from the inception of the Soviet Union. Even now, it is possible to hear highly educated persons confidently assert that Chechen delegates met with Hitler and presented him with the gift of a white horse. Hitler must have had a herd of white horses, because similar stories were spread about other North Caucasian peoples expelled together with Chechens: the Ingush, Kabardians, Ossetian, Balkar, and Karachay, Crimean

Tatars, Ukrainian nationalists, Cossacks, and others.

In response to our professor's statement, I asked all the students in his course to walk out of the auditorium in protest against such false accusations leveled at the entire Chechen nation. Only three out of fifty-one stayed, two Russians and a Chechen, on the grounds that they felt sorry for the old man. Our protest spread to several departments and became the first mass action at our university. Teachers who did not renounce their agreement with the deportation were shunned.

Historical Note

Soviet history had to record the eviction of the Chechens as a logical decision of the Soviet government. Therefore, several generations of Chechens were brought up in the post-war era with a sense of shame for their ancestors who, we were told, refused to fight when conscripted. It is only with public access to state archives after the break-up of the Soviet Unionthat it become clear that those accusations were a false.

The Soviet state had correctly calculated that the accusation of treason would fall on fertile ground in a country that had lost tens of millions of people in WWII. No one challenged the charges or questioned how Chechens could have assisted Nazis when there was never any contact between them. Furthermore, the Soviets made it clear that the charge could not be discussed or denied.

Military archives revealed that on the first day of the war Chechen troops bore the brunt of the invading army: two hundred Chechens defended the Brest fortress, which became a symbol of wartime resistance. Yet a plaque in honor of the Chechen heroes who defended it with their lives was allowed only sixty years after the event.

Military archives also divulged that the percentage of Chechen participation in the war was much higher than that of many other USSR nationalities. Furthermore, the scores of recommendations for the award of Hero of the Soviet Union, denied to Chechens, testified to their heroism. Chechens were the first to meet the enemy in Brest and the first to meet the Americans on the Elbe, led by Major Mavlid Visaitov, a Chechen who was awarded an American decoration. Thousands of Chechens had been withdrawn from the front to be deported, but many, ashamed of the withdrawal, were able to remain on the frontlines by changing the nationality listed on their documents. Archives of German legions organized by Soviet prisoners of war showed only a few dozen Chechen volunteers. The majority had been prisoners in Nazi concentration camps. None of these facts were ever made public.

Deportation is not simply a period of Chechen history; it is a historical memory that will always remain. A Chechen would never speak of those tragic years saying, for example, "it was in 1947"; rather, he would say that it was in the third year of deportation. People who have been expelled have a memory of the exile that evokes events of those years in all their nuances.

Alexander Solzhenitsyn wrote in The Gulag Archipelago *that "there was a nation that did not succumb to the psychology of submission—not individuals, not rebels, but the whole nation. They were the Chechens."* [1] *In Solzhenitsyn's words they were mutinous, and the government sometimes had to give way to them. At a time when millions in the Soviet Union were persecuted as traitors to the Communist government, Chechens forced the authorities to reckon with them and taught others how to survive Soviet repression. Much of the credit for this belongs to the Sufi tradition, which taught secrecy and group survival in an environment that threatened death.*

After Stalin's death and their thirteen years in exile, many Chechens returned with the bones of their relatives who had died in the steppes of Kazakhstan. This was contrary to the precepts of Islam but, for Chechens, it was unacceptable that family members remain buried in foreign soil.

However, return was difficult. Chechens found their homes occupied by migrants from Central Russia, many of whom refused to leave. For months they lived in the open at the gates of their former homes. In order for some settlers to vacate the premises, they had to be bribed with the few possessions Chechens had been able to retain; others had to be subjected to moral and psychological pressure. Physical violence was not an option as perpetrators could be sent back to Siberian labor camps.

Tens of thousands of people died in the horrific conditions of transportation; and thousands of families, failing to acclimate to a new and harsher climate, did not survive the cold and hunger of the early years of exile. When Chechens speak of deportation, they speak of genocide. There is not a family that has not lost someone. Deportation is for Chechens what the Holocaust is for Jews: They do not forget or forgive.

Knowing this Chechen historical memory ignored by the Russians is

---

1. Solzhenitsyn, A. *Arkhipelag Gulag.* M., 1989, p. 401.

necessary to understand the Chechen consciousness. This memory makes Chechens persist in fighting for their existence. Russia's refusal to admit to a Chechen genocide is a substantial obstacle in Chechen-Russian relations.

Conflict with the KGB

The protests at the university drew wide attention. To cool passions, the dean of the history department, the department's Party secretary, the Rector (president) of the university, and other administrators negotiated with me to find a solution to the stalemate and allow professors, who refused to recognize the deportation as a crime, to resume their classes. However, my most important discussions were with a KGB lieutenant colonel, a Chechen. He began by giving me a long speech about international imperialism, particularly American imperialism, trying to destroy our country before he came to the real point of our meeting, that my present activities might affect my future. In the end, he proposed that we work together and hinted that all Komsomol members in my department were already cooperating with him.

If my dealings with the administration made me feel important and excited, my meeting with the KGB officer deflated me. At a gathering of the university's Communist and Komsomol delegates, I asked to speak. After summarizing our achievements in the deportation controversy and before anyone could stop me, I demanded to know why the KGB was recruiting collaborators among the students. The audience of a few hundred went silent. The president of the university asked, "Vatchagaev, why must your speeches always be scandalous?" He was referring to my having broached another Soviet taboo, the KGB recruitment of informers. My decision to speak publicly about such matters was not a rush to heroism but an attempt to protect myself from further contacts with the KGB. To make sure that the KGB would never seek me again, I exposed another scandal, stating that, according the officer who had sought my collaboration and asked me to sign an agreement to that effect, various former and present departmental and university Party secretaries cooperated with the KGB. Cries of "It's not true; we did not collaborate; we are not informers," echoed from several corners. I replied, "Let's ask KGB Captain Afanasiev sitting in the last row of the auditorium, and whom we all know, why he is here and why he behaves so cavalierly in our university." Captain Afanasiev ran out of the room so fast that he probably set a world record for obstacle courses.

After the meeting, in front of everyone, the KGB lieutenant colonel approached me and told me, "All you have done and said in this room today will remain forever a problem for you." He turned and left the building. I did not feel heroic but depressed because I knew that retribution would surely be coming; the only question was: how and when? Still, I had declared war on the all-powerful monster of the KGB. Over time, when I faced a variety of troubles always arising as if on orders out of nowhere, I remembered that conversation with the KGB officer in a hallway of my university.

Chapter 2

THE BEGINNING OF
THE GREAT ADVENTURE

Leaving Chechnya

After graduating from college with honors, I was one of three students admitted to the regional research institute to begin a career as a professional historical researcher. To join such an institute immediately after college was like winning a major lottery since most graduates were sent to teach in middle or high schools. Continuing my subversive activities at the institute, I proposed disbanding the institute's Komsomol cell on grounds thast it was completely uselessness. Although the delegates voted unanimously to disolve the cell, most later withdrew their signatures under pressure from their parents and the institute's director. The fact remained that for the first time a unit of the Chechen-Ingush Komsomol organization voted itself out of existence. The seriousness of the matter is demonstrated by the fact that the entire leadership of the institute was summoned to the regional Party committee to receive a rebuke. The administration of the institute, finding me uncompromising, pressured students by warning parents that their children's future could be compromised if they stayed under Vatchagaev's influence.

My next battle centered around my research topic. In an institute devoted to the humanities, I was denied the research topic of my choice, the Caucasian War or the Russian colonization of Chechnya in the late eighteenth through the early nineteenth centuries. The study of such themes was denied to members of indigenous nationalities that had been involved in that war because of their alleged bias. Studies of Russian-Chechen relations were reserved for Russian researchers because they were believed to be internationalists and, therefore, objective. Nonetheless, after consultation between the institute's director and the regional Party committee, I was allowed to pursue the topic of my choice. The patience of the director and the Party came to an end when I attempted to set up a secret Chechen-Ingush social democratic party.

After that, my earlier inquiries into the possibility of joining a graduate program in Moscow leading to a Ph.D. in history were denied. But later, following my last effort at politics, an opening was found in a graduate school in order to isolate the institute's young researchers from my harmful influence, and I was sent to Moscow.

The university in Grozny did not offer graduate programs. Chechens who were authorized to study for a Ph.D. had to move to cities outside of the Republic, mostly to Makhachkala, Rostov, Tbilisi, or Moscow. Places in graduate schools in Moscow were allocated by the Chechen-Ingush Regional Party Committee. Every year, the committee granted two places for historians, one reserved for a Russian and the second shared alternately by a Chechen and an Ingush. The ratio of Russians to Chechens in the republic was one to four, but Chechens were granted places in institutions of higher education six times less often than were Russians. The sending of students to Moscow was planned years in advance. My acceptance to graduate school in my first year at the institute showed the involvement of the higher echelons of the regional Party committee. I attribute this most welcome and unexpected outcome to the Russian wife of the Party secretary who participated in distributing seats in post-graduate studies. It is worth noting that the probable influence of a Russian wife was a route to the highest echelons of power. It was believed that by marrying a Russian, a Chechen became an internationalist and broke with his Chechen past. Therefore, top officials of the Republic often had Russian wives.

Getting to Know Moscow

The move to Moscow opened a new chapter in my life. My level of education increased significantly; the Russian Academy of Sciences, where I was admitted, was a dream come true for those wanting to follow an academic path. Settling in Moscow had been my secret aspiration: I had wanted to leave home, to feel independent, which was difficult to achieve for a Chechen with a large and conservative family living by traditional standards.

To climb the career ladder, one needed contacts, a college degree, and, of course, to join the Communist Party. Education and skills were not enough. The Party was a tough clan system. To join, one had to prove commitment; they had no interest in independent thinkers. Aspirants needed to learn and understand the works of Karl Marx and Vladimir Lenin and demonstrate an understanding of Party policy and ideology as demonstrated in their research.

The results of such prerequisites were ludicrous. Graduate students in physics, chemistry, or mathematics had to learn Marxist-Leninist works and, more important, to apply them in their research! We students in the humanities wrote introductions for these poor scientists describing how Lenin foretold their research and searched for appropriate quotes in Marx and Engels' writings.

Moscow, I realized after my arrival, was not just the largest city in the USSR; it was also a world separated from the rest of the country. The best educational institutions, libraries, archives, culture, and politics were all concentrated there. Even the mentality of Muscovites was unlike that of people elsewhere in Russia. The residents falsely stereotyped everyone else in the country. Those living in Moscow did not know Russia, and Russia did not understand Muscovite psychology. Whatever happened in Moscow did not apply outside of the Garden Ring encircling it.

The advisor appointed to supervise my dissertation was a Jew from Baku, Dilara Ibragimovna Ismail-Zadeh, an intelligent, sweet, and kind-hearted woman. I was lucky to meet such an extraordinary person whose refined behavior bespoke a different era. When we became better acquainted, she laughingly told me of her fears upon learning that she would have to advise a Chechen student. Our first meeting, however, dispelled all her reservations, when I began talking about my research topic. She believed (showing typical Muscovite stereotyping) that I would not know Russian and that she would have to communicate with me in sign language. But she later told her colleagues that her Chechen student knew Russian as well as a native. Chechens speaking Russian do not have the accent of most non-Russians. Only two other nationalities have the same skill, the Ingush, related to the Chechens, and the Kalmyk, a nation from the steppes. Although Dilara formally served as my supervisor, she became my longtime mentor and friend. For me, she was a member of my family, and I really miss her.

Historical Note

The most distinctive feature of Chechen society is spelled out in the nineteenth century Russian Encyclopedic Dictionary, "At the time of their independence, Chechens … had never known feudal institutions or class divisions. In their independent communities, managed by public meetings, all members were absolutely equal. We are all Uzdeni (i.e. free) claim the Chechens."[2] The absence of class structure complicated contacts between Chechens and their neighbors since policy was determined by each community and not by individual leaders. Many researchers, incorrectly interpreting this phenomenon, concluded that Chechens preserved features of a patriarchal society. Chechens traditionally had a governing institution, loosely analogous to the parliaments of free societies, called in Chechen Myahhk Khhel or Council of the Country, which regulated many issues. It was not a survival from a patriarchal society but resembled the scheme devised by the free (independent) cities of Europe.

The Chechen nation emerged from a military-political alliance of nine consanguineous tukhums (unions of kindred clans).[3] Each of these tukhums is, in turn, an alliance of kinship teips (i.e. clans). As Chechens descended from their mountains to settle on the plain, members of specific teips coalesced into blocks (klup) within rural communities. As teips grew, they began dividing on the basis of large interrelated families, forming a new structure within the teip, the gar (i.e. branch of teip).[4] Each gar then divided into neks; each nek divided into tslas or patronymic families (father, sons, and grandchildren). The last cell of the social structure is the

---

2. *Entsiklopedicheskii Slovar'.* Brokhaus and Efron. 1903, T. 38A.

3. Accepted by Chechen society and by many experts in the field of ethnography, those *tukhums* are the following: Akkii, Mialkhii, Nokhchmakhkakhoi, Terloi, Chantii, Cheberloi, Sharoi, Shotoi, and Orstkhoi.

4. For example, the Tsikaroi *teip* (a clan of the Cheberloi *tukhum*) sub-divided into five *gars*: Topin *gar*, Arbole *gar*, Makhin *gar*, Guchin *gar*, and Taimazin *gar*.

dlozal or nuclear family (husband, wife, and children). Thus, the social structure can be represented by a diagram: klam (the people)—tukhum (union of teips)—teip(clan)—gar (branch)—nek—tsla (patronymic family)—dlozal (nuclear family).

Some teips, accepted today as Chechen, derived from other nations, or as the Chechen saying goes, "they do not have their own mountain"; a Chechen without his native mountain has roots somewhere else. Some are of Georgian origin, two of Russian ancestry, and one each of Abaza, Circassian, Kabardian, Tatar, Nogai, Turkish, and Jewish heritage.[5]

My First Trip to the West

I did my graduate work at the Department of International Relations (inter-ethnic relations) of the Institute of Russian History of the Academy of Sciences in Moscow, where the team was ethnically diverse. My fellow students included an unassuming Dagestani, an intelligent Balkar, a cheerful Ossetian, a cautious Armenian, a cold Latvian, a clever Russian, and a noisy Tatar.

I established the warmest friendship with Alim, the Balkar, who, although he had lived in Moscow for twenty years, did not consider himself a Muscovite and always referred to himself as Caucasian (from the Caucasus). It was thanks to him that I took my first trip to the West. He knew that an international conference on Imam Shamil and the Caucasian War was to be held in Oxford. More interested in transnational challenges than in history, Alim suggested that I contact the organizers to let them know I was writing my dissertation on that specific topic. Urged by my North Caucasian friends—who, unlike me, did not find the idea silly—I wrote to Oxford without expecting any response. To my astonishment, shortly before the beginning of the conference, I received an invitation signed by Marie Bennigsen-Broxup and Moshe Gammer, two historians with whom I would come to collaborate closely; but their names and professional activities then meant nothing to me.

---

5. The origin of the Ardaloi, Batsoi, Gurzhii, Mekhaloi, Chartoi and Shoi *teips* is Georgian; the Arseloi and Orsi *teips* is Russian; Abzoi is Abaza; Cherkazii is Circassian; Glebertloi is Kabardian; Gezloi is Tatar; Nogloi is Nogai; Turkoi is Turkish; and Zhugtii is Jewish.

Only a few days remained before the start of the conference, and I had to get authorization to leave the country. It was then for the first time I felt the reality of the warning issued to me in Grozny by the KGB lieutenant colonel. As I was a student of the Academy of Sciences, my passport had to include an exit permit issued by the KGB department of the Academy of Sciences. Hoping Moscow was unaware of my subversive activities at the university in Grozny, I submitted my request and received it back within a day stamped "travel prohibited" in red ink across the passport. In other words I was politically suspect. It was not only a rejection, but it also meant the destruction of all my hopes for the future since from now on I would be totally dependent on the KGB for permission to travel to professional meetings.

On the advice of my student friends, I resolved to try to get my paper to Oxford to represent my participation in the international conference. However, there were only two days left before the opening of the conference, and the Internet was years away. Then by chance I learned from some Dagestani graduate students that the President of the Dagestan Academy of Sciences planned to attend the annual meeting of the Academy of Sciences of the USSR in Moscow the next day, before flying to London to join the conference on Shamil. I decided to try to approach him at the meeting and ask him to carry my paper to Oxford—although chances of meeting him would be slim as security for that event was very tight.

Security agents blocked the streets leading to the building where the annual meeting of the Academy of Sciences was held. The first police post let me pass after I pleaded my case, being sure that KGB security would not allow me into the building. To my great surprise, after protracted explanations and deliberations, a KGB major agreed to take me to the President of the Dagestan Academy of Sciences and accompany me out after I delivered him my paper. As we entered the building, I chanced to see a Chechen, Salambek Khadzhiev, Minister of Industry of the USSR. I told the KGB major who accompanied me that I needed to talk to Khadzhiev. He took me to him, and I immediately began telling the minister my story in Chechen. Surprised, he asked me how I had been able to be invited to the meeting; and after hearing my explanation, laughing at my resourcefulness, he took me to the Vice-President of the Academy of Sciences of the

USSR[6] and asked him why he did not allow one of his Chechen countryman, namely me, to go abroad to a conference. Of course, the Vice-President did not know me. Khadzhiev explained that the KGB department of the Academy of Sciences had denied my request to go to Oxford and that he, as a Vice-President of the Academy of Sciences, should cancel the ban. He tried to leave; but the Minister, holding him by the arm, would not let him go until he gave me permission. While the Vice-President wrote his consent, I heard him mutter irritably, "and they say there is no Chechen mafia; here it is!"

The personnel at the KGB office, where I arrived just before closing, were stunned and initially refused to believe that a Chechen student was able to secure an authorization from someone like the Vice-President of the Academy of Sciences. I had to bluff and assure them that I could produce him and the Minister in person. They finally caved in and issued me a diplomatic passport for a single trip. And the following morning, at Sheremet'evoairport, I joined the delegation travelling to the conference.

Oxford

In Soviet times, the ruble had no exchange value, and people traveling abroad did not carry currency. Instead, members of the delegation took brandy and Russian souvenirs. My friends had given me a bottle of Armenian brandy. I was delighted to be flying to Oxford to an international conference even without a penny to buy anything in the West. A Ukrainian immigrant who worked in the dining room of St Antony's College gave me ten pounds for my brandy. I do not know whether he took pity on me or really believed that Armenian brandy was the best in the Soviet Union. My esteemed colleagues had brought bags full of expensive cognac, but in the end they had to sell them to the Ukrainian immigrant for five pounds a bottle in order not to carry them back to Moscow.

With my ten pounds, I decided to open a bank account at the local Lloyds Bank. Even today, I cannot explain why. I never used

---

6. Vladimir Kudriavtsev was Vice President of the Academy of Sciences of the USSR and also Chairman of a Legal Commission of the Supreme Soviet of the USSR.

it and do not know what happened to the account. However, my standing rose sharply in the eyes of my colleagues, who until then had condescended to me because of my youth. I helped seven of them to open accounts at Lloyds Bank.

The conference was a landmark in my life. Talking to Marie Bennigsen-Broxup, one of the organizers of the conference, I disclosed that Chechen students at the university in Grozny hand-copied all they could find written about Chechnya in the West and distributed it among themselves. There were two historians we secretly worshiped, a Chechen, Abdurahman Avtorhanov, who lived in Munich, and a Frenchman, Alexandre Bennigsen. Surprised, she repeated "Bennigsen?" I began to tell her about Bennigsen, an expert on Islam in the Soviet Union, and telling her that someday I hoped to thank him personally for all he had written about us. Marie then told me that he had died two years before. When I asked her if she had known him, she surprised me by saying that he was her father! Later she told me that it was that conversation about her father that inspired her to begin to use her maiden name in her professional activities.

The other organizer of the conference was Moshe Gammer, an Israeli historian with an encyclopedic knowledge of the Caucasian War that he used with great sensitivity. In Oxford I also met with another future specialist of the North Caucasus, Anna Zelkina, a student of Gammer, then just starting her career. When I see her today, I always feel ashamed that Soviet customs confiscated a packet of cookies I was to pass on to her husband back in Chechnya.

I have often thought that had it not been for that conference, I might not have continued as an historian. Contacts in Oxford made me understand that history could be the vehicle through which the West could comprehend and appreciate my people, and that I should strive to present historical events as viewed by Chechens.

With a sense of pride in my three days in Oxford, I returned to Moscow. I had to return the diplomatic passport to the KGB who, of course, wanted details of the conference. I politely informed them that "all the participants asked me to convey to you their heartfelt greetings." I read malice in their eyes, but I innocently thought I would never have to deal with them again. But it so happened that until 1991, although our paths never directly crossed, they continued to do me harm, and I often felt their scrutiny.

Little Chechnya in Moscow

I arrived in Moscow a year before the collapse of the Soviet Union; it was a wonderful time. Hundreds of Chechens were studying there in both graduate and post-graduate programs. For this I could only rejoice. Drawn to the Chechen community, I met with its leadership and taught a course on Chechen history to children in its Sunday school. There I encountered Shamil Beno, a competent and energetic Chechen from Jordan. A post-graduate student at the Institute of Oriental Studies, he helped me with my work. Unfortunately, at that time Chechens had a rather bad name in the country because some were involved in criminal activities. Several of them dabbled in Chechen politics.

Criminals using revolution for their own purposes have always existed. Unfortunately, this happened in the Chechen revolution as well. The revolutionaries for the most part were members of the intelligentsia whose commitment to changing the system derived from their belief that it was good for their people. However, a number of criminal offenders exploited developments in Chechnya, combining illegal activities with politics. Some lasted a long time on the political scene; others left fairly soon. In the process, they all strengthened their positions in the criminal world and increased their wealth.

Criminal leaders used Chechen students to build up their power. Some students, mostly fellow villagers or clan relatives, were willing associates; others were unwitting collaborators. When gang leaders needed help with their dirty work, they appealed to students to help defend Chechen honor, generally through their associates. Hundreds of students went courageously to do battle when, in fact, they were helping criminals build their illegal businesses.

A representative of Chechen lawbreakers in Moscow was the apparently respectable Khozh-Akhmed Nukhaev, who in the 1980s dominated the illegal automobile market in the capital. By 1990, his standing well established in the Russian underworld, Nukhaev decided to dabble in politics. Understanding the potential for exploiting the changes taking place in the country, he promoted the idea of Chechen independence. He financed the publication of nationalist underground newspapers, thus acquiring a reputation as a man wanting to distance himself from his criminal activities. Even though he would never be able to entirely shake off his criminal past, he was able to gain status among prominent political figures of the Chechen revolution. He would eventually become a minister in Dudaev's government, but only briefly.

Criminal Chechnya

Not only Chechen criminals from Moscow played a role in Chechen politics, a number of local criminals also became participants. Ruslan Labazanov from the town of Argun was one. A year younger than I, he attended my school in Argun. Not even in a nightmare could we who had studied with him have imagined what the harmless boy would become. For five years, those he considered rivals or thought had underestimated his capacities for violent behavior were made to tremble. He regarded himself as a Chechen Robin Hood, but he was nothing more than a murderer and racketeer. At first a member of the president's guard, he moved to the opposition mainly because Dudaev forbade him to engage in criminal activity. In Argun, he bought an entire block and erected fortress walls around it; then he moved to Grozny where he acquired numerous apartments in a high-rise building. Like the Ukrainian anarchist Nestor Makhno from the early Soviet period, he traveled the country defiantly provoking reaction from the authorities. He would not submit to them, and the security forces were unable to cope with him.

Bislan Gantamirov was another criminal on the Chechen scene. A minor figure in the underworld, he was unknown in Chechnya in the early 1990s. However, the pride of an ambitious youth from the village of Gekhi caught Dudaev's attention. In the early days of the revolution, President Dudaev, because of his long absence from Chechnya, looked idealistically upon all Chechens as principled people like his parents. One of Dudaev's favorites, Gantamirov would eventually become a main tool of Russia's policy in Chechnya, even if his unpredictability could at times get him into trouble with his masters in Moscow. He claimed that his break with Dudaev was over policy; however, his criminal activities may have been the real reason for the split. When Russians captured Grozny in 1995, he was named mayor but was soon removed for criminal behavior.

It is important to point out that those who opposed Dudaev and his policies were not, at least at first, particularly vocal. Most feared his support among the population and possible reprisals. Characters such as Gantamirov or Labazanov were not afraid; they did not hesitate to openly attack Dudaev, even speaking on television, which may explain Moscow's reliance on them.

Yet another anti-hero was Alavdi Khamzatov, a native of the village of Guni. He had no ambitions in national politics, but his behavior put him on par with the likes of Labazanov. Khamzatov was an indiscriminate killer, and some of his murders could sometimes be related to politics. He assassinated a minor anti-Dudaev leader, who had allegedly not shown enough patriotism during a conversation with Khamzatov. He also murdered his mother-in-law because of rumors that she had been trying to feed him a witch's brew to bedevil him. For many years Khamzatov and Labazanov did not meet, Labazanov making sure their roads did not cross to avoid attempts to slaughter each other. Khamzatov was probably the only man Labazanov feared. Only at the end of the first Chechen war did their paths meet, ending in the death of both.

Chapter 3

THE ROAD TO INDEPENDENCE

The Chechen Revolution

Gorbachev's Glasnost and Perestroika inspired demonstrations in Chechnya. Activists pioneered new trends. The first protesters were environmentalists who opposed the construction of a biochemical plant in the city of Gudermes. Their marches and rallies politicized the environmental movement. The intelligentsia followed suit, and new underground intellectual circles, such as *Kavkaz* and *Prometei*, attracted many young adults interested in their people's history. Well-known historians founded *Kavkaz*, and acclaimed poets founded *Prometei*. Aspiring revolutionaries probed such bitter issues as the government's depiction of Chechens as enemies and surreptitiously searched archives, so jealously protected from Chechens, for documents that gave rise to new historical interpretations. In that cauldron of ideas, many came to view coexistence with Russia as only temporary. Therefore, thinking of the future, they began devising political schemes and rules that would make Chechens the decision-makers in their own republic.

Political demonstrations began in April 1988 and took place almost weekly. Starting in Gudermes, they gradually moved on to Grozny. It became obvious that the leading officials of the regional Party committee were unable to connect with protestors—perhaps they were afraid of them. The committees had to consult with Moscow on minute details, thus confirming that they were not allowed to make decisions without Moscow's approval. They seemed more concerned about what Moscow would think than how to respond to demonstrators. The press, equally an instrument of government, ignored the rallies because it did not know how to report them. To counterbalance the popular meetings, the government tried to conduct its own rallies. An instructor of the Central Committee of the Communist Party flew in from Moscow to lead negotiations and teach local Party leaders how to handle such situations. Several attempts to ban public protests were made, but a people impelled by unprecedented freedom could not be stopped.

Demonstrators became increasingly specific in their demands for the overhaul of Party and government positions. Nominations for all positions were the prerogative of the regional Party committee. Since the inception of the Soviet regime, a Chechen had never headed the regional Party. According to an unwritten law the First Secretary of the Party Committee (the most powerful position in the Republic) had to be a Russian; the President of the Supreme Soviet (the second most important position) had to be an Ingush; the only office open to a Chechen was that of the chairmanship of the government, a minor rank that did not carry much patronage. The Chief Prosecutor, Chief Justice, Chairman of the KGB, Minister of Internal Affairs, and others posts were reserved principally for Russians who reported directly to Moscow. At the lower level, the first Party secretaries of districts could not be Chechen. Presidents (or rectors) of institutions of higher education were never Chechen. Chechens, the largest nationality in the republic—larger than the Russians and the Ingush combined—were understandably unhappy with the situation. Would-be revolutionaries in the newly formed underground circles and parties made much of Moscow's unfair cadre policy.

The 1989 appointment of a Chechen, Doku Zavgaev, as First Secretary of the Chechen-Ingush Party Committee was an attempt by authorities to catch up with events. Against the background of the Communist Party's fading glory, that nomination no longer quelled the unrest; Chechens now wanted more than just one of them in the first job of the republic.

In the early 1990s, encouraged by the militant politics of the Baltic States, Latvia, Lithuania, and Estonia, Chechnya challenged the multi-layered constitutional organization of the Soviet Union. The USSR consisted of fifteen Soviet republics, including the Russian

Federation, which had the theoretical right to secede from the Union. The Russian Federation was subdivided into autonomous republics, regions, districts and territories, among them the Chechen-Ingush Autonomous Republic. None of those subdivisions had the right to leave the Federation. Chechen activists demanded equality between Soviet and autonomous republics. Such an elevation of status would allow Chechnya to leave the USSR legally and proclaim its independence. This occurred in 1990.

In the context of the power struggle between the USSR and the Russian Federation, the President of the Soviet Union Mikhail Gorbachev proposed a law equalizing the status of autonomous republics with the status of the Soviet republics. The purpose was to undermine the chairman of the Supreme Soviet of the Russian Federation, Boris Yeltsin, as the Federation was the only one among the Soviet republics to have several subordinated autonomous republics. The law adopted by the Supreme Soviet of the USSR and signed by Gorbachev became a watershed legal confrontation. Its publication on 26 April 1990 in the Official Journal of the Supreme Soviet of the USSR made it the law of the land.[7] Chechen separatists based their claims on this law. Hoping to enlist the support of autonomous republics, Yeltsin, while on a trip to the Autonomous Republic of Bashkiria, uttered his famous phrase "take as much sovereignty as you can swallow"; and this is the legal basis upon which all those who wanted to break the shackles of Russian federalism derived their claims.

Chechen revolutionaries were then willing to remain in the USSR with the status of a republic of the USSR, but not under the dual control of the USSR and the Russian Federation. Russian politicians, rejecting the Chechen position, argued that the law was not binding for the Russian Federation because the Russian Supreme Soviet had not approved it. The Soviet Constitution, still operative at that time, clearly stated that in cases of legal conflicts between the USSR and the Soviet republics the laws of the USSR superseded those of the republics. This is the essence of the legal battle between Russia and Chechnya since 1990. That law considerably weakens Russian legal

---

7. "On the division of powers between the USSR and the subjects of the Federation." *Bulletin of the Congress of People's Deputies and the Supreme Soviet of the USSR*, № 19, 1990, page 329.

arguments denying Chechnya the right to break away. Any politician, historian, or analyst debating Chechen separatism without mentioning that law is deliberately misleading.

When the Soviet Union collapsed in 1991, the standoff between Chechnya and Russia was still an issue: Chechnya proposed abandoning independence if it were recognized as a full-fledged Soviet republic, a compromise Russia could not afford. Numerous experts at the time endeavored to prove that Chechnya's exit would be fatal to Russia because of the importance of Chechen oil and oil industries, pipelines and refineries, and because of many other non-existent problems.[8] The real issue was Moscow's fear of the domino effect: that following Chechnya's example, other autonomous republics monitoring the controversy between Grozny and Moscow, especially Tatarstan and Bashkiria, would make similar demands.

In fact, scarcely any republics were ready to follow Chechnya. Tatarstan, against the background of complicating relations between Chechnya and Russia, was bargaining to extract as much power as possible for itself from the Russian government. For experts, Tatarstan exemplified the practical way of dealing with Russia, making substantial gains in the process. Whereas Chechnya typified the unrealistic approach by risking military confrontation. Few of those specialists like to remember that ten years later Tatarstan lost everything it had achieved in the 1990s.

Meanwhile, in the early 1990s a real revolution was taking place in Chechnya that resulted in the overthrow of Communist rule and the capture of the Interior Ministry, the KGB, and other centers of power. Encouraged by Chechen unrest, the Ingush people in the west of the republic launched their own protest in March 1990 demanding the restoration of the Ingush Republic, which had existed prior to 1934.

The Historic Year 1990

Political developments and the radical transformation of the population's mood made 1990 a watershed in the history of Chechen people. The most noteworthy event was the National Congress held

---

8. Among the experts were Sergei Shakhrai, Valerii Tishkov, and the Chechen Ruslan Khasbulatov.

in Grozny 23 to 25 November. The Chechen totem, a wolf—symbol of the future Republic of Ichkeria—made its first appearance there.

Deputies to the National Congress, elected on the basis of one deputy for one thousand Chechens, debated issues brought up at numerous prior meetings held in Grozny. In the presence of delegations from diaspora communities in the United States, Jordan, Syria, and Turkey, the Congress issued a declaration on the State Sovereignty of the Chechen Republic Nokhchich'o (Chechnya in Chechen). It stated that Chechnya respected the union of nation states and was ready to become a full member of the Union of Soviet Socialist Republics.

The Chechen-Ingush Supreme Soviet, basing its decision upon the declaration of the Congress, approved a change of name for the Republic from the Chechen-Ingush Autonomous Republic to the Chechen-Ingush Republic. In this act, not only the name of the republic, but its very essence, had been altered. In its initial decision, the Supreme Soviet referred to the Chechen-Ingush Republic as a subject of the USSR, completely ignoring the Russian Federation. However, at the request of Ingush deputies the language was softened. However, it was quite clear that Chechnya saw itself as only a member of the USSR and not of the Russian Federation. Ingush deputies had asked for the change of language because of a land dispute with North Ossetia. After Ingush were deported together with Chechens in 1944, part of their ancestral land had been given to the North Ossetian Autonomous Republic. The Ingush saw in the political ferment of the country their first real hope of regaining the lost territories. They were afraid that the declaration by the Chechen Supreme Soviet that the Republic was a member of the USSR would hinder the recovery of these territories, since North Ossetia in its own affirmation of sovereignty had made it clear that it was a member of the Russian Federation.

Article fourteen of the Declaration of the Supreme Soviet clearly indicated that the Chechen-Ingush Republic looked upon itself as a sovereign state, even before the signing of any kind of treaty with the Russian Federation or the USSR. Thus, following the Baltic States before the collapse of the USSR, in December 1991 Chechnya declared its independence. Already in December 1990 the Supreme Soviet had renamed Grozny airport to honor the great Sheikh Mansur in response to public pressure. The Sheikh's name had been banned from history because it personified the struggle of Chechens and other North Caucasians against the Russian Empire in the eighteenth century.

Historical Note

Russian colonization of the North Caucasus began in the second half of the eighteenth century. In an early stage Sheikh Mansur led the resistance of all North Caucasians, regardless of ethnic identity, against the Russian Empire. Those who followed him in the anti-colonial struggle never achieved the same unity.

The Sheikh, a native of the small village of Aldy that stood on the site of present day Grozny, was born in 1760 into the Elistanzhi clan of the Nokhchmokhkakhoi union. According to Russian historians, his exceptional intelligence and oratory skill got him elected imam of the mosque in Aldy. His solitary life dedicated to prayers generated interest in his preaching. He called for moral purity and the return to the path of Islam.

Sheikh Mansur still lives in the North Caucasian memory. Songs, legends, and myths have been associated with his name. Imam Shamil, a leader of the resistance to Russia in the nineteenth century, called him his teacher and spoke of him with admiration. Sheikh Mansur provoked controversy in the East from Istanbul to Mecca and in the West from Italy to England. Many wondered who was really hiding under the name of Sheikh Mansur. Turks saw him as their great man; Bashkirs considered him their tribesman who had left to fight in the Caucasus; and Italians declared him to be the adventurer Giovanni Battista Boetti, a native of Italy, the offspring of a family of lawyers.

Captured by Russians, the legendary Sheikh Mansur died on 23 April 1794 in a dungeon of the Shlisselburg Fortress near Saint Petersburg. He was buried anonymously near the fortress walls so that his grave would not become a place of pilgrimage.

In Search of a National Leader, 1991

Once the revolution began, it needed a champion. First wave nationalists were not aggressive; they had lived too long with a self-image as second-rate citizens and feelings of alienation from the state. They wanted to obtain for Chechens the rights enjoyed by other peoples. The old stigma that Chechens never considered Russia or the USSR as their state was partly correct; but it was the state that had deliberately placed Chechens in opposition with its disregard of everyone and everything Chechen.

Nationalists of the 1980s and early 1990s were most often members of the intelligentsia, young writers, poets, artists, or just romantics. One of the early meeting places of those intellectuals was the private club *Prometei*. There they shared their discoveries, mostly historical documents they had uncovered in various archives, and read their poems dedicated to Chechnya and the Chechen people. Nothing in their statements was intended to insult the Soviet state. For official Russia, however, such poetry in the 1980s was tantamount to a political crime, in which nationalism was undermining the foundations of the Communist system. The authorities appointed their own poets to glorify the friendship between the various peoples of the USSR.

Prometei had existed for several years when the KGB disbanded it, and its members were recorded as potential troublemakers. Rumors spread that the activities of the club had been denounced to the KGB by one of the official poets dissatisfied because club members underestimated his work. Maybe there was some truth in those rumors since that poet later became an architect of the collapse of the nationalist camp and the formation of the intelligentsia's ultra-reactionary wing.

The escalation of the rivalry in Moscow between Mikhail Gorbachev and Boris Yeltsin encouraged Chechen revolutionaries to believe that events were moving closer to the historic moment when they could seize power from the local Communist elite. Finding a leader who could unite all Chechens was imperative. However, no charismatic figure existed. There were many interesting personalities, but none that could inspire the majority of people or at least a vocal minority. Thus, nationalists who had prepared for revolutionary changes suddenly discovered that no one among them could become the standard bearer of the revolution. Since they had operated exclusively underground; when they surfaced, only those who were interested in similar issues knew them.

Potential leaders of the revolutionary movement were few. For a time, the Green movement head Khokh-Akhmed Bisultanov, who organized the first mass rally in the 1980s to protest the construction of a biochemical plant in Gudermes, was popular. After he accepted a position equal to that of minister (director of Vtorchermet) from the Communist authorities, he quickly lost his appeal and left the political arena. Personalities like Lema Usmanov, Lechi Umkhanov, Isa Arsamikov, all members of the intelligentsia, were unwilling to lead the revolutionary movement. Nor did the well-known scientist and minister of the chemical industry of the USSR Salambek Khazhiev show much enthusiasm. The well-known lawyer Aslanbek Aslakhanov and the Ph.D. Andarbek Iandarov, a grandson of a prominent Sufi sheikh, both lacked charisma. Yandarov, in particular, was too soft for the difficult job of asserting Chechnya's claims against Moscow.

The best candidate for leadership appeared to be Dzhokhar Dudaev, the only Chechen-born general of the entire Soviet era. For people proud of their military history, he seemed ideal. Dudaev, the commander of strategic aviation in the Soviet Baltic, rapidly gained popularity. He became an icon because he had achieved something incredible for a Chechen, becoming a general despite Soviet racism. Soldiers who served under him revered him: he helped them and spent time with them. They even told of occasions when he had participated in fistfights with people who denigrated Chechens.

A delegation of prominent nationalists met with Dudaev in the Baltic States. Nationalist revolutionaries wanted reassurance that he would not abandon or betray the revolution. Dudaev agreed to lead the revolutionary movement and become head of an independent Chechnya. This choice ended his military career.

Dudaev had charisma. In the broken Chechen of the mountain Orstkhoi dialect he boldly threatened Moscow, the city that most Chechens felt was eternally at war with them. Chechens were enthusiastic about his energy, courage, and determination to confront Moscow. A rough military man, he would never be comfortable with the nationalist intelligentsia that had invited him to lead the revolution. He saw the intellectuals as part of the Soviet past, too prudent, unable to understand the revolution, and not real patriots. He would eventually sideline them. Dudaev emerged rather quickly. Moscow was probably too busy neutralizing potential strongmen from Chechnya to recognize the possibility of an outsider heading the movement. Furthermore, the Russian rulers may have doubted that he had the character to become a Chechen paladin.

The attempted coup against Mikhail Gorbachev in August 1991 accelerated the rise of the nationalists. The Chechen Supreme Soviet, whose chief executive was Doku Zavgaev, did not support Gorbachev, and this enabled nationalists to demand Zavgaev's removal. His unwillingness to hand over power led to mass meetings, some turning into clashes with security forces.

During this crisis the Chechen National Congress set the date of the Republic's presidential election for the 27 October 1991. A National Guard was organized to counterbalance untrustworthy elements of law enforcement. Its task was to maintain order in towns and villages. Communist officials opposed the elections, as did Boris Yeltsin's representative in Chechnya Akhmed Arsanov, son of a famous Sufi sheikh. But the momentum for self-rule could not be stopped. In the evening of 27 October it was announced that out of 640,000 eligible voters 470,000 took part in the elections, 430,000 voted for Dzhokhar Dudaev. Observers from the Baltic States and the Republic of Georgia gave a press conference reporting that they had seen no evidence of fraud.

Historical Note

Twice in the last century, Chechens believed they had a chance at independence: at the collapse of the Russian Empire in 1917 and at the collapse of the Soviet Union in 1991. In 1917, the small Chechen political elite fragmented over the ultimate nature of the state and the choice of allies: The Mensheviks of Georgia, the Bolsheviks of Russia, and religious groups demanding reconstruction of the theocratic structure that had existed under Imam Shamil from 1840 to 1859.

The Chechen Tapa Chermoev headed a wing of the national movement that wanted a pro-western state. In November 1917, together with other North Caucasian leaders, he set up the Mountain Republic. However, having called for the creation of state institutions, the Mountain Republic's government did not follow through with implementation. In opposition to Tapa Chermoev, the Chechen Sufi sheikh Uzun-Haji tried to form an Islamic state, the Emirate, which was short lived and lasted only until his death. A small faction of revolutionary socialists, with close ties to Russian Bolsheviks, sought to create a state in partnership with the new Soviet Russia. Finally, there were a few Mensheviks sympathetic to the Provisional Government, and even some monarchists.

At times between 1917 and 1921, the Northern Caucasus had three simultaneous governing entities: the Mountain Republic of the Northern Caucasus (local political elite), the Mountain Autonomous Soviet Socialist Republic (allies of the Bolsheviks), and the religious Emirate of Sheikh Uzun-Haji in Chechnya. Thus, the divided national movement was unable to coalesce to struggle against Soviet Russia.

My First Work for Independent Ichkeria, 1992

Immediately after his election President Dudaev welcomed Zviad Gamsakhurdia, the deposed President of Georgia, to Grozny. Unlike other heads of state, Dudaev received him as the legitimate president of Georgia. He also remained faithful to promises to ease Gamsakhurdia's exile and allowed some of Gamsakhurdia's cabinet ministers, the parliament, and Georgian priests to join him in Chechnya. Similarly, Dudaev offered protection to the former head of East Germany, Erich Honecker. If welcoming Gamsakhudia had been an act of friendship, the invitation to Honecker was an act of defiance against Russia, which did not want to give him refuge. This gesture also gained instant visibility to obscure Chechnya.

In early 1992, I came home on leave. Dudaev had appointed my friend from Moscow Shamil Beno foreign minister in December 1991. I decided to visit him in Grozny. He greeted me cheerfully and asked for my help in future diplomatic exchanges with Moscow. Thus, I was appointed coordinator[9] of the upcoming negotiations between the Chechen Republic and the Russian Federation. I accepted Shamil's request with some apprehension. As a coordinator, I would have to meet with the leadership of the Russian delegation headed by Iury Iarov, First Deputy Chairman of the Supreme Soviet of the Russian Federation.

Upon my return from Chechnya to Moscow, I contacted Iarov's staff and suggested a meeting. The encounter took place at the Gaidar Library on October Square. The choice of location was odd but understandable. Since Moscow did not want to publicize preparations for negotiations, it picked the obscure office of a children's library for the meeting. I met with Sergey Smitiushenko, an assistant of Iarov. Smitiushenko asserted that Russia wanted to start negotiations

---

9. Ministry of Foreign Affairs, order № 02-153, 8 April 1992.

as soon as possible and, to keep the meetings out of view of public attention, proposed holding the talks in the resort town of Dagomys, a part of Greater Sochi, in southern Russia. In order to compensate for locating the conference in an obscure small town, he offered to assume the cost of the meeting, including the transportation of the Chechen delegation to Dagomys. I responded that we were able to provide for ourselves during negotiations. However, aware of the young Republic's deplorable financial situation, I suggested that Russia pay for the first round of negotiations conducted in Russia and that Chechnya assume the cost of the inevitable second round held in Chechnya. Smitiushenko agreed. Because negotiations could last for months, a group of experts would work out details for the Russian side, although Iarov would preside over them. Moscow had already identified several experts to assist him.

What would happen, Sergei Smitiushenko pointedly asked, if suddenly Chechens were to remove Dudaev? Were such a removal orchestrated from the outside, I replied, it would be considered an act of aggression that would end diplomatic discussions. Therefore, I suggested that Russia stop exacerbating the situation by supporting the Chechen opposition to Dudaev. Furthermore, I inquired why Chechen nationals were barred from Moscow hotels. Smitiushenko tried to dismiss the issue as some kind of periodically recurrent phenomenon, but I warned him that it might cause a backlash against Russians in Chechnya. He then promised to find out personally who had ordered evictions, to reverse that decision, and to inform me of the results.

I reported back to Shamil Beno that the location for the conference was not an accident and recommended that Chechnya insist that negotiations be held in Moscow. In the provincial city of Sochi there would be no independent journalists to cover the proceedings; the Chechen delegation would be isolated. Furthermore, I found out that negotiations would be overseen by Ruslan Khasbulatov, the Chechen-born Speaker of the Supreme Soviet of the Russian Federation, well known for remarking, "neither Chechnya, nor Dudaev." Lastly, I warned Beno that Smitiushenko obviously had some information about tensions between Dudaev and the Speaker of the Chechen Parliament Khussein Akhmadov over ministerial appointments and lack of consultation. There could be a leak either from staff of the president or of the speaker. My overall impression had been that

Russia was not interested in those negotiations; that it was actually waiting for the situation to deteriorate enough so that it could help the opposition take power, an opposition that would opt for a close collaboration with Moscow.

Beno had asked me to establish contacts with Iarov and to organize the negotiations; he then broadened my responsibilities. In practice, I was to be a representative of the Chechen Ministry of Foreign Affairs in Moscow. In that capacity, I met with the Turkish Ambassador to the Russian Federation. I was received by him but had more meaningful discussions with his first secretary. Turkey, it was clear, was interested in Chechnya as a base for spreading Pan-Turkic ideas among the Turkic peoples of the North Caucasus.[10] In exchange for that, it was ready to help the new republic in a number of ways.

The Republic wanted to change the alphabet, from Cyrillic to Latin. Chechens believed that the Cyrillic alphabet was introduced by Russia in order to isolate them. For centuries Chechens had adopted the Arabic alphabet. Latin script was introduced in 1926, and in 1936 Stalin imposed Cyrillic, the forty-nine-letter alphabet that did not suit the Chechen language. Turkey, I was told, would be willing to provide expertise and financial assistance in the transition to Latin. The secretary also conveyed his government's wish to set up a television center in Chechnya to promote the spread of Turkish programs among Turkic ethnic groups. We discussed other assistance concerning independence from Russia.

Excited by my meetings at the embassy, I immediately contacted my minister, who at once reported our conversation to the president. The nature of my discussion at the Turkish Embassy was obviously best kept secret. Imagine my dismay when I found out that Dudaev had revealed everything on television.

The following day, I was asked by the Turkish Embassy to come to the ambassador's residence. I was hopeful he had not yet heard of Dudaev's indiscretion. Alas, that was not the case. A different secretary explained that the ambassador had been summoned to the Russian Ministry of Foreign Affairs to hear a formal complaint about conducting separate negotiations with breakaway Chechnya.

---

10. Kumyk, Nogai, Balkar, and Karachai and also among Crimean Tatars, who had stayed in Ukraine after the break-up of the USSR.

Therefore, I was informed, all proposals of cooperation were tabled; Turkey was not going to have contact with Chechen authorities behind Russia's back. I tried to explain that we were just learning our way in politics, that our institutions and politicians were inexperienced and wanted to be transparent, and that any errors were not due to a wish to offend. The secretary's behavior, however, clearly showed his reluctance to discuss the issue further. Thus, the approach to Turkey ended ingloriously before it had even begun.

My next trip as representative of the Foreign Ministry was with Beno to Kazan, capital of the Autonomous Republic of Tatarstan. He was to speak at the State Council of Tatarstan to request recognition of Chechnya's independence. Tatar nationalists, who thought Tatarstan should follow Chechnya's example, had invited him. However, on arrival, we found ourselves in a crossfire: on one side the Tatar nationalists who had invited us and on the other a group headed by Mintimer Shaimiev, the speaker of the State Council who did not like the strained relations between Moscow and Grozny. Shaimiev implored us not to appeal to the State Council. Most delegates, he alleged, would not support Chechen independence; our request would only harm Tatarstan's negotiations with Moscow. In fact, Shaimiev was manipulating Moscow: he maneuvered for increased autonomy for Tatarstan—de facto following Chechnya's path—asserting that the more Moscow gave to Tatars, the faster Chechens would understand the benefits of negotiations with Moscow. Of course, Shaimiev was aware that such bargaining was not agreeable to Chechnya, but it allowed him to wrest concessions from Russia that other republics did not receive.

After deliberation, Beno decided not to address the Council, and he presented to our Tatar nationalist guests this decision as his own idea and not as a result of Shaimiev's request, putting him in debt to us. I remember regretting that we would miss our plane to Moscow since there was only an hour before our departure, when Shaimiev reassured me he would make sure the plane would wait for us, so afraid was he that we would spend the night in Kazan.

After my trip to Tatarstan, I began to realize my differences with Chechen reality. My perception of events conflicted with Grozny's views; we proceeded from different perspectives. I worked for Beno because I thought it helped Chechnya, but the government of Dudaev did not seem interested in negotiations. Moreover, not being part of any political clan, I had no influence. Therefore, I decided to resign from the foreign ministry and concentrate on my dissertation.

In February, the parliament barely approved the first cabinet of ministers, which was destined to be a short-lived one. Before his nomination could be approved, Beno resigned. His resignation was a loss for Chechnya because he was energetic and professional, the latter quality lacking in early Chechen politicians. Shortly afterwards local groups seeking booty stormed several military bases that were still in Russian hands, forcing Dudaev to impose martial law. These thefts may have been incited or committed by criminal elements in order to acquire arms. Violations worsened after the break-up of the Soviet Union, since the Chechen government was unable to replace Soviet security forces. Martial law, however, did curb crime.

Some developments in this period were positive, particularly in airport traffic and trade. The Grozny airport began running at full capacity. An agreement was reached with Armenia so that all flights to and from Yerevan would land in Grozny to refuel.[11] Markets in the city were now working around the clock near the Petropavlovsk highway. They were packed with buyers from Cherkessk, Nalchik, and Makhachkala. Grozny was gradually becoming a trading center in the North Caucasus.

Such improvements in Chechnya's situation could only worry Moscow. In consequence, imported automatic weapons were distributed to Dudaev's foes, and rumors circulated that the Russian Vice-President Vladimir Rutskoi had approved arming the opposition. On 31 March, the opposition violently seized the television and radio station, but in the evening the National Guard ejected the opposition troops. Perhaps the anti-Dudaev group was misled by the brief capture of the station. That incident was the first in a series of clashes. In the summer friction escalated between Parliament and

---

11. Deprived of its gasoline delivery through Georgia because of a conflict between Tbilisi and Sukhumi and through Azerbaijan because of the war in Nagorno-Karabakh, Armenia was choking from lack of fuel. Chechnya did not have an air fleet. In exchange for the favor, Armenia reserved thirty seats for Chechens on each of its flight. If on arrival in Grozny the reserved seats were occupied, those passengers stood in the aisle for the remainder of their journey. Flights looked more like crowded trams than aircraft but there was no option but ignoring violations.

President; ultimately Dudaev disbanded Parliament. The members, mostly from the nationalist intelligentsia, had expected mass support but they miscalculated their influence. People identified with the populist President and his aggressive stance against Russia rather than with Parliament's moderate approach in dealings with that nation.

Chapter 4

POLITICAL CONFRONTATION BETWEEN MOSCOW AND GRONZY

A Conversation Between Two Men, One Deaf and One Mute, 1993

During 1993 I was busy with my dissertation. Dividing my schedule between archives and libraries, I was content to immerse myself in historical documents. The topic of my thesis, "Chechnya in the Caucasian War," had been studied exhaustively in dozens of theses and monographs and thousands of articles, almost all written from the viewpoint of military history or about Imam Shamil. My goal was to reveal for the first time Chechnya's role in that war, a subject ignored by most scholars. Every time I found an important document read, but not cited, by some eminent historian, I was delighted. In the Russian archives, everyone who requests a document must sign out for it on an open list, so one can see who used a particular document and when.

I reconstructed the progress of the Caucasian War in Chechnya almost month-by-month and sometimes nearly day-by-day. In the draft of my dissertation, I did not realize that I was frequently using the expression, "a small Chechen detachment." Amused, my supervisor told me to diversify my style. Later, during the 1994–1996 war, she often commented, "How right were you to use those words in relation to the Chechen opposition and the Russian army."

Meanwhile, the situation in the Republic was troubling. Tensions even affected my Chechen community in Moscow. We vigorously discussed which side was right. The opposition sympathizers among us were rare, one or two percent; we nevertheless often criticized the authorities, who, in our opinion, made ill-advised policies. Our conversations wandered because we did not listen to one another and frequently contradicted ourselves.

Debates focused on independence. Nearly everyone wanted an independent Chechnya, but opinions varied on how to bring this about. Some thought that Chechnya should sever all ties with Russia. Others felt that freedom should proceed gradually; still others argued that, as a first stage, Chechnya should remain associated with Russia and develop at its expense. The smallest group believed that it should remain an integral part of Russia, which to the rest of us who believed in independence, seemed crazy.

The Battle of Gekhi: A Turning Point, September 1994

The situation in Chechnya seemed to be approaching a military confrontation. It would never have happened had Moscow not relentlessly pushed the anti-Dudaev camp into a conflict with the supporters of independence. Armed agitation supported from Moscow rapidly moved from a nuisance to a tragedy. Surrounded on three sides by the Russian Federation, Chechens found that movement into and out of the Republic was controlled by Moscow. The Russian government was convinced that a blockade of Chechnya would force concessions. Chechen authorities, however, sustained by the vigor of pro-independence sentiment, would not be diverted. This unyielding stance impelled Moscow to encourage the opposition to intensify confrontation with Dudaev's government.

Since the beginning of 1994 clashes of varying degrees of violence between the pro-Russian and independence factions occurred almost continuously in the towns of Argun, Urus-Martan, and Grozny. A tense situation gripped the villages of Tolstoi-Iurt, Znamenskoe and Beno-Iurt on the river Terek. An extreme example was the fight in September between Dudaev's forces and Bislan Gantamirov's clique in the village of Ghekhi in the Urus-Martan district.

Bislan Gantamirov was the main recipient of military equipment generously supplied by Russia. His base was a military compound inherited from the Soviet era and transformed into a fortress. From there he led punitive forays against independence groups. He terrorized the suburbs of Grozny. The Chechen military command resolved to disarm Gantamirov and, if necessary, to destroy his base in the outskirts of Ghekhi.

Chief of Staff Aslan Maskhadov launched a special operation. According to the plan approved by Dudaev, Gantamirov's fortress was to be attacked from three sides. At the designated time, however, only detachments commanded by Maskhadov were engaged. The remaining units headed by Ruslan Gelaev arrived after the battle was over. Gelaev's absence gave Gantamirov the advantage of concentrating his forces against one group of assailants.

In Chechnya nothing remains secret. Chechens make fun of themselves saying that all secrets can be discovered in the marketplace; women in the bazaar usually discover them before anyone else. Indeed, Gantemirov had been warned of the assault and was waiting in ambush. From the start everything went wrong for the government troops. At the intersection of the roads to Urus-Martan and Gekhi they first came under a fire from Gantamirov's fighters who hit a truck with tank ammunition. In the night the scout leading the way missed the country road that Maskhadov should have taken. By the time he arrived at the compound it was daybreak, and the element of surprise had been lost. An armed personnel carrier with Maskhadov's bodyguards was hit at the entrance to Gantamirov's base, and almost everyone in it sustained injuries. The old-fashioned carriers, with high and narrow windows, were like iron coffins on wheels. The wounded had to be pushed out the windows before the survivors could jump out. Lastly, when Maskhadov's forces finally took up their positions, they realized they had no support. According to one participant, there was a minor panic. Carriers were hit, tank ammunition destroyed, and tank turrets jammed. The situation was like an anarchist brigade only waiting the order to turn and run.

At that point Aslan Maskhadov spoke to his troops, telling them that it would be a shame to return to Grozny without capturing the base given the casualties they had sustained, and that it would embolden the opposition if they were to retreat. His counsel was to begin the attack immediately without waiting for support. Then he pulled out his gun, summoning all those who considered themselves real men to follow him; and without looking back started walking across the field toward the base. After a moment's indecision, seeing

Maskhadov walking alone toward hundreds of well-armed fighters, the column slowly advanced. It must have been a strange spectacle: a man, pistol drawn, striding alone followed by a strangely silent convoy with tank guns aiming in random directions. After a brief exchange of fire, Gantemirov's ranks inexplicably fled, abandoning their arms. While the battle was winding down, the long-awaited Gelaev and his units drove up to the village to support the audacious men led by the little known leader Maskhadov. No exact body count existed; but hearsay estimated hundreds dead. Maskhadov's adjutant probably gave the most accurate toll when he said that he personally helped to load about twenty corpses from each side into a personnel carrier.

In their own words, those who fought in Gekhi were not elated; they felt bitterness and guilt. It was the first real battle in which Chechens fought Chechens over the issue of the country's future. A beneficial result was that the victory would help the pro-independence forces deal with later conflicts. As the government crossed the threshold of war, disruptive elements, such as Labazanov or the Russian puppet leader Avturkhanov, did not dare exploit the situation as openly as they did before the battle. With Chechen blood spilled, everyone now wanted to negotiate, not fight. Even Avturkhanov announced that he was ready to recognize Dudaev's government.

Unfortunately, the government failed to secure the advantage it gained over the opposition. The interior ministry and the prosecutor's office did not punish those who took up arms against the government. Consequently, the opposition recovered its strength. The defeat at Gekhi had another result. Moscow made up its mind to hasten the overthrow of the president.

The anti-Dudaev faction was demoralized; it realized that it could not win without the help of Russia. Even though faction members understood the role Russia played, they still believed that with Dudaev gone agreement with Russia would be possible and independence secured. They failed to recognize that Russian assistance would be accompanied by Russian control.

In Moscow the Chechen politician Ruslan Khasbulatov put a totally different spin on the events in Gekhi. Forced to resign as Speaker of the Parliament after a failed coup against Yeltsin, Khasbulatov chose to play peacemaker in Chechnya. Perhaps he thought his credentials entitled him to interfere in Chechen affairs. He had been Yeltsin's deputy, Speaker of the Russian Supreme Soviet, and for a while the second most powerful man in Russia after Yeltsin. He was an academic and an internationally acclaimed economist. In fact, the authority his political and academic positions had earned him was thwarted by exaggerated self-importance, contempt for others, an inability to listen, and a philistine outlook. His break with Yeltsin was the result of an escalating clash of egos.

What could average Russians be expected to think when a man with Khasbulatov's credentials could spread horrific stories about events in Chechnya? Describing the battle in Ghekhi, Khasbulatov wrote in a Moscow newspaper: "armed men in civilian clothes made their way in buses to a military base of the Provisional Council near Urus-Martan and shot staff officers and civilians at point-blank range." "Armed men in civilian clothes" stood for Maskhadov's troops, "buses" for his personnel carriers, and "military zone" for Gantamirov's base. The Provisional Council, a rival of Dudaev's government, had been set-up by Russia to give legitimacy to the opposition leader Umar Avtorkhanov, who in the late 1980s had been dismissed from the Abkhazian Interior Ministry (MVD).

My opinion of Khasbulatov had changed earlier, when during the constitutional crisis of September 1993, he was besieged in the White House (Russian Parliament) by tanks loyal to Yeltsin. While surrounded, he still naively assumed that Russia would rally to him. Chechens of the Moscow community, including students, professors, doctors, and businessmen, told him that they were ready to fight for him. He refused our help, however, saying that he did not want to be accused of having Chechen ties and that he needed the support of Russians not Chechens. We were offended by his attitude. Khasbulatov was wrong in 1993 when he believed Russia would rise up against Yeltsin; a year later, he was wrong in assessing Chechnya. Serial miscalculation raises a question: was this academic that smart?

During interviews Khasbulatov divulged information better kept secret. He reported Dudaev's attack on his friend Ruslan Labazanov (the bandit), who had been in the uniform of an FSK major (Federal Counterintelligence Service, formerly the KGB). On 22 September he related to the newspaper *Nezavisimaya Gazeta* how Dudaev's forces had surrounded his native village and destroyed a tank of the militia defending it. Militiamen with tanks! Dudaev, he shamelessly lied, had rocket launchers, two-dozen tanks, and dozens of armed personnel carriers protecting him. His own popularity in Chechnya would be manifested, Khasbulatov proclaimed, when the Chechen government collapsed, and for this the Provisional Council needed only adequate armament. The Russian army need not invade Chechnya since the forces of the Provisional Council would be sufficient to unseat Dudaev. Were the Chechen people to understand that Russia would not help the opposition, Khasbulatov asserted, they themselves would depose Dudaev. Khasbulatov had been a top politician of the Russian Federation, but he seemed unable to grasp the reality in Chechnya.

Moscow now decided to defeat Dudaev. But this time, instead of relying on the opposition, it sent Russian mercenaries and military advisors, who would fight without thinking of far-reaching possibilities. Thus, the battle of Ghekhi presaged Moscow's direct involvement in Chechnya.

The Onset of the Bloody Tragedy, November 1994

On 22 November, a few days before alarming reports arrived from Grozny, members of the Chechen intelligentsia gathered in the Moscow office of the lawyer Aslanbek Aslakhanov to discuss holding a conference on the Chechen problem. The gathering was impressive: Among those present were Salambek Khadzhiev, academic and former Soviet Minister of Industry; Andarbek Iandarov, professor of philosophy and former education minister in the Dudaev government; Abuiazid Apaev, head of the Chechen community in Moscow; Salman Vatsanaev, professor of philosophy; Mahmoud Esambaev, internationally acclaimed dancer; a representative of Ruslan Khasbulatov; and many others who viewed Chechnya's situation as extremely dangerous. I was there as a representative of the Chechen diaspora.

Even though those gathered in Aslakhanov's office had different opinions about Dudaev's legitimacy, all felt that Chechnya was on the brink of war, but that problems should be solved through dialogue between Grozny and Moscow. It was decided that the conference should be held within days. Aslakhanov offered to organize the event, Khadzhiev took on the financing, and Iandarov agreed to develop the program. The conference would be dedicated to avoiding an armed confrontation. My role was to notify students and encourage

Chechens living in Moscow to get involved in helping our homeland in this crisis. As a supporter of independence, I wanted to ensure that the conference would express no pro-Russian sentiment. I had not felt any such undercurrent at the preparatory meeting, and I was proud that, at such a time, the eminent Chechens presented a united front.

The conference was set for 28 November at the Writers' Central House on Hertzen Street in the center of Moscow. The program included six reports and discussion sessions led by people with different opinions of developments in Chechnya.[12] The conference was to produce three documents: an appeal to the Chechen people; an appeal to parliaments, governments, and peoples of the world; and a conference resolution.

The mayor of Moscow Yuri Luzhkov increasingly made Chechens unwelcome. Policemen began looking upon them as bandits, regardless of whether they were respectable citizens, students, or belonged to criminal gangs. Luzhkov's discrimination tactics—at first directed against Chechens—gradually became a handbook in inter-ethnic relations in the capital. The goal was to force Chechens to be submissive citizens of Russia, but police brutality fostered an even greater thirst for independence. Many actions of Russian politicians seemed irrational; therefore, it was decided to invite Muscovite leaders to the conference so they could hear how Chechen scholars, politicians, and artists viewed the growing danger. We were naive in believing that our opinions would be taken into account. While we were looking for a peaceful way out of the crisis, preparations were underway for a military invasion of Chechnya.

For Chechens war began on 26 November 1994, two weeks before Russian troops officially entered Chechnya. Early in the morning anti-Dudaev forces entered Grozny, coming from different directions. Three days earlier on 23 November, Russian planes destroyed equipment parked in Shali, leftovers of the Soviet army, in total twenty-one tanks and four armored personnel carriers. On the morning of 26 November, the air force bombed the military airfields in Khankala, Kalinovskaia,

---

12. Reports were to be made by Andarbek Iandarov, Aslanbek Aslakhanov, Dzhabrail Gakaev, Vakha Mezhidov, Iusha Aidaev and Khassan Musalatov. Discussions were to be conducted by Doku Zavgaev, Isa Munaev, Kazbek Tamkaev, Salambek Khadzhiev, Zaindi Shakhbiev.

and Grozny airport.[13] When anti-Dudaev forces entered Grozny, the Chechen army had lost its aircraft, tanks, and personnel carriers.

It is important to note that hardware abandoned by the Soviet army and air force in 1992 had been rendered useless prior to their departure; generators, batteries, and navigation devices had all been removed or destroyed. Therefore, the November bombings had no effect on the Chechen army, especially as it was not a traditional force. Pro-independence units were individual detachments or squads—Basaev's squad, Gelaev's squad, etc.—although, taken together, they represented the Chechen army.

As became clear, the armed incursion into Grozny had been planned by Russia to overthrow Dudaev. For this assault Russia called up mercenaries from different parts of the country, gave them brief training at a military base in Astrakhan, and deployed them to Chechnya. The appearance of military vehicles on Grozny streets was aimed at breaking the pro-independence resistance. Moscow actually expected to demoralize Chenchens with a few dozen tanks, which proves again it had little insight into the situation in Chechnya.

The invading columns were composed of T-72 tanks manned by Russians and armored personnel carriers transporting forces of the Provisional Council. Mi-24 armed helicopters provided air cover and Su-27 aircraft were used to create psychological pressure. It became obvious that the tank crews were not Chechen when they had to ask passers-by for directions. Tank crews were recruited from the Moscow military district and were under contract to the Federal Counter-intelligence Service for nine million rubles (about three thousand US dollars) upon signing. Captured tank forces all told the same story: they trained near Moscow; were transferred to Astrakhan; and were then taken to Mozdok, on the border of Chechnya and North Ossetia. On the Mozdok military base, the Russian First Deputy minister of Defense addressed them.[14] The soldiers for the coup

---

13. Altogether were demolished: thirty-nine combat-training aircrafts L-39 Albatross, eighty L-29 Dolphin, three pursuit planes MiG-17, two training MiG-15UTI, six aircrafts AN-2, and two helicopters Mi-8 –leftovers of the Soviet air force. At the Khankala airbase, only seventy-two L-39Albatrosses and sixty-nine L-29 Dolphins were left intact.

14. General Mikhail Kolesnikov was the First Deputy Minister of defense.

numbered about 1,200. All the anti-Dudaev leaders were present.[15]

In an interview with British Lord Rea and French researcher Marie Bennigsen-Broxup, who in December 1995 had arrived in Chechnya from Georgia, Maskhadov gave the figure of 187 armored vehicles (tanks and carriers) and 4,000 soldiers, Russians and anti-Dudaev Chechens. The total she gave were three times higher than those officially released. I prefer to believe Maskhadov. He was a military man serious about numbers and not in the habit of conscious deception. He reluctantly spoke about his battles, but when he did he was honest.

The assault had begun in the morning on 26 November. Columns converged on Grozny from the north along the Petropavlovskoe highway, from the east from the Tolstoi-Iurt-Petropavlovskoe Road, and from the west from Urus-Martan-Aldi. News of the invasion spread like wildfire. From every corner of Chechnya, people hurried to Grozny to help their government and their president.

At about 8:00 a.m. in Argun my sister's husband Aiub Dzhokharov, learning that tanks had entered Grozny, grabbed a grenade launcher and a Kalashnikov and rushed to the city leaving his wife and four children, the youngest twins only five years old. He did not even assemble the militia he commanded: He ordered his neighbor to assemble it. Half an hour late, he was in Grozny on Minutka square in the October district. There he met a column of tanks moving toward the avenue that led directly to Liberty Square and the Presidential Palace.

There were no presidential troops in that part of town, but the battle could be heard from the other side of the river Sunzha. Aiub stood in front of the column of tanks, his armed grenade launcher ready to fire. It was a crazy move but he had no time to think since the advancing tanks were on their way to surround the Presidential Palace.

The news Aiub had heard was that anti-Dudaev forces had entered Grozny and that it meant fighting other Chechens. According to witnesses Aiub hesitated to fire; he did not know who was in the leading tank, Russians or Chechens. In Chechen, he called on the tank crew to get out in order to avoid being shot. A moment of confusion led him to understand that Chechens were in the tank. Again, he appealed to them to step down, saying he did not want to spill Chechen blood. In response the tank shot point-blank and tore him

---

15. Among them Avturkhanov, Gantamirov, and Labazanov.

and his grenade launcher to pieces. The tanks continued toward the Palace, but the explosion at Minutka Square warned the government forces that the enemy was coming from the south. At the cost of his young life, Aiub, not yet thirty-five years old, had prevented the enemy from getting through from the south. On that day, I also lost an unarmed friend Sultanbek who rushed to the Presidential Palace but was struck by machine gun fire from a tank entering the square from the Staropromyslovskii highway.

At first, people did not realize that they were at war. They believed the Russian media that anti-Dudaev forces had entered Grozny, but no one took the opposition seriously; no one thought he would die at their hands. There was anger but no fear.

On that bloody day, the Chechen defense lost twenty men. The Russians had twenty-one tankers captured. Each side gave different casualty numbers; Chechens claimed they had killed hundreds of Russian soldiers, while the Russian Ministry of Defense admitted only fifty dead and twenty-one captured. Some sources alleged five hundred dead among the invaders. Perhaps the truth lies somewhere between the two figures. There were more than two dozen burned tanks and as many captured. The attitude of the Russian Minister of Defense, Pavel Grachev, and the Head of the Federal Counterintelligence Service (FSK), Sergei Stepashin, who categorically refused to take responsibility for the actions of the Russian troops, shocked many. Abandoned by everyone, captured soldiers and officers became a commodity: Russian politicians would go to Grozny to return with at least one prisoner in order to increase their favorable rating in the polls.

The results of the battle of 26 November proved that Chechens could beat Russia. They had defended their freedom and accepted the loss of loved ones. Chechens had won a moral victory over Russia; many Russian citizens and most of the world were on their side. Neither casualties nor the defeat of skilled forces by untrained separatists, however, changed Russia's determination to end the conflict with Grozny by force.

A journalist for the French newspaper *Le Monde*[16] witnessed Russian pilots strafing the funeral procession in Argun that carried my brother-in-law Aiub to the cemetery. They continued shooting people

---

16. Sophie Shihab was the journalist for *Le Monde*.

who fled to hide; and they killed two children and their mother, who were buried in the same grave since it was difficult to identify the remaining body parts. Chechens were appalled by Russia's war to crush their independence movement. The behavior of the Russian Army on that 26 November changed many minds: scores of those who had sided with the opposition now favored an independent Ichkeria. On 27 November I arrived in Argun, where my entire family was at Aiub's funeral. My sister Aishat's first words to me were, "Do you think this sacrifice will not be in vain in the end?" I was unable to give her an answer.

Thus, that day became the prologue to the Chechen war. Russians, surprised at their failure, continued the bombings. Moscow had tried to end the conflict using the local opposition, but it had been misled by those who had argued that military vehicles on Grozny streets would suppress forces loyal to Dudaev. The Russians remained confident, however, that they could crush Chechnya as a warning to others. Since 1991, Russia had gone through radical changes; the resolution of the Chechen problem had to be postponed, but was becoming a major threat. Chechnya was an example for other border regions, many of which closely monitored Moscow's response.

Chapter 5

THE RUSSIAN ARMY
IN CHECHNYA

The Russian Invasion, December 1994

Although for Chechens the war had begun on 26 November, the Russian official date is several weeks later. The failed gamble seemed to have cooled heads in the Kremlin; Chechnya, however, experienced the opposite effect.

Chechens were riveted to their televisions and radios. They listened to every word and paid attention to every gesture that might indicate the Russian authorities. All expected a sequel to the 26 November, even if they hoped for a miraculous peaceful conclusion.

Officials in Grozny tried, through journalists, to approach the Russian authorities with a proposal for a dialogue. Moscow pretended not to hear; Grozny responded by vilifying the Russian army and the leadership of the Russian Federation. Television channels repeatedly showed disabled tanks and dogs eating corpses of Russian soldiers; and against this background the Minister of Defense denied any involvement in the invasion. More and more frequently fighter planes appeared in the skies over Chechnya; flying low over populated areas, they instilled fear.

Moscow concluded that the defeat of the 26 November was due to inadequate allocation of resources in engineers and troops. The final decision to send the army to Chechnya was taken at a meeting of the Russian Security Council on 1 December. The leadership, it seemed, was not united. The resignation of all the Deputy Ministers of

Defense and the Minister of Justice came like a bolt from the blue.[17] Later, the reason of the Minister's resignation became clear; he was the only member of the Security Council to oppose the invasion.

Pavel Grachev, Minister of Defense, made a statement that clung to him for a long time afterwards. To solve the Chechen quagmire, he claimed "he only needed seventy-two hours and a single airborne regiment." He insisted that before sending troops, Grozny should be wiped out. A veteran of the Afghan war, he disregarded civilian casualties and casually talked about leveling a city in his own country. To deal with Chechnya, Moscow needed a ruthless man.

Meanwhile, in early December, Russian politicians—from all factions of the State Duma—began descending upon Grozny. They had one goal: to free at least one Russian soldier to boost their political career. Deputies, among them Iuschenko, Iavlinski, and Loginov, offered themselves as hostages in exchange for soldiers. The Chechen command allowed them to leave with the prisoners of war, on the condition that they do their utmost to protect the rescued from persecution in Russia. Each politician departed with one or two prisoners. The decision of the Chechen authorities to let the soldiers go generated sympathy for Chechnya that the Russian propaganda machine was unable to neutralize totally; and probably hastened Moscow's invasion plans.

Against the background of pro-Chechen sentiment in Russia, Moscow could not ignore the proposal for negotiations made by Grozny. On 6 December in the village of Ordzhonikidzevskii, talks took place between the Russian defense minister and Dudaev. The meeting was tense, made worse because the Chechens disarmed Pavel Grachev's guard and returned their weapons only after the end of discussions. Asked what had been agreed upon, Grachev replied unequivocally, "We will fight!"

Another negotiation took place on 7 December in Vladikavkaz between the Russian Federation's Minister of Nationalities and the Chechen Attorney General/Minister of Justice. Although the conference was held at the ministerial level, after what passed between Grachev and Dudaev, it achieved nothing. The Russians tried to

---

17. Deputy Ministers of Defense were: V. Mironov, Boris Gromov, and Vladimir Semenov. Minister of Justice was: Iuri Kalmikov.

convince the Chechens to give up independence, the Chechens argued that they would defend themselves to the end.

Up to that point the president of the Russian Federation had avoided any public statement of his position on Chechnya. Acting upon the advice of deputies who had visited Chechnya in the first two weeks of December, the State Duma issued a resolution recognizing that the situation in Chechnya was not under the control of the Federal government.[18] Furthermore, a group of deputies sent a telegram to Boris Yeltsin, cautioning him that any bloodshed in Chechnya would be his responsibility and demanding a public declaration of his position.

Yeltsin's answer left no alternative to war. On 9 December, Presidential Decree Number 2166 stated that the Chechen government had organized illegal armed groups persecuting those opposed to its policies and that the Federal government had to intervene to curb those military groups.[19] For the first time the Federal government acknowleged military intervention in Chechnya. On the same day, government resolution number 1360 assigned responsibility to several ministries and agencies for implementing and maintaining a special regime in the Chechen Republic, although no formal declaration of a state of emergency or martial law was made. The uncertainty about war was now over. On 11 December at 7:00 a.m. three columns of armoured vehicles decorated with flags of the former Soviet Union moved toward Grozny from Mozdok (North Ossetia), Kizliar-Khasaviurt (Dagestan), and Nazran (Ingushetia).

Hostility in the border areas, before the entry into Chechnya, surprised the Russian army. Local inhabitants blocked the Kizliar armor column in the Dagestan district of Khasaviurt. The first deaths took place in the village of Barsuki in Ingushetia where local residents also tried to halt the army. Attempting to negotiate, the Ingush Minister of Health, Tamerlan Gorchakhanov, was killed for having obstructed the path of the convoy with his car. Four other Ingush died, crushed on

---

18. The resolution was entitled: "On the situation in the Chechen Republic and the measures taken to resolve it."

19. The presidential decree was entitled: "On measures to curb the activities of illegal armed groups in the Chechen Republic and in the zone of the Ossetia-Ingush conflict."

barricades they had erected. The columns were delayed, and the plan to encircle Grozny in the early hours of the operation was disrupted.

Chechens were surprised by the announcement of order number 247 of the Ministry of the Interior setting up detention camps in Mozdok, Stavropol, Piatigorsk, and later Grozny, in which detainees from the war zone would be interrogated and the degree of their involvement in combat against the Federal forces determined. Thus, the first act of Russian internal affairs had been to establish concentration camps.

Few people believed that the army was ready to destroy the Chechen capital. The capture of Grozny that planners had expected would take only a few hours dragged on for days. Russian commanders were surprised. They were prepared to fight armed men but not an unarmed population. Women, children, and old people lying in the path of tanks and armored personnel carriers confused senior officers. Their indecisiveness infuriated the Minister of Defense and on 15 December he dismissed a group of officers who had refused to move their tanks against civilians. The overall command of the forces was entrusted to the Commander of the North Caucasus Military District Colonel-General Mitiukhin.

On the same day the N. Egorov, appointed head of a new Territorial Administration in Chechnya met with his power structure in Mozdok and alleged that the "bandits" would be finished in a day. On 16 December, Russian troops took up positions on hills around Grozny. Moscow must have viewed the encirclement as a critical accomplishment. Grozny is situated in a valley, and the occupation of strategic heights in the north (Terek Ridge) and in the south (foothills of the Khankalskii canyon) would allow troops to control the city. The first Russian tanks reached Grozny on 16 December. The distance from the village of Ordzhonikidzevskya on the Ingush border to Grozny is just 65 kilometers or 40.4 miles; that is, the average speed of the military convoy was 11 kilometers or 6.8 miles a day!

As the columns advanced, the victims multiplied. If on the first day rumors that somewhere someone had been killed were difficult to believe, by 16 December deaths were reported everywhere; and no one was surprised any longer. The dread of war turned into contempt for the invaders. Chechens could not comprehend why women and children were killed, strafed by aircraft, or why the elderly and enfeebled were tormented by those who for seventy years had been their fellow citizens.

Again on 16 December, Russian Prime Minister Viktor Chernomyrdin announced that he was ready to meet with President Dudaev at any time or any place. He promised humanitarian aid, especially sugar, which in those days was rationed in Russia. His statement, however, was clearly made without consultating Yeltsin; because on 17 December the latter issued an ultimatum to the Chechen authorities to meet with his representatives in Mozdok. In other words, he ordered Dudaev to surrender at the military base in Mozdok. Throughout the campaign there was an obvious lack of coordination between the Russian President and his Prime Minister. Beginning on 19 December air strikes above Grozny, but also throughout Chechnya, became a daily occurence. Chechens wryly ridiculed them; they called bombs and cannon fire from diving aircraft "the promised humanitarian aid." "Behold," they said, "here comes Chernomyrdin's sugar."

The Russian military was in turmoil. Generals who refused to storm civilian targets were retired; Colonel-General Mitiukhin, who had been named head of the expedition only a week earlier, was removed. Eduard Vorobev was appointed to take his place, but refused. The situation was becoming tragicomic. The army was in semi-rebellion. Trained to fight external foes and having forgotten how to fight internal enemies, the dissatisfied army was becoming an important asset to democratic forces; if, of course, it could be manipulated. The former Soviet General Dudaev was well aware of the situation, which is why the Chechen army was made accessible to the Russian opposition and journalists. A permanent figure in Dudaev's headquarters was the most prominent Russian human rights activist—after the death of Andrei Sakharov—Sergei Kovalev. Thus, the world heard of the destruction of Grozny not from the Chechen authorities but from human rights activists and journalists who witnessed the brutal bombing of civilian targets. Dudaev's strategy undoubtedly hindered Russian propaganda.

Russian authorities then pretended that Chechnya was under their control and carved the territory into fictious managerial units. News footage showed meetings of those units allegedly taking place in liberated parts of Grozny, when in fact they were filmed on the military base in Mozdok. Russian actions seemed ad hoc adjustments to unanticipated problems.

On 20 December Russian government decree number 1411 instructed ministries and Federal services to open executive offices in the Chechen Republic and to entrust their management to deputy ministers. On the tenth day of the invasion, the Russians at last found generals willing to obey Moscow: Lieutenant-General Kvashnin was made commander of the Federal forces operating in the Chechen Republic, and Lieutenant-General Shevtsov his staff officer. Their first act was to close the southern border between Chechnya and Georgia by landing troops on the heights overlooking Georgia.

With each passing day Grozny increasingly resembled the German city of Dresden destroyed in World War II. To protect against potential attacks from ground to air missiles, Russian planes struck from high altitude. Many had hoped that only selective pockets of insurgents would be bombed. After the heavy night raid of 23 December that wiped out the "Children's World" store, the bank, and started fires throughout Grozny, a mass flight occurred among the 405,000 inhabitants.

On 23 December Yeltsin's Foreign Minister Andrei Kozyrev approached Sergei Kovalev, the human rights activist, to inquire about the Chechen authorities' conditions for negotiation. Dudaev's reply was clear: immediate cessation of hostilities and negotiation on all issues. He was even prepared to discuss disarming his own forces. Kovalev forwarded the conditions to Kozyrev, but no reaction came from Moscow. In all likelihood, Moscow judged Dudaev's response as proof of weakness and evidence that the Chechen army was crumbling under the strikes of the Russian air force.

According to Russian propaganda the conflict was between different Chechen factions and not between Russia and Chechnya. Tensions between Dudaev's forces and the opposition had turned into an armed confrontation, and the Russian federal government had to intervene to prevent the loss of life. To sustain this new version of events, on 26 December, Moscow set up a government of "national revival," gathering all those disgruntled with Dudaev and headed by Salambek Khadzhiev, academic and former Soviet Minister for Industry. I was surprised at Khadzhiev's presiding over this puppet government. He had been at the meeting held in Moscow in November to organize a conference on Chechnya and open a dialogue with the Russian authorities. In answer to a query about the possibility of his joining the opposition, Khadzhiev had noted, "Only a political prostitute will now play these games under the Russian flag." A month later, he had apparently found such prostitution irresistible.

The remarks of Russian politicians were characterized by their duplicity in the conflict. For instance on 27 December, while Grozny was subjected to non-stop bombing, Yeltsin appeared on television claiming that "For the sake of saving people's lives, I have ordered the exclusion of such bombing as could produce casualties among the civilian population." After Yeltsin's statement, the air attacks intensified on towns and villages. Yeltsin was well aware of what was happening. His speech undoubtedly was designed to improve his image at home and abroad.

Secretary of the Security Council Oleg Lobov on 28 December announced that Grozny was surrounded; seventeen days after the beginning of the war, the Russian army finally managed to encircle the city. To rationalize this rather unimpressive achievement, it invented a fairytale in which it fought tens of thousands of Chechens. The Chechen army actually consisted of a few units, each under the control of a commander. The total number of combatants could scarcely have exceeded two to three thousand at the beginning of the conflict; and many quietly left for home to await better times now that the struggle was becoming a real war. Volunteers organized in individual villages: the "man with a gun" was the most important element of the fighting forces. In military reports of those years we come across names of individual commanders[20] and names of villages' units, such as the Naur battalion from the village of Komsomolsk in the Gudermes district. I believe that because of their scorn for Chechen fighters Russian military planners did not know the composition of Chechen forces. They believed that the power of the army of the Soviet Union would rout any foe. The achievement of Chechen fighters was to destroy this myth. The world became aware that the new Russian army was weaker than its Soviet predecessor because of disorganization and diminished combat skills, but also more dangerous to civilians because of its lack of discipline.

---

20. Shamil Basaev, Ruslan Gelaev, Vakha Arsanov, Khunkerpasha Israpilov, and others.

Historical Note

The Caucasian War began in XVIII century and continued without much interruption until 1859. The earliest battles took place in Chechnya. Chechen legends praise such events of that war as General Aleksei Yermolov's expedition against the village of Dadi-Iurt on 15 September 1818. To support their men in battle, the legend tells us, young women danced on the village's square. After their men were killed, women and young girls took up arms and, rather than endure captivity or abuse, cut their own throats. By nightfall the village was destroyed, and forty-six wounded women were taken prisoner. As they were being ferried across the river Terek, these women hurled themselves on their Russian jailers, shouting "kill the enemies!" and holding them in a death grip threw themselves into the river. Only a few children survived the nightmarish event, one of them, Petr Zakharov, destined to become a prominent figure.[21]

The New Year's Assault On Grozny

The assault on Grozny of New Year's Eve 1994 was one of the most absurd battles in Russia history. For several days prior to the attack, artillery and tank shells hit the city. Casualties were heavy, but civilian deaths only made the armed defenders more determined. According to various estimates on 31 December about 250 Russian armored vehicles entered Grozny, and four to five thousand soldiers were designated to storm the Presidential Palace and raise the Russian flag over it.

What motivated the Minister of Defense to choose that specific date? One popular opinion claimed that it was Pavel Grachev's birthday, and the commander of the expeditionary force wanted to ingratiate himself by making him a present. This operation, however, could not have been possible without the Minister's approval and, thus, could not be a surprise to him. More probably, the planners hoped that people would be distracted by the holiday and public outcry would be lessened over what was taking place in Chechnya. For Chechens, expecting death, the holiday had no meaning. Yet another explanation was that Yeltsin wished the Chechen problem resolved as quickly as possible in the New Year.

---

21. Petr Zakharov became a scholar at the Russian Academy of Fine Arts.

Grozny was bombarded for three days prior to the assault. Artillery and tank shells emitted a terrifying whistle that created the sensation they were flying at you. Each explosion brought a moment of relief as you realized that you were still alive. The consciousness that someone else had been killed came only later. It is the strange sensation of war: survival crowding out the awareness of death.

Many Chechens who fled Grozny could go to their villages in the mountains or the foothills. The Russians of the city had no place to go. Some left with their Chechen neighbors; but, overlooking the fact that bombs do not sort out victims by nationalities, most Russians thought they would be safe because it was their army taking over the city. When they collapsed, multi-story buildings in the vicinity of the Presidential Palace became mass graves for Russians hiding in their cellars.

A number of Russians lived in my hometown, many of them school teachers. Some who could depart remained nonetheless. No argument could persuade my elderly and respected middle school teacher to leave. She promised her Chechen neighbors to look after their apartments, safe-guarding them from marauding Russian soldiers. Russians were the last to flee, only after bombs and rockets destroyed their faith in the army they had viewed as their protector. The Russian army decimated the Russian population of Grozny and forced its survivors to become refugees in Russia, where no one was waiting for them and no one helped them. Russian nationalists clamoring about Chechen barbarity or going on at length on the Internet about the "Russian soul" did not lend a hand to their repatriated countrymen who had lost everything. Twenty years later, these refugees have not yet received any support from the authorities.

We had anticipated the last day of the year with anxiety. In Avtury we heard the thunder of cannons hitting Grozny, some twenty-three miles to the north all day long, and the night lit up in a bloody glow of fire. That day brought death to almost every village. Funeral rituals were simplified to bury the dead within the twenty-four hours as Muslim custom requires. The closest hospital to treat the wounded was in Shali, four miles from my village; but hospital personnel had been considerably reduced after being targeted by Russian shelling. The bombardment had killed or wounded hundreds of people; after that most of the medical staff vanished. It is hard to blame them; they were ordinary Chechens. Nursing the wounded was left to families, to people who had little or no knowledge of medicine. Veterinarians assisted, but they were few and in high demand. To evacuate the wounded to hospitals in neighboring republics meant going through numerous Russian military check points. It could be dangerous since the wounded could be suspected of having been involved in the fighting. Thus, people suffered at home. Only in the spring of 1995 was a temporary military hospital set up in Vedeno; and after its capture by Russians, that relocated to Tsatsan-Iurt. Headed by Umar Khambiev, it eventually became a rural health clinic.

The only source of news in those days was Radio Liberty. Every half-hour it broadcasted news directly from the field of battle. Radio Liberty had two journalists in Chechnya whose names, Andrei Babitski and Khasin Raduev, are forever linked to the first Chechen war. We listened to the radio and passed on information, since we needed confirmation of what we heard. Many were coming to me because they naively thought that I, a graduate student at the Academy of Sciences, would be able to add something they had missed. In those days I did not console or soothe them. On the contrary, I tried to prepare my countrymen for the worst possible outcome rather than encourage them to expect a miracle. Maybe it was unkind, but I thought it my task to make people face reality. With time, my circle of listeners became more extensive and diverse. After the war, I was told that people joked, "Let's go to Mairbek to hear the black truth from him ... though it is already evident that nothing positive is happening." The Chechens attitude did not reflect pessimism; I would say they were grasping reality.

During the bombardment of Grozny, it was decided to organize a corridor for refugees. Therefore, on the morning on 31 December, Sergei Kovalev, carrying a list of residents wanting to leave, came to the Presidential Palace to meet with the Vice-President, Zelimkhan Iandarbiev. During their meeting the Russian artillery barrage began on the Palace, and further discussion of refugees was made impossible. Kovalev had to remain in the Palace because no one could get out and survive under the fire aimed at the executive mansion.

The story of Khusein Iskhanov, Maskhadov's adjutant, shows how bad the situation was. Khusein's wife was killed by Russian fire as she was looking for her husband, since he had not been home for several days. She did not know that the artillery salvos on the Palace would start just as she was approaching it. She had been listening to Russian official television that claimed that all was quiet on the Chechen front. She was confident that nothing more would happen beyond what she could see from her window and decided to go in search for her husband. Family burial is a fundamental ritual of Chechen society and Khusein could not leave the Presidential Palace to attend his wife's funeral because he feared he would be suspected of desertion.

Another battle was developing at the same time in the railway station district, not far from the Palace. Two Russian battalions of the 131st motorized rifle brigade[22] advanced to that district. The station itself was unimportant; no troops or equipment would move by rail. But the area had strategic value because of a bridge connecting the southern part of Grozny to the center of the city. Chechen fighters still battling in the center of town could use the bridge to attack the rear of the Russians who were storming the Palace. Chechens, of course, understood the importance of the district and had no intention of giving it up, even as tanks were moving against them. The battle lasted for several hours during which one of the two Russian battalions ceased to exist. The official Russian casualty count for the whole brigade was only seventy-four soldiers and officers killed, including its commanding officer.

Dozens of Russian soldiers and officers were captured on that New Year's Eve. Treatment of prisoners was unconventional. Chechens did not regard their captives as enemies; they pitied them and felt guilty for having arrested them. All prisoners—officers, soldiers, or pro-Russian Chechens—were kept together and treated the same. Any attempt by officers or Chechens to command the soldiers was stopped, and perpetrators were threatened with death.

Russian media reported the superiority of Chechen forces. They were not aware that the Chechen fighting strength was a tiny fraction of that of the Russian army advancing on Grozny. The blocking of a Russian elite paratrooper unit in the district of Andreevskaia dolina and of the 693rd motorized rifle brigade in the western part of Grozny were similarly described as being surrounded by a Chechen army of several thousand, who prevented Russian troops from deploying in the center of Grozny. In fact, about one hundred Chechens held against the Russian army in the western part of town.

---

22. The 131st motorized riffle brigade, also known as the Maikop Brigade, had its headquarters in Maikop, capital of the Adyge Republic.

Movements of Russian army units within Grozny were increasingly chaotic. They did not know where to make their stand or when or how to retreat. Chechen fighters assigned such tasks among themselves, for example who would be responsible for disabling tanks. They also divided weapons seized from tanks and armed personnel carriers. Many Chechens coming to the battle were unarmed but wanted to hunt a tank.

It was evident that the operation to capture Grozny was failing. The Russian Minister of Defense, unable to justify a defeat, declared, "These eighteen year old boys died for Russia, and they died with a smile. A monument should be erected in their honor; instead they are defamed.... This peace-maker deputy ... Kovalev ... is a double-crossing bastard. He is an enemy of Russia, a traitor to Russia ... and everywhere he is given a grand welcome. This Ushenkov, this vile creature! There is no other name for him; he criticizes the army that gave him education, gave him skills. Unfortunately, according to regulation, he is still a colonel in the Russian army. And he, that foul creature, defends those villains who want to destroy the country." The fact was that the spokesmen for the Chechens were Sergei Kovalev, Duma (parliament) deputy and human rights activist, and Sergei Ushenkov, Duma deputy and chairman of its committee on defense. Both were in the thick of the battle in Grozny and, via journalists' satellite channels, reported what was going on in the city. Understandably, Grachev and his generals were angered by the broadcasts and abhorred their two presenters who, in some sense, were themselves hostages of the Russian policy in Chechnya. Kovalev and Ushenkov did not defend Chechnya because of any sympathy for its cause, but due to what they witnessed.

Grachev's outbursts were sacrilegious. The world had seen horrific pictures from the streets of Grozny: dead Russian soldiers everywhere, as no one collected their bodies for days, and stray dogs ate the corpses. The images were a silent reproach to the Russian authorities. The dead did not have smiles on their faces, as the minister claimed, but frozen expressions of horror and pain.

Regarding the dead, no international humanitarian organization was present in Grozny, a fact that is a terrible trademark of the first Chechen campaign. It was clear that no one cared for those corpses lying in the streets for days and weeks; only the frost saved the city from possible epidemics. Their burial was left to the residents who survived in that hell. Between bombs and rocket attacks they dug pits in the frozen ground deep enough for the bodies to be out of reach of hungry dogs. They interred the Russians in the home backyards and schoolyards and in hedges, but not in cemeteries because of the danger of being shot in open spaces.

Urban warfare revealed the weaknesses of the Russian army. Tanks and armed carriers were a hindrance and easy targets for Chechen fighters who shot at close range from corners, windows, and ruins. Having drawn lessons from these battles in 1996 Maskhadov would set his ultimate combat for Chechnya's independence in Grozny.

Historical Note

The issue of rebellion has always been relevant in Chechen society, even during communist years. The last Chechen Robin Hood to fight the Soviet regime was killed as late as 1976.

The Archives of the Ministry of Internal Affairs of the Chechen-Ingush Autonomous Republic disclosed that Khasukha Magomadov was involved in 194 attacks and killed more than thirty people. His victims were mostly KGB members, including its regional head, Party and Soviet workers, and police and other security services' employees. For more than thirty-five years, Khasukha was an abrek.[23] It is rumored that he planned his own death. Old, sick, lonely, and tired of life on the run, at seventy-one he made his last stand in the mountains around Shatoi. In March 1976 Magomadov set up his camp in a canyon near the village of Benoi. Forces of the KGB, Ministry of Internal Affairs, and the army took part in his capture. The last abrek was killed fifty-four years after the establishment of Soviet power in Chechnya and eighteen years before the beginning of the Russia-Chechen war in 1994.

An Underrated Victory

The successful defense of Grozny on 31 December gave us a ray of hope that Russia would agree to negotiate. Sergei Kovalev's voice, shaking

---

23. In Chechnya, an *abrek* is a «bandit of honor» fighting his own guerilla war against the infidels.

with emotion at what he had seen in Grozny, echoed throughout the world, appealing to the international community and above all to the Russian leadership to stop the bloodshed. We believed that the world would demand an end to the murder of Chechens. How naive we were.

The actions and rationale of Russia leaders defied common sense. They claimed they were restoring order for Chechens, but they were killing those to whom they allegedly were bringing stability. They said they came to save Chechens from "bad" Chechens, but they massacred indiscriminately. To rescue us, according to such logic, it was necessary to slaughter us first. Corpses lying in the street of Grozny or the outskirts of villages did not need law and order. So why would we need justice from Russia. I want to live, to enjoy life, and to work. I want to see my home, my relatives, and my family. I want to love the world. I want to see the sun and the moon. And who are you, Russia, to deprive me of all this?

Only with the Chechen war did I begin to comprehend why our ancestors had tried to teach us that Russian rule would never be legitimate. Alienation from Russia was a lesson taught by Moscow to Chechens of my generation, who were born in the Soviet Union and came of age at the time of its collapse. Moscow made it clear why we should not love and respect its authority. It became the most important lesson of my life.

Strangely enough, in conversations with my fellow countrymen, I had not sensed hatred for Russians; but I was aware of contempt! Even in the midst of that awfulness, there were some who felt sorry for the dead Russian soldiers, unwanted and unclaimed by their army or their country. During a discussion in the street with a group of neighbors, an elderly relative of mine came up to curse us for being cruel to the "poor and weak" Russians and for not burying their dead. He demanded to be taken to Grozny to arrange funerals. We listened, so as not to hurt his feelings, but no one volunteered to go under the bombs to bury those who had invaded us.

Briefly, news from Grozny had made us hope that Russia would refrain from occupying us. Almost every household hosted refugees from Grozny. People fled the city once they understood that the Russian army did not value human life. They were the first internal refugees of the war, and we in Avtury would also become refugees if the army were to approach our village. The behavior of the army had ended any illusions that it might leave peaceful citizens alone. Its deeds had made it clear that Chechnya's population was to be treated as the enemy. Infuriated by its failure, the Russian army became dangerous not so much to the armed resistance as to ordinary people.

On 3 January war came to my village. A few miles away, in the town of Shali, Russian aircraft bombed the district hospital that had been there since the 1917 October Revolution. Chechens claimed hundreds of civilian dead, Russians acknowledged only fifty-five. The bombing could not have be a mistake because on all civil and military maps a red cross indicated the hospital. The hospital shelling may have been carried out to prevent it from treating wounded Chechen fighters. The realization that the Russian air force could target a civilian hospital and kill on the suspicion that it was treating rebels was a sobering thought. In Avtury we buried several people slain in the destruction.

From that day forward, Chechens learned to run at the appearance of Russian aircraft. In the early days of the war, many lives were lost because people spilled out into the streets to look at the bombs and missiles. Chechen honor also discouraged men from running and showing fear, especially in the presence of women and children. President Dudaev went on television to tell his fellow citizens that there was no shame in hiding to save their lives during air strikes.

After the hospital bombing, escape began, but Shali residents did not go very far; they moved into neighboring villages, in particular Avtury and Serzhen-Iurt. Those refugees needed a place to weather the storm before returning to their homes as soon as possible. People did not want to lose everything for the third time in a few generations. Thus, they clung to their homes, farms, and land. The general deportation of 1944 had deprived Chechens of their possessions; whatever they had been able to acquire during the years in Kazakhstan and Kyrgyzstan, they had to abandon before returning home. Once again, Chechens faced losing everything.

It became obvious that Avtury was the next target. My family decided to leave. After a brief discussion, it was agreed that I would stay in the village to guard the house and the rest of the family would move with its belongings to neighboring Dagestan, wherein Khasaviurt, local Chechens were taking in many refugees. I would remain at home because I was the most able to move around and had a safety net. My papers confirming that I was a graduate student at the Academy of Sciences in Moscow had always acted magically upon Russian soldiers. They may not have known what a graduate student was, but they had heard of the Academy of Sciences of Russia.

My family moved to Khasaviurt at the end of March; the Russians were expected in Avtury at anytime. Only one man per household stayed behind. Men stood by the gates of their homes for hours, staring into space. Hardly anyone slept that night; it was not fear that kept us awake but anticipation of the enemy. We did not expect mercy, but we dreaded mockery. If we were destined to die, we wished it would be without humiliation.

In the morning instead of the Russians, my cousin Kharon, who lived nearby, came running to let me know that my father's second cousin had died during the night. Dumbfounded, all I was able to say, unfortunately out loud, was, "Couldn't he have chosen another time to die?" We had to deal with his funeral and, because no other relative remained in the village, burial was physically and emotionally difficult. My cousin and I had to dig a grave two meters deep in the frozen ground and to honor all the Islamic traditions, namely to utter the formula *"La Illah Illa Lahi"* (There is no god but God) 77,000 times, which took several hours. Fortunately, we did not have to carry the body to the cemetery a few miles away as a neighbor was able to drive us. By the time we had finished, it was late afternoon. We were exhausted and had not realized that Russian troops had entered the village.

In the morning, the streets began filling with Russian military hardware. We developed a warning system. Anyone threatened with death or arrest should alert the rest of us by shouting in Chechen as loudly as possible. We would then try to prevent his being taken away; otherwise, finding him alive later would almost never happen. Russian soldiers went from one household to the next looking for something to steal. The most desirable items were carpets and all sorts of electronic equipment. Tanks and personnel carriers were packed with goods looted or received in exchange for a life. I was lucky; the lieutenant who came to my house was from Moscow. When he found out I had a Moscow residential registration, he asked me where I lived; and it turned out we lived from the same part of town. When he realized I was at the Academy of Sciences, he spoke to me respectfully, and quietly led his soldiers out. It was sheer good fortune. On that day in my village, the Russians did not kill anyone; it was surprising. There had been several detentions and a few men were taken away, allegedly for identification, to the military camp set up near the village. The looting did not bother us, we were happy to be alive.

We knew that on 5 February in Staraia Sunzha, a suburb of Grozny, drunken soldiers went on a rampage and, without any reason or accusation, killed Chechens who had stayed to protect their property. Children testified that they were also looking for guns. Finding no gun and not much to loot, they shot most of the adult males; they also shot and abused old women. News about these atrocities spread from village to village; after that, people fled not so much from bombs, but from drunken soldiers and their officers. Later, it became known that the Russian authorities had amnestied and released criminals and sent them as contract soldiers to Chechnya.

On 9 February, in the town of Argun where he lived, an exploding projectile injured my older brother Aslanbek. That day Russian tanks methodically obliterated the city; within small squares of a thousand square meters, they exploded shells in staggered rows. My brother and his family finally agreed to come to my village, where the situation was less dangerous. He received treatment with herbal drugs; and then they departed to become refugees in Dagestan.

Grozny Falls and Chechnya Is Overrun, March-May 1995

The Russian army entered Grozny in early January; it was only a question of time before Chechen fighters had to retreat. However, after two weeks of assaults the Presidential Palace was still in Chechen hands. On 13 January the Russians threw in their special forces in hopes that they would do better than the regular army. But over and over again their attacks petered out.

Psychological warfare played a role in the contest. The Chechen flag flew over the palace during battles and the Chechen anthem sounded continuously through speakers set on the roof. When Russians shot down the flagpole, Colonel Taimaskhanov, Staff Commander for Grozny, climbed under fire to raise the flag and reconnect the broken speaker wires. These symbols defied the Russian assault. After the Russians captured Grozny and hung their flag over the ruins of the palace, it was often replaced with the Chechen one at night.

Chechens clung to the Presidential Palace because they believed its fall would inspire a Russian of triumph. However, on 16 and 17 January Russians used bombs that cut through the concrete of the upper floors and reached the basement bunkers used by the staff. President Dudaev decided to abandon the palace before it became a mass grave for its defenders. By midday on 18 January Chechen fighters had left the palace, crossed the Sunzha River flowing to its left, and set up headquarters in the movie theater *Iunost'* (Youth), located only a few hundred meters from the burning palace. The location testified to the Chechen reluctance to go far from the palace. The theater, however, turned out to be a difficult target to defend, and headquarters moved again, further south, near Minutka square, into the bombed Second City Hospital. The last seat of the general staff was the ruins of the maternity hospital on Musorova Street.

On 5 March all Chechen army units left the capital; only Shamil Basaev's troops remained to cover the withdrawal. Basaev went on the defensive in southwest Grozny. His position was hazardous because of the Russian advance along the Urus-Martan-Grozny route and the possibility that the Russian ring around Grozny could be closed at any moment. Dudaev had to approve the retreat. After Maskhadov met with the president—relocated in the mountains of southwestern Chechnya—the order was given for the remaining troops to leave. For reasons that remain unclear, the Russian army never completed its encirclement of the city. It allowed the last Chechen combatants to escape through the narrow southern opening and seek refuge in the mountains. It is possible that the Russians had left that gateway open to force Chechen fighters out and to be able to claim victory.

Grozny held out for two and a half months. Having failed to win a decisive victory over the irregular Chechen troops in the streets of Grozny, the Russians destroyed the city. Block by block, they obliterated all high-rise buildings. For this reason, Russian television did not show films of captured Grozny. The city, built in 1818, lay in ruins. Later the famous western photo-journalist Thomas Dvorzhek said that in Grozny it was easy to film incidents of war since the material was available everywhere, that the devastation was total, and that he had not seen anything similar in any wars in which he had been involved: Afghanistan, Iraq, and Bosnia. Stanley Greene, another renowned photojournalist, commented that in Grozny he had had only two problems: to escape Russian bombs and to select what to film, as material was over abundant!

Upon leaving Grozny the general staff initially set up quarters in the town of Argun, ten miles from the capital. The command had not yet admitted the futility of fighting the Russian army in regular battles; with no aircraft or armored vehicles it still believed it could defeat the Russians in an open clash. Realization that this could not be done came in Vedeno, where for the first time Chechen forces avoided a formal battle in order to preserve their forces. In the next few months, Maskhadov and his staff changed course.

The behavior of people from Grozny was different from that of people in small rural towns and influenced Maskhadov's strategy. The Chechen population of Grozny was a recent migration. When the city was assaulted, Chechens returned to the villages of their origins, where they had family ties and most still possessed houses and land. In rural communities, on the other hand, people had no bonds outside of their villages. Forced into exile, they would have to go into unknown situations. In battles for Argun, Shali, and Vedeno, townspeople reluctantly supported the combatants. By bringing the war into villages, the Chechen army was losing civilian support. In order to force Chechnya to surrender, Russia terrorized civilians, as demonstrated by the brutality of Interior Ministry units in Samashki on 6 to 8 April, where hundreds were killed and injured, including children. Therefore, from March to May, Maskhadov rethought his strategy. He moved the general staff from Argun to the mountains, avoided set battles, and adopted classic guerrilla warfare.

Fighting in Grozny became a learning experience for Chechen patriots too young to have served in the Russian army. The main lesson was that the army feared by the whole world could be resisted. Fighting in Grozny was also a new experience for Russians. Their army was unable to perform simple tasks or achieve goals. It did not know how to react to civilian resistance. The army in Chechnya was made up of new recruits from all over Russia, who did not understand what they were doing there. Desertions in the early stages of the war reached two thousand, and high rates lasted through the first Chechen war.

My Thesis

My dissertation defense got entangled with the war in Chechnya. I had completed my work in 1994, but the Director of the Institute where I was a graduate student refused to set a date for my defense. He was fearful of a political repercussions were he to permit the defense of a thesis whose theme was the nineteenth-century Chechen resistance to the Russian conquest at a time when Russia was engaged in another war with Chechnya. To offend the Kremlin could have negative results for the Institute. This denial, for non-scientific reasons, angered my supervisor who, after a heated conversation, called the director a coward in the presence of many witnesses. For her it had not been easy; she had been at school with him. But she perceived my rejection as a personal challenge and as an expression of distrust of the Institute leadership toward her. After such a scandal, I had nothing to do at the institute and, as the war claimed the life of my sister's husband, I returned home.

Amidst problems of survival in Chechnya, I did not have time to think about my dissertation. So great was my surprise when Moscow journalists reaching Chechnya brought me a message from a Chechen friend. She had found out from my Caucasian fellow students that my supervisor was looking for me to give me urgent information. Via the satellite phone of foreign journalists, I was able to contact Dilara who, upon learning that I was alive, broke out in tears of joy then told me that I should come to Moscow without delay because my defense had been scheduled for early May! My Institute had a new director who, surprised at the decision of his predecessor, allowed my defense to proceed. He could not believe I was in Chechnya and not in Moscow.

By the end of April my family, unwilling to remain in Dagestan, returned to our village. My mother was reluctant to accept the charity of people unrelated to us for too long. As soon as the house-to-house searches were over, many decided to come back, my family among them. My decision to travel to Moscow was received with ambivalence; the farther I was from Chechnya the better, but I would also be out of reach.

I arrived in Moscow in early May and had little time to meet the bureaucratic standards required for the defense. Without the help of my Caucasian friends, I would have been overwhelmed. Some

67

typed my text, others, not trusting the mail, delivered my thesis. With their assistance, I managed to complete all formalities a day before my defense.

According to the rules of the Academy of Sciences, each defender had to have two "devil's advocates." My supervisor had been looking among her colleagues for a Caucasian specialist to be the main advocate. Upon arriving in Moscow, I learned that seven professors had refused the role without even having read my thesis! Against the backdrop of the war in Chechnya, they were afraid to be seen as supporting my work. We were losing hope when a sponsor presented himself. Dilara had been recounting her misfortune to a colleague from a different department, who had stepped into her office for a cup of tea. He told her that, having published work on the Caucasus, he could stand as my main advocate, if we were willing to accept him. His offer was like winning a lottery!

At the same time, my friends were searching for a secondary "devil's advocate" among North Caucasian junior professors. An Abkhazian, a fellow at the Institute of Ethnology, offered his services upon learning that a number of experts and specialists did not want to serve. Academics who I respected for their expertise refused to be on my panel. I tried to comprehend their motivation, but deep down I was angry at them. After all, I was presenting a dissertation, not a plan to capture Grozny; and scientists should hardly have anything to fear. Seven professors and eleven junior professors declined to participate in my defense because of the war.

Finding academics willing to be my advocates did not guarantee my passing the defense. A party in my institute, made up of supporters of the former director, had mobilized itself against my candidacy, wanting to punish me for bypassing his decision. One of them, a historian, claimed that my chance to become a doctor of philosophy was almost nil.

On the morning of the defense my supervisor told me to pay close attention to her as her expressions would be an indicator of how the defense was going. She seemed to be more worried than I, who was by then reconciled with the idea that I would fail. An unwritten rule at the Institute was that a new Ph.D. must provide food and drinks for members of the jury. I did not even bother to supply a table. Twenty-three out of twenty-four members of the jury—all members of my department—showed up. The former director recused himself, giving ill health as a pretext. Those who had vowed to ruin my defense sat in front rows of the jury room; all my Caucasian friends sat in the back.

A thesis defense at the Academy is a protracted event with ancient rules. I was asked first to present an overview of my study but, setting aside my prepared text, I talked only about what I believed were the strong points of my work. After I finished, the new director of the Institute unexpectedly said that my work was worth listening to attentively. My devil's advocates then spoke of my research's pros and cons and read an external reviewer's opinion from a member of the Institute of Oriental Studies. I had answered all their questions when the director, who was carefully looking through my text, made a startling remark to the jury: "Had we let Vatchagaev defend this thesis last year, maybe the Kremlin would have understood that it should not start a war in Chechnya!" This comment was a sign that the director was happy and, thus, that I had a chance to pass. I gestured to my Caucasian friends to run to buy drinks and something to eat. I realized from my supervisor's radiant face that what had seemed implausible a few hours ago had come to pass.

Moreover, the historian, who had predicted that my defense would have more votes against than in favor of passing, asked me for an article for the prestigious academic journal *Voprosy Istorii* (Issues of History). The jury even recommended publishing my thesis at the expense of the institute. Twenty-two members of the jury voted to pass me with only one abstention!

I had not expected such incredible success. I could not wait to get to my room to shout, I did it! The students at my dormitory gave me a feast. I felt I had passed an important hurdle, but at home there was a war and I knew that, after finishing the post-defense bureaucratic paperwork, I would be going back to Chechnya. I returned feeling like a victor, although the state of the Chechen forces was anything but victorious. As I arrived, the Russian army announced the capture of all mountain districts.

Chapter 6

ICHKERIA AT WAR

The Army of Ichkeria and the Influence of Sufism

Before leaving Moscow, I got all available publications on Chechnya. Sadly they revealed that few people understood who and what Russia was fighting. Most articles talked about the large and well-equipped Chechen army. They gave some incredible numbers, such as thirty to fifty thousand Chechen fighters.

From the beginning, of his tenure President Dudaev, a professional officer, tried to talk about the various Chechen military formations as part of an army. In fact, they were squads of individual commanders. For Dudaev and his chief of staff Aslan Maskhadov, also a military professional, to incorporate independent units into a single army structure was a matter of primary importance. They understood the danger for a young state of autonomous paramilitary units. Individual squads could be manipulated to intervene in political quarrels or to support vested interests, as in the case in the disputes between the Grozny mayor's office and the President in 1992 or between the Parliament and the President in 1993. In each case, some units, following their commanders, sided with forces opposing Dudaev.

Russian authorities regarded those multiple militias as the unified army of Ichkeria. Thus, they could claim that the Federation forces were facing a professional army and not individual fighters who had come down from their mountains to defend their freedom. How else could they explain the Russian army failure until at least the middle of March 1995?

Chechens typically fought without coordinating their actions with their general staff. Referral to the general staff occurred mainly when units ran out of ammunition, because `the general staff oversaw distribution. In theory, almost all military formations were under the flag of the general staff, but in the field they were mostly autonomous. Lack of coordination was most evident during the battle for Grozny. Men came from their villages to volunteer for fighting assignments. But those volunteers did not consider themselves conscripts and might (and did) withdraw at any time for any reason. This situation was confirmed by Dudaev, who after listening to undeserved reproaches from individual commanders would say, "I did not summon you to fight, you may leave at any time..."

Maskhadov tried to make combatants give up the habit of calling individual detachments by the name of their commanders. Instead, he urged them to start talking about the Armed Forces of the Republic of Ichkeria. But at a time when the general staff could only distribute a few bullets, the desire of its chief was seen as misrepresenting reality. When Chechens were forced to retreat from Grozny, they lost their largest source of arms from Boronovk base, which further complicated relationships between Maskhadov and the commanders, as well as between the various units.

Some units were known by the name of their well-known commanders, such as Basaev or Gelaev. But many of the forces fighting in Grozny volunteered either in groups, with or without a leader, or as individuals. Some joined existing detachments, but more often they took on a section of the front and led independent action. If they named their units, it was generally after some Sufi Sheikh.

Young men from the village of Komsomol'sk in Gudermes district came to Grozny and fought together anywhere help was needed, most often from Minutka Square to the Presidential Palace. Their commander was a prominent Moscow businessman who had left his business to fight for his country. Being wealthy, he could afford to buy unlimited quantities of weapons and ammunition and supply his squad with proper food and gooduniforms. The original feature of that unit was that it took the name of a sheikh of the Sufi Qadiri *tariqa* Ali Mitaev.

One idiosyncrasy of the first Chechen war was the importance of the Sufi factor. Following the example of the men from Komsomol'sk, many combatants gave their outfits the names of Sufi sheikhs, by that act showing themselves as disciples of the Sufi order following the precept of that sheikh. In Grozny there was a Kunta-haji detachment (after the Qadiri sheikh), a Tashu-haji of Sayasan detachment (after the Naqshbandi sheikh), an Iusup Koshkel'din detachment (after the Naqshbandi sheikh), and many more. Some fighters wore paraphernalia distinguishing them as followers of a specific Sufi *tariqa*. Tashu-haji disciples wore red bandanas over the Chechen hat, or *papakha*; Vis-haji followers wore white *papakhas*. Not all Sufi disciples displayed visible emblems; and some, Kunt-haji members for example, wore a distinctive skullcap or *pias* in the warm season only.

The Sufi element was of great importance. As most Chechens identified themselves with Sufi orders, the war for independence fought under Sufi banners got the support of almost the entire population. There were a few notable exceptions. Followers of the Naqshbandi order Deni Arsanov refused to accept the war for independence as a holy war, and therefore did not take arms against the Russians. In 1991 Boris Yeltsin had appointed the grandson of the founding sheikh Deni Arsanov as his representative in Chechnya. Failure of the Chechen government to recognize him as such led the active members of that order to side with the opposition to Dudaev.

The case of the Qadiri order Ali Mitaev is also atypical. Members of the Mitaev family, descendants of the founder of the order, Ali Mitaev, did not align themselves in the war with Russia. The head of the family was Shamil Mitaev, whose interests ranged from poetry to business; he had close ties to Chechen businessmen in Moscow. Shamil Mitaev did not come out in support of the war; nevertheless, he did not give the Russians an excuse to use him against Dudaev.

Shamil's lack of commitment to either side was interpreted in different ways by the followers of the Ali Mitaev order. Some, mostly older members, construed his silence as disapproval of the war and, therefore, decided it was not their war, because the descendant of their sheikh did not call them to war. Others concluded that, as Shamil did not denounce Dudaev, he supported independence. Shamil Mitaev considered that talks and declarations would not build a state, and he was unhappy with some of Dudaev's choices for ministers. Furthermore, having businesses in Moscow, he probably did not want to compromise his assets. After the war, he claimed to me that he had always been for an independent Chechen state, but that he opposed the government striving to achieve that goal because of its lack of professionalism in both politics and economics. He concealed his views to avoid exacerbating the descent into war.

The Sufi orders' backing of the government in Grozny was of prime importance to the political leadership of Ichkeria. It is incorrect to say that the two *tariqas,* Naqshbandi and Qadiri, found themselves on opposing sides. The Naqshbandi Tashu-haji and Iusup Koshkel'din orders were supporters of Dudaev, whereas the Naqshbandi Deni Arsanov order opposed him. Furthermore, many who considered themselves followers of Sheikh Deni Arsanov fought on Dudaev's side. Similarly, not all Qadiri disciples sided with the independence forces. The conflict was not between *tariqas* but between ideas—independence versus federalism; therefore, it is inappropriate to talk about a division of Chechen society along Sufi lines.

Historical Note

Opinions vary as to when Chechens adopted Islam. The dissemination of Islam stretched over many centuries. No Muslim grave predates the campaign of Tamerlane at the end of the fourteenth century; and no pagan burial is dated after the Imamate of Shamil in the mid-nineteenth century. Islam gradually penetrated Chechen society through voluntary acceptance, community after community. As Islam advanced, paganism receded. In the twelfth century, under the sway of neighboring Georgia, Christianity influenced Chechens. The decline of Georgia after the Mongol invasion in the thirteenth century led to the decline of Christianity among Chechens. By the end of the fourteenth century it had disappeared from Chechen mountain regions.

Islam in Chechnya is of the Sunni Shafi'i School. It is dominated by two popular tariqas, the Naqshbandi and Qadiri tariqas.[24] Each is divided into virds or orders. In present day society, the Naqshbandi tariqa is represented by twenty-three orders,[25] while the Qadiri tariqa

---

24. *Tariqa*: is a school or order of Sufism.

25. The Naqshbandi orders are known by the name of their founding sheikhs. The most active orders are: Tashu-haji of Sayasan, Iusup-haji Koshkel'din, Deni Arsanov, Doku-sheikh Shaptukaev, Abu-sheikh Aksai, Usman-sheikh Khantiev, and Solsa-haji Iandarov and others.

is represented by six orders. [26]

Sufi orders in Chechnya, remarkably, have kept the military structure they adopted during the Caucasian War of the nineteenth century. Depending on its distribution among the population, each order is divided into thousands, hundreds, and tens. An elected leader heads each subdivision. This system makes it easy to respond to events, be it war or peaceful political processes such as elections. In each settlement, leaders of the order control the organization of all matters.

Russian Prisoners of War

In the treatment of prisoners of war (POWs), nations show their level of culture and morality. Over the centuries Chechen society had developed its own way of dealing with captives. Because of the absence of class distinctions in Chechen society, POWs were most often kept with Chechen families. Such dispositions could be burdensome if they were not rapidly exchanged for fellow tribesmen. On the other hand, there were times when Chechens took prisoners and sought ransom. However, because present day society has integrated representatives of many nations, some were former prisoners who stayed within Chechen communities. Over time, they were given the same rights as Chechens and allowed to marry Chechen women.

Historical Note

Dozens of Chechen clans have assimilated representatives of neighboring nations. For example, a branch of the Tsikaroi clan bears the name of a Georgian, Taimuraz. Captured during a skirmish with Georgians, Taimuraz remained with the Tsikarois, became a full member of their clan, and married a Chechen woman. His descendants continue to be called the offspring of Taimuraz. Similar stories can be found among almost all mountain clans. In mountainous settlements, it is not uncommon to find "Georgian"

---

26. The Qadiri orders are also known by the name of their founding sheikhs. The undisputed leader, according to the number of its disciples and its dynamism, is the Kunta-haji of Ilskhan-Iurt order. The remaining five orders are: Bamat-Giri-haji, Ali Mitaev, Chimmirza Taumirzaev, Mani-sheikh Nazirov, and Vis-haji Zagiev.

quarters, a section where live Chechens whose ancestors came from Georgia.

During the colonization of Chechnya, Russians admitted that Chechens showed unusual compassion to their prisoners of war. Deserters had gone over to the Chechen side and settled in the villages of Dargo and Vedeno. Chechens refused to extradite them, even when threatened with the destruction of their villages.

During the revolutionary turmoil in 1917 and the outbreak of the civil war, Denikin's White Army took prisoner many North Caucasians. They were treated as slaves and often left to die of hunger and cold, circumstances unacceptable to Chechen culture. The military council of the Mountain Republic, after referring to the shocking conditions of Caucasians prisoners in Denikin's army, required their forces to share their last piece of bread with their prisoners.

The Russian army that invaded Chechnya in 1994 behaved toward POWs in a way similar to Denikin's. The capture of Chechens was an act of retaliation. Torture and murder were the norm for those prisoners.

Early in the war Russian POWs were already more afraid of their own compatriots than of their Chechen captors. Before the attack on Grozny, prisoners were kept in the basement of the Presidential Palace. Chechen and Russian wounded lay side by side, and no one ever thought to separate them. All were nursed by the mother of one of the Russian prisoners of war, who had come to Chechnya in search of her son. Russians and Chechens alike called her "mother." On the eve of the New Year, when a group of human rights activists came to Grozny to ask for the release of a few Russian prisoners, her son was the first to be freed. When she left with her son, she cried for the wounded she would leave behind.

Concern for prisoners' safety led to unexpected problems for Chechens. Most soldiers pleaded with their captors not to be returned to the Russian army. This request disturbed Aslan Maskhadov. He understood that in this unconventional war it was impossible to harbor POWs in safety because Chechen fighters and their command moved constantly to avoid being trapped. To drag prisoners along was dangerous and expensive; the larger the group, the harder it was to go unnoticed by the Russians.

The Chechen command wished to get rid of the burden. But Maskhadov could not bring himself to return prisoners when he knew that most would be jailed for desertion. He made it known that were parents of POWs to come to Chechnya, their children would be released into their custody on the condition they would never again show up in Chechnya bearing arms.

Although doubting such promises, most parents were reunited with their children. Back home, however, many former prisoners were prosecuted for treason. News of what former POWs faced at home spread rapidly. It made the situation worse for Chechens. Parents reunited with their children now refused to return home and begged Maskhadov to allow them to stay with their children. They were afraid that Chechens would be forced to turn their sons over to the Russians.

When in July 1995 General Vladimir Shamanov surrounded the village of Chiri-Iurt, where the Chechen general staff was stationed at the time, he demanded the POWs. The soldiers and their parents were held in the village school. The military commander, Isa Madaev, tried to delay a response to the ultimatum. In the end, however, he decided to give up the prisoners to save thousands of Chiri-Iurt residents. Maskhadov reacted angrily by this decision of Issa; he considered Madaev's action unacceptable, even if it saved Chechen lives. Maskhadov also argued in support of POWs with the Russian command. At each of his meetings with the Russians he insisted that they were not deserters, but prisoners of war.

Some of the Russian soldiers wanted to stay and fight for the Chechens, but they were dissuaded so as not to endanger relatives in Russia. This chivalry was not extended to members of the riot police, Special Forces, or contractor fighters who came to kill Chechens for money, or even to officers. The POWs killed in that war were from these groups.

Numerous stories have been published in Russia distorting the reality of those days. They refuse to recognize that Chechens behaved more humanely than those who came to teach them integration and friendship of peoples with bombs and fire. Such authors had obviously never been to Chechnya, confusing mountains and plains, names, events, villages, and years. Their goal was to erase the memory of what happened in Chechnya.

The issue of POW exchange was raised in 1995 during the first negotiations held between Russians and Chechens after Shamil Basaev's raid on Budennovsk. Negotiations took place on the Khankala military base near Grozny. A joint commission was created to address the exchange of prisoners. Aslan Maskhadov's adjutant took part in the talks and reported directly to Maskhadov, but agreement was not forthcoming. Russian authorities were looking for ways to circumvent the commission; therefore, Chechen POWs were charged as criminals in Russian courts.

Unfortunately some Chechens helped Russians to dodge the commission. Seeing one of them in Khankala, the Chechen delegation protested, but *was told that the man was paid to search for prisoners. Since Maskhadov insisted from the beginning that any exchange of prisoners should be according to the principle of "all Russians for all Chechens," the commission achieved nothing. Many times he demanded that General Romanov stop those sham negotiations and accused him of creating a slave market in Chechnya. The purchase and sale of people, therefore, began as early as 1995, fostered by Russian authorities.*

The Chechen Raid on the Rear Guard of the Russian Army, Budennovsk, June 1995

Shamil Basaev in an interview in early May stated that Chechen fighters should adopt guerrilla tactics. The successes that followed showed that such a strategy made sense against one of the most powerful armies in the world. The appearance of Chechen combatants in the city of Budennovsk was an incredible development. Budennovsk in the Stavropol' region is located 217 miles north of Grozny and 137 miles north of Chechnya's northern border. How could armed Chechens pass through as many as fifty-two military roadblocks! Their papers allowed the movement of loads issued as "cargo 200," that is as dead soldiers. Some saw this as a conspiracy between the militants and the Federal government.

The significance of Basaev's raid has not always been correctly interpreted. It has been described most often as an act of terrorism. Basaev's unit had been created to attack military targets in the rear guard of the Russian army. Its assault in Budennovsk was actually an attempt to pressure Russia to end the war by showing that Chechen fighters could appear anywhere. Later Basaev boasted that his real destination had been Moscow. A raid on Moscow was a fiction, but Basasev liked flamboyant speeches.

The original plans for an attack behind Russian lines were probably limited to the borders of the North Caucasus where numerous military objectives existed. Two-dozen Russian air force bases—out of a total of 245 for all of Russia—were there. Budennovsk's airfield housed warplanes and helicopters of the type used in Chechnya, making it an attractive target.[27]

---

27. The Budennovsk Air Base 6971 housed the 7th Aerospace Defense Brigade.

On 14 June 1995, Basaev's commando unit commenced operations at the Budennovsk air base and the police station. These attacks shocked the country. According to the official press, rebels in Chechnya had been eliminated, and Russian constitutional order had been restored. People could not comprehend the appearance of 100 armed Chechens outside of Chechnya doing battle deep in Russian territory. Basaev's forces eventually retreated to the hospital and took hostage the medical staff and patients. Later they justified their retreat by the need to get medical attention for their wounded, but helpless people had been made captives. In disbelief, Russians watched their government go down on its knees (in their opinion) in front of Chechen fighters and heard their Prime Minister on live radio hysterically begging Basaev to listen to him.

Legendary Russian Alpha and Vega commandos brought down from Moscow bogged down in their attacks against the hospital and caused casualties among the medical staff. The detainees, who thought they stood a greater chance of dying from Russian bullets than being shot by their Chechen captors, asked the Russian forces to leave.

Basaev was criticized for seizing the hospital; but should they have bargained with the Russians while standing in an open field to make it easier for the Russians to shoot them? His fighters were not martyrs. They had not gone on the raid to die, although they were well aware they could be killed. Their aim was to make Russia realize that Chechens could strike anywhere. Their demand for ending the stalemate in Budennovsk was the withdrawal of Russian troops from Chechnya. Basaev's unit suffered the loss of fifteen men plus sixteen wounded. The official casualty count was 129—of which thirty-five were acknowledged to be policemen and airmen from the base—with 415 injured. The media described the victims as mostly local civilians, while the Chechens suspected that most of those killed were servicemen and policemen. The victims' graves demonstrated that the Chechen assessment had been correct since most of the listed military or police ranks. Russian authorities promised to start negotiations, which began shortly after the end of the attack. They let Basaev and his men, hiding behind hostages, return to Chechnya where they were welcomed as heroes.

After the raid the minister of Russian internal affairs, the director of Special Forces, and a number of deputy prime ministers resigned.

The political consequences of the raid nullified all of Russian's victories because it led to the signing of the Khasaviurt Agreement according to which Russia de facto and de jure lost sovereignty over Chechnya. The raid also revealed the unpreparedness of the Russian government, security services, army, and society for attacks on their territory. The Russians at last dealt directly with the Chechen government and stopped putting forward Chechen puppets brought down from Moscow. Among Chechens the raid sparked the idea that, because Russia had initiated it, the war could be taken into its territory. And finally, it gave Chechens a respite before hostilities resumed.

Many questions about the raid remained unanswered. How could Basaev have managed to organize a military operation in the Russian rear guard in such a short time? It is probable that the original plan was more modest. The group had to have contacts in the area, connections with, if not all of the military checkpoints, at least with some of the largest, plans of the military base in Budennovsk, and much more.

Negotiations as an Indicator of Russian Politics

Negotiations began shortly after the raid. Moscow tried to spin its point of view by insinuating that it had defeated the Chechen fighters and that it was now negotiating with them to get their recognition of a Russian victory. Chechens believed that forcing the Russians to negotiate with the combatants was a concession from the Kremlin, which had repeatedly insisted on "no negotiations with rebels."

The whole process was arduous. Chechens of all ranks and levels had to learn to negotiate. The Chechen delegation had to travel every day from the mountain village of Benoi to Grozny. It had to pass through dozens of military checkpoints where conflicts arose, despite Russia's promise not to hinder Chechen movements. The checkpoints tried to obstruct the delegation headed by Aslan Maskhadov in a number of ways, but backed down when confronted by Maskhadov's guards. Nonetheless, getting to Grozny took hours.

The delegation was generally accompanied by large numbers of fighters. As a result checkpoints began ignoring their movements. In Grozny the population grew bold as well. Any vehicle or military equipment displaying the Chechen symbol was met with enthusiasm.

Russian troops, on the other hand, waving to screaming children were greeted with raised middle fingers.

A detachment of Dudaev's presidential guard set up quarters in a garage a few hundred yards from the Russian military base on the road to Khankala. Soldiers from the base fired at the garage; and initially the guards felt uneasy, but eventually they became inured to the fire. The guard's presence in Grozny was important as a symbolic return of Chechens to their city.

A mission from the Organization for Security and Cooperation in Europe (OSCE) organized the conference procedures. The mission came to the village of Benoi to meet with Maskhadov and was present at the first meetings with the Russians. It was an important moment for the Chechens, who had insisted on the presence of international organizations at the proceedings to give them international recognition.

Heading the Russian delegation was the Commander of Russian Forces in Chechnya, General Anatoly Romanov, a tall, slender, and arrogant man who posed as the conqueror of the Caucasus. He never acknowledged the guards accompanying Maskhadov, even though the talks took place in one large room with all present. One day, after hours of discussion, he took leave of Maskhadov and was about to depart when he saw through the window a group of protesting Chechens moving toward the building. The Russian's attitude changed instantly. His pride forgotten, he shook hands with everyone he had previously ignored, while glancing furtively toward the window. Shaken, his face reddened, he obviously was playing for time. Were he to leave, his armored personnel carrier would have to drive the short distance to the Khankala base through a crowd of angry people whose intentions were unclear. The crowd shouted slogans aimed against Russian troops and against the General personally. They demanded the removal of Romanov and and his troops from Chechnya and an end to the killing. As the farewells were dragging on, Maskhadov, in Chechen, asked his guard to escort Romanov through the screaming crowd and to accompany him and his vehicle to the gates of the base. He had not wanted it understood that he had guessed the General's fright. Like Romanov, most Russian generals, when they first met Chechens showed their contempt; but they eventually revised their attitudes.

Russian officers who came to negotiate with Maskhadov dropped their condescending attitude within an hour of meeting him. They rapidly understood that they were dealing not just with a former Soviet officer, but with a man who was impossible to frighten with threats. One day, in a canvas tent set up on the outskirts of the small village of Malye Atagi, talks took place between the Russian generals Tikhomirov and Pulikovski and the Chechens Maskhadov and Saidaev, the latter a former major in the Soviet Army. Discussions centered on the attacks on civilians. Angrily listing numerous violations of the truce, Mumadi Saidaev repeatedly used the familiar form of address when speaking to the generals. After a while, Pulikovski turned to Maskhadov requesting, "Aslan Alievich, would you please ask him [Saidaev] not to address me as thou." That exchange made clear the generals' opinion of their Chechen counterparts. Recognizing Maskhadov's authority, they talked to him with civility. They referred to Saidaev by his surname, but with Maskhadov they used the formal patronymic form of address. Maskhadov was conversant with the etiquette and followed its rules during negotiations.

While awaiting agreement on the issues under discussion, we had to pass the time; and some of us managed to have informal conversations with the staff officers accompanying their generals. A major bitterly complained to us that for everyone the day would end in two or three hours, while he would have to sit up all night redrafting minutes of the meetings. Puzzled, we asked why the minutes had to be revised after the heads of the two delegations had signed them. He explained that after each meeting with Maskhadov, he had to rewrite the minutes, rephrasing what the generals had said and how they had said it. It turned out that all those respectful patronymic addresses such as "Aslan Alievich" and good will references such as "we are all officers" or "let's agree" had to be replaced by "I order you, Maskhadov," "no one will bully the Russian army," and "if you are sitting here, it is only because we allow it." The text had to include remarks such as "then Commander so and so slammed his fist on the table," "the commander abruptly stood up to leave the negotiations," "the commander said 'son of a bitch,'" and similar descriptions. The new draft had to show that Russian officers dominated the talks.

Historical Note

Listening to the staff major I was reminded that in the nineteenth century Russian commanders, defeated by Chechens, reported their campaigns in such a way that Saint Petersburg rewarded them with decorations and promotions. At the battle of Dargo in 1845, Prince Mikhail Vorontsov lost his army and barely escaped capture by Chechens. The report he presented to the Emperor of his operations against mountain Chechens earned him an elevation from Prince Vorontsov to His Serene Highness Prince Vorontsov, and Nicholas I let him rule over the Caucasus as viceroy for another nine years.

The display of the Ichkerian flag by negotiating commissions maddened the Russians. One day, members of the Commission for Missing Persons had to go to Shatoi to verify information about Russian POWs held there. After the village of Starye Atagi, at the entrance to the Argun canyon, the commission was stopped at a checkpoint manned by paratroopers. They demanded the removal of the Chechen flag displayed on its car to allow the commission to proceed into "their" territory. The commission's chairman pointed out that Russia did not have power over Ichkeria and that Chechens could move freely in Chechnya, no matter the Russians' desire. As the paratroopers refused to budge, a member of the commission, Maskhadov's adjutant, demanded to be put through to their commanding officer. The commander began talking about "their" territory, but the adjutant told the commander that he was violating the truce agreement and threatened to report him to his superiors in Grozny. The commission was allowed to proceed to Shatoi with its flag flying. Balavdi Beloev, the Chechen commander from Borzoi, alongwith several cars full of armed men, joined the commission on its journey back to Grozny. No Russian checkpoints, including the paratroopers' post, dared to stop them. In occupied Chechnya, it was a psychological victory over the Russian army.

Russian troops in Chechnya behaved in a way reminiscent of the anarchist brigades during the civil war following the collapse of the Russian Empire in 1917. Soldiers decorated their tanks and armored personnel carriers with symbols of the Soviet Union and not of the Russian Federation! It was their way of protesting against the collapse of the Soviet Union and the new Russian Federation. It was amusing and repulsive at the same time to see that they did not even know under which flag (Soviet or Russian) to fight.

Grozny after Budennovsk

In the summer of 1995, Sophie Shihab, a well-known journalist from the French newspaper *Le Monde*, arrived in Chechnya. We drove to Grozny where negotiations had begun. At the delegation's head-quarters we met Il'ias Akhmadov with whom I had worked in 1992 at the Ministry of Foreign Affairs when Shamil Beno was minister. Akhmadov was an interesting conversationalist in that his analyses of events were thoughtful and he had a sense of humor. We learned afterward that he was seriously ill but that the situation did not allow him to leave the Republic to seek treatment. Akhmadov introduced us to Khusein Iskhanov, Maskhadov's adjutant, with whom I later went through many ordeals.

To my surprise, one of my relatives turned out to be a friend of a close companion of Shamil Basaev. My relative organized a meeting at his home. Having learned about the presence of a French journal-ist, two members of Basaev's inner circle joined us. Sophie Shihab and I were enthusiastic since all three had taken part in the raid on Budennovsk. In particular they claimed that the fighting began on the military base where their side killed many pilots and only later continued into town with the local police.

Listening to these stories along with Sophie Shihab, I often won-dered how much truth was in them. I had the impression at times that what we were told was, to put it mildly, unreal. At a meeting of Chechen women, for example, one woman tearfully reported how Russian soldiers had snatched her one-year-old son from her bosom and smashed his head against their personnel carrier to kill him. I was horrified, but I later learned that she had no children! Why the need to invent such tales when thousands of real stories were enough to plunge listeners into a state of terror. Some invented events to be in the spotlight; but one must realize that people can easily lose their sense of reality when confronted by the horrors of war.

Chapter 7

ASLAN MASKHADOV

My Acquaintance with Aslan Maskhadov

After our introduction in Grozny my acquaintance with Khusein Iskhanov developed. He wanted me to meet Maskhadov and several times offered to organize an encounter. I did not want to visit Maskhadov just to meet him, but Iskhanovev entually got his way. He claimed that Maskhadov had asked to see me. I wondered what he could want from me if, of course, it was not a fabrication by Iskhanov.

We drove for a long time from my village to the godforsaken village of Gansolchu in the Nozhai-Iurt mountain district where Maskhadov had settled temporarily. The village consisted of a few houses scattered on the slopes; it had no paved streets or roads. We arrived at the house of one of Maskhadov's guards, where women were busy preparing food for Maskhadov and his guests. It was getting dark, and I wondered how I would get back home since the Russians often erected temporary roadblocks at night.

In the late afternoon Maskhadov summoned me. He greeted me with a smile, but it turned out that he met everyone who came to him with a smile. He said that Iskhanovhad had spoken of me and had told him that I was a professional historian educated in Moscow. I explained that I defended my dissertation during the war. He replied that not everyone had to fight, some had to help. He was obviously trying to put me at ease. Throughout the night Maskhadov asked me questions about history, particularly about earlier Chechen wars with Russia. He could not comprehend why some Chechens cooperated with the Russians. I explained that collaboration was not rare, that in all wars some allied themselves with the Russians to gain power, confident that having power they could marginalize the Russians. Few succeeded. He was also interested to know about the Moscovites' reaction to events in Chechnya. Maskhadov seemed to me naive and a bit of a romantic in his belief that this Chechen war would change the course of history.

At dawn, we broke for prayer and a few hours of sleep. What I saw in the guards' rooms so surprised me that Maskhadov smilingly told me, "I have more faith in God than in my guards." The sentries were asleep! I questioned Maskhadov about security measures because there were Russians all around. He took me behind the house and showed me a height occupied by Russians. Had they known how slack Maskhadov's men were, they would have arrested him a long time before.

Maskhadov asked me, if it was not against my principles, to help him organize the propaganda department of the general staff. The title sounded impressive; it really meant helping him prepare texts, letters, and statements. I had always been anti-militaristic and did not want too close an association with the military; but that job was agreeable to me, and I accepted. Maskhadov smiled; and that time it seemed to me that his smile was sincere, not simply for the sake of civility and respect for Chechen etiquette.

Before leaving, I asked Maskhadov why he chose that specific village as a safe haven. The answer was logical from a military standpoint. The Russian military used old maps of Chechnya made in Soviet times. None of those maps indicated a road leading to the village. Russians did not expect him to be there and obviously had not verified that the maps were up to date. This allowed him and his men to travel along paths without being fired upon.

My Work at the General Staff of the Ichkeria Armed Forces

It was actually presumptuous to talk about a general staff. The staff only consisted of Aslan Maskhadov, his adjutant Khusein Iskhanov, and two men responsible for funds and electronic communications respectively, Islam Khalimov and Ali Dimaev. In practice the General Staff of the Chechen Armed Forces was Aslan Maskhadov himself.

My job originally consisted of preparing material on issues that interested Maskhadov, such as the history of relations between Chechnya and Russia, Sufism in Chechen society, the status of Russia in world politics, the standing of various international organizations, and their possible involvement in Chechnya. I did additional work, of a more sub-versive nature, with Khusein Iskhanov. I did not report to Maskhadov daily since I did not need his approval on every detail. If approval was needed, he was consulted and never challenged our activities.

My other duties were mostly self-defined. One consisted of writing leaflets, a half-page maximum on various subjects, which Iskhanov and I distributed in Grozny and at checkpoints while standing in line for inspection. A set of flyers, for example, called the Russian soldiers' attention to their officers who "were eating their money." Iskhanov and I invented orders of the Ministry of Defense, allegedly directing that soldiers serving in Chechnya be paid twelve to fifteen thousand rubles and be given two weeks leave. We hoped to sow doubt about their officers in their minds.

Another set of leaflets, printed in a thousand copies, had an unex-pected effect. The text claimed that on the Khankala base an officer tortured and humiliated his own soldiers. Shortly after we handed it out, in a meeting with Maskhadov, General Pulikovski put the pam-phlet in front of Maskhadov and asked him to stop its distribution. "We served in the same Soviet Army, Aslan Alievich," he implored. "Order your people not to do such nasty things." I wondered what might have happened on the base for Pulikovski to have made such a request of Maskhadov. We did not stop our subversive activities. The only person who disagreed with my method was the staff member responsible for funds, a Salafist who argued that Muslims should not stoop to the level of Christians! Maskhadov did not object and we proceeded with the work. We organized a support group in Grozny and replicated and spread our flyers throughout the city without the risk of carrying them through checkpoints.

In early 1996, individuals or individual groups carried out most of the attacks on Russians in Grozny. Nonetheless, Maskhadov received reports from different commanders taking responsibility for those operations, and often for the same ones. This was not because money was allocated to the most active units, but mostly due to a lack of coordination between squads, and also because the real attackers shared information with members of other units. The perpetrators themselves remained in shadows. Living in a Grozny full of Russian troops, they had to hide their presence and identities.

Drawing on these episodes, Iskhanov and I decided to create a mythical, non-existent squadron with a resounding name, which would help the attackers remain unnoticed and stop the contradictory reports reaching Maskhadov. We made it known that a new Hezbollah commando unit had been created. We did not mention that in the Middle East Hezbollah was a pro-Iranian Shia organization; we simply liked its meaning, Party of Allah. We spread stories about Hezbollah in our leaflets. Our imaginary squadron quickly gained popularity in Grozny. Its heroic deeds were recounted in colorful wording, and people even swore to us they knew some of its members. Our aim had been achieved. Maskhadov stopped receiving ambiguous reports; the only ones reaching him were those emanating from commanders whose men had truly taken part in some action.

To step up psychological pressure, our imaginary commando unit passed fictional death sentences on Russian officers. Our handouts alleged Hezbollah had in its possession the home addresses of pilots, which of course was impossible. They also announced a false operation conducted in Russia to eliminate an officer who had fought in Chechnya and who had been accused of crimes against humanity. Interestingly, no one ever called our bluff on these stories.

Most of my work on the General Staff was propaganda aimed at undermining the Russian military. We had proof of the effectiveness of our tactics when Russian generals brought our flyers to the negotiation table and begged Maskhadov to stop the actions of our fake commandos. Twice, our pamphlets were brought up at meetings—those concerning pilots' addresses and the shooting of former officers.

I was also responsible for organizing Maskhadov's interviews. Journalists learned that to see Maskhadov, they had to contact me. In that way, I became acquainted with many journalists from around the world.

A Delegation from Europe to Aslan Maskhadov

In early December 1995, an unofficial foreign delegation met with Maskhadov. It was composed of a member of the British House of Lords, a well-known French journalist, a doctor, a retired British army officer, and Marie Bennigsen-Broxup. I met the delegation in Moscow, and we boarded a flight to Makhachkala, capital of Chechnya's neighbor, Dagestan. Iskhanov was waiting for us at the airport; he had procured false papers and brought an escort to accompany us to Maskhadov. The escort consisted of Chechens from the pro-Russian administration's police. Iskhanov knew them well and was sure that they would not betray us. On the road to the Chechen border there were several permanent military checkpoints. Because the Chechen pro-Russian police in a marked police car accompanied us, the delegation got to the border without incident.

Even the police could not guarantee that in Chechnya we would not encounter an FSK (former KGB) checkpoint along the main highway; therefore, we took a road through the mountains to our meeting with Maskhadov. With difficulties—because mountain tracks were treacherous—we reached our destination by evening. The delegation's accommodations were on the outskirts of the village of Alleroi where Maskhadov was also staying. It was housed with Maskhadov because it was a way of honoring the members, but also for safety. Should Russian troops move against the village, the delegation could slip away. Maskhadov was happy to welcome such guests. They talked most of the night about Chechnya, the war and its outcome, and future prospects. Maskhadov wanted to understand why the West was afraid of Russia when a handful of Chechens had showed the world that there was no effective Russian army.

After two nights with Maskhadov, I took the delegation to Avtury, where it settled in at my family home for the rest of its stay. The living arrangements, food, and other social customs were strange to my guests. They were amazed that my mother set the breakfast table as if it was for dinner. But they quickly got used to our hearty morning meals.

Our first trip to Grozny shocked my guests. It was one thing to watch the few news reports of Grozny's destruction on television and another to ride through the streets. It was like driving through a Hollywood movie set. Roads were blown apart, and we had to wind our way between blasted armored vehicles and destroyed houses. There was no gas, electricity, or basic amenities. Frankly, the people did not care; they were happy to be alive. In that devastation they went on with their lives, selling, buying, trading, or looking for jobs. People were even generous to the dirty and hungry Russian soldiers begging for food and cigarettes at checkpoints.

During trips to the countryside Marie Bennigsen-Broxup observed that the army was not interacting with the population. You never saw officers or soldiers talking to local people. She was amused by what she witnessed at the market in Argun. We stopped at a small market right off the highway to find something to take to my mother for dinner; and we were buying jars of cucumbers at fifteen rubles a can, when a Russian officer barged in and told the vendor "quick, give me a can of cucumbers for fifteen rubles." Without raising her voice, the woman replied, "Fifteen rubles is not for you, you murderer; it is for Chechens. You can have it for twenty or get out." The officer left, and Marie asked her if she was not afraid he might come back and harm her. "And what else can he do besides what he has already done to me and my people? We have ceased to be afraid of them."

When visiting a market in Grozny, the French journalist was surprised that it was well supplied even offering bananas. She had expected to find Chechens lying in the streets dying of hunger. That, however, would not be Chechnya; war or not, life did not stop and customs did not change. It was incomprehensible to me, and somewhat offensive, when she began to cry over a legless dog. I was shocked. I had seen hundreds of people maimed for life by Russian bombs and bodies unburied because people had no strength to dig graves in the winter. I had seen thousands of displaced people; and I could not accept those tears for a wounded dog, which, of course, was no less to be pitied than a man.

Grozny is sitting on a field of petrol. The British lord had heard me saying that in Grozny oil comes to the surface. He did not believe me and asked me to show him. Iskhanov and I took him to the basement of a ruined building that was bathed in oil. In a nearby ruined factory we came upon two men who became flustered at the sight of us. After we explained what we were looking for, they showed us how oil sprang like a fountain if you dug only a few meters. They told us that they fill large cans and drive them to villages, where the oil is distilled into gasoline. The last information struck the British lord as doubtful since he knew that it was not possible to refine gasoline directly from raw petroleum; and he questioned the men's story. To his annoyance, we reminded him that he had not believed that oil surfaces in Grozny.

Next, we took the lord to a location where oil was refined in the fields using artisanal methods. In one field we saw more than two-dozen smoking devices. The owner of one of those mini-plants confirmed how fairly good gasoline could be produced using primitive techniques. The oil was put into pits, ten feet deep and twenty-three to thirty-three feet wide, and burned for days to separate the refined fuel. In blockaded Chechnya, where no gas was imported, cars were running on that homemade gasoline.

The lord went from one pit to another. No one in London would believe that there was no need for refineries; a large pan was enough to distill gasoline! These primitive methods created an ecological disaster because the residue remained in the soil, which was permanently destroyed, and the whole area poisoned with black smoke. People living in the vicinity of those primitive plants had major health issues, and the death rate among infants was the highest in the country.

The Chechen Raid into Kizliar-Pervomaiskoe, January 1996

Negotiations were periodically interrupted by Russian army maneuvers. The Russians could not forgive Shamil Basaev for the raid that forced them to the table. Some Chechens, however, were also resentful of Basaev's success. Salman Raduev, a former district Komsomol leader and son-in-law of President Dudaev, coveted Basaev's national laurels. Only his envy could account for the second raid to the Russian rear guard in January 1996. A Chechen detachment commanded by Raduev was to attack a helicopter regiment quartered in the outskirts of the Dagestan town of Kizliar, actually a large village with a population of slightly more than 40,000 that bordered on Chechnya.

On 9 January, world news agencies began reporting the Chechen attack on Kizliar; but Raduev's raid only vaguely resembled Budennovsk. Raduev entered the town with two hundred fighters. Everything went wrong. The helicopters, except for two that were out of service, had left the base. Since destroying broken helicopters would not bring him fame, Raduev decided to seek action in the town itself. He tried to capture the hospital; but instead he encountered the police in a shootout in which he lost two-dozen fighters and decided to retreat. Taking hostages, he withdrew towards the village of Pervomaiskoe, where he was stopped by Russian troops with whom he unsuccessfully attempted to negotiate a safe passage to Chechnya.

Both sides prepared for battle. The Chechens managed to dig a network of trenches all over the village, forcing residents as well as captured riot policemen to participate in the work. On January 15, Federal Special Forces stormed Pervomaiskoe. Ten helicopters appeared above the village and launched missile strikes at a position held by Chechens. They were followed by a salvo of 85-mm guns, which in a similar situation had been found to be ineffective; as a result, some shells flew over the village and hit the Russian troops. The attack was repulsed.

The next day Pervomaiskoe was again under fire. Raduev would never be a second Shamil Basaev; on the contrary, he evoked pity. His command was taken over by Khunkerpasha Israilov and Turpal-Ali Atgeriev. They prepared for the next battle while looking for a way out. Meanwhile, Yeltsin claimed on television that every Chechen fighter was being watched by a Russian sniper; "if a fighter moves, so does the sniper," he claimed, miming a sniper aiming his gun. Yeltsin's performance was widely ridiculed.

On the morning of 17 January, the Air Force fired missiles at the village; and Alpha Special Forces moved in and began house-to-house searches, during which two Alpha men were killed by friendly fire. Eventually, the village was razed to the ground. The Chechens, to the Russians complete surprise, were able to escape being encircled by crossing the Terek River helped by the presence of a gas pipeline. As usual, the Russians had acted according to the principle that Chechens could not perform as an experienced armed force. During all that time, in Gudermes, the Chechen district bordering on Dagestan, fighters gathered to help their comrades trapped in Pervomaiskoe.

Thirty-four people were killed in the town of Kizliar and thirty-one died in Pervomaiskoe. Aslan Maskhadov announced the losses suffered by Raduev's commando force. This bungled operation cost the lives of fifty-three fighters. Many were buried in the cemetery of Tsatsan-Iurt, where there was later erected a memorial in honor of victims of Chechen wars fought for freedom.

The only good result of Raduev's raid was that members of his squadron had shown courage. Surrounded and without communications with home, they did not surrender; and they were enthusiastically welcomed home. However, there was a difference between the welcome given Raduev's men and the reception that had greeted Basaev's commandos. People rejoiced to see Raduev's men alive, but they did not receive them as champions. Basaev's men had been hailed as heroes because they forced Russia to seek an armistice.

In Moscow, Doku Zavgaev, head of the Russian-backed Chechen government, commented on the raid insisting that there should be a dialogue within Chechnya to resolve the crisis by peaceful means. Few were interested in his opinion. President Dudaev in one of his televised speeches disingenuously thanked Zavgaev, but noted that his only service to his country was the money he was diverting to the rebels from the budget allocated to him by the Federal government for his administration. Although, Dudaev's insinuations may have been an attempt to discredit Zavgaev, everyone understood that there was some truth to his words.

Chapter 8

THE POLITICAL
FORCES IN PRESENCE

The Pro-Russian Chechen Opposition during the War

When the war started in December 1994, it was obvious that Moscow did not intend to rely on its former protégés, Avtorkhanov, Gantemirov, or Labazanov, who had proved to be disappointing. When Russian tanks moved into Chechnya, people who had fallen into oblivion after 1991 followed them. Moscow relaunched the old Communist guard, most particularly, the last Secretary of Chechen-Ingush Regional Party Committee, Doku Zavgaev.

It was an understandable choice. The social and intellectual standing of the old guard was much higher than that of the likes of Avtorkhanov, Gantemorov, or Labazanov. Former Chechen Communist leaders owed a debt to Moscow for the carefree existence they had enjoyed after the collapse of the Soviet Union. And for a not unimportant reason: through them Moscow was establishing continuity with the former legitimate power of the USSR. This continuity was selective of course; Moscow had been overturning most of the laws that the Soviet Parliament adopted in the last years of its existence, keeping only those that helped the Russian Federation establish control over breakaway regions.

Most Chechens saw the "second coming" of Doku Zavgaev as a bad joke. Chechnya had been experiencing a revival of Islam, and the return of an atheist former Communist leader was seen as an insult to religious feelings. Moscow may have made a mistake by getting Zavgaev out of retirement, but it seemed that it had no one else in reserve. The pool from which Moscow could select ministers for its new pro-Russian Chechen government was so limited that it had to assign people working as advisers or assistants in the various organs of the Federation Council and the Federal Parliament.

Members of the pro-Russian Chechen government generally viewed themselves as hostages in Moscow's game with pro-Dudaev Chechens. None dared to move freely within Chechnya. They lived in a temporary city built especially for them within Grozny and were guarded by the army, FSK (former KGB), and Interior Ministry forces.

The head of the pro-Moscow government was in no better position. Doku Zavgaev was flown daily from Mozdok in North Ossetia, where the largest military base of the Northern Caucasus was located, or was driven from Severny (Grozny airport) to appear on television. For safety reasons, most of his meetings and appointments were held at the Grozny airport, and the road to it was guarded by Russian troops. Among Chechens, Zavgaev became known as "Doku airportovich."

It was a time when all sorts of scammers made fortunes. A scheme run by the trade minister, a brother of Doku Zavgaev, consisted of buying second-grade fabrics, bringing them to Mozdok, and selling them at high prices. The Rebels were subsequently accused of attacking warehouses and burning the remaining stock, which allowed the swindlers to fake bills for fabrics already sold. Unsold fabrics were sent to Siberia, where the scam started again and high prices were also blamed on Chechen militants. Con men made hundreds of millions of dollars in just a few such schemes.

Akhmad Zavgaev became trade minister during the second coming of his brother. In his village of Beni-Iurt in the Nadterechny district, he was not a poor man. In the period of revolutionary upheavals, he had suffered at the hands of his fellow villagers who plundered his property. Rumor had it that when Doku Zavgaev was appointed head of the pro-Moscow administration in early 1995, his brother opened the door of his house and told his fellow villagers they had twenty-four hours to return his stolen items or he would denounced them for robbery committed in 1991. He seemed to regain quite a lot of property.

Former members of the Communist nomenclature knew why they had come back to Chechnya, to take revenge. They believed that the time had come to avenge themselves for all the wrongs inflicted upon them by supporters of independence. Members of the pro-Russian administration can be divided into several categories. First were those who sought power to make money from their own people. At a 1997 hearing of the State Duma considering the economy of the North Caucasus and Chechnya especially, the numbers presented astounded Chechens, who had never heard of funds invested by Moscow for the restoration of their destroyed economy. A second category consisted of those who had to go along with the Russians. They or members of their families, for example, had committed some criminal offense. Often they had been recruited in Soviet times and were unable to get out of their entanglement. They seemed more compassionate than the first group. A final category was made up of those who saw nothing wrong in staying in their jobs, no matter who was in power. Most often, they were part of the creative intelligentsia. In Chechen public opinion members of that last group, while disliked, were not viewed as enemies.

Following Russia's example, the pro-Moscow government took from Dudaev's decrees and regulations what they could use, even if officially they rejected all of them. Such was the case of the Chechen Academy of Sciences. During the Soviet period, there was no Chechen academy nor any branch or institute associated with the Academy of Sciences of the USSR. Dudaev created the Chechen Academy of Sciences, and the new authorities had never declared it illegal. To this day, it is operating on the basis of Dudaev's decree. The fact was that many in the pro-Moscow administration wanted the title of academician, even in a modest Chechen academy. Thus, the Academy had members who, under normal circumstances, would not be allowed to teach secondary school, not to mention being associated with higher education.

Remarkable also was the behavior of those the pro-Russian authorities had nominated as the heads of towns and districts. Many of them subsequently refused their assignments, claiming they had been appointed without their knowledge, which was hard to believe. Many who served moved to the Grozny quarter erected for the pro-Moscow political elite, under the protection of the FSK.

In Grozny, according to the Minister of Information of the pro-Russian government, the central office of FSK had more than 800 employees. Their task was not to hunt all over the mountains for Dudaev and Maskhadov, but to restore the former KGB network of agents, since the lack of a functional network impaired the FSK's work in the republic. The FSK had lost data when in 1991 Chechen revolutionaries destroyed the archives of the KGB. There were rumors that copies of the primary database were preserved in Moscow. Nonetheless, Chechens were not particularly aware of the FSK's activity during the first war.

The pro-Moscow administration did not even pretend to act on behalf of Chechnya. As a result, everything that Russia's henchmen tried to do alienated Chechens. Even the government's attempts at presenting itself as "independent," by criticizing the actions of the Russian Army were pathetic. In the first months of rule, members of the pro-Russian administration realized that it would never be possible to return to the old days. For the majority of Chechens they were traitors. Realizing their own futility, many tried to resign and flee Chechnya.

Salafists in Chechnya

The first Chechen war was a turning point for local Salafists who had first appeared in Chechnya in 1987, but had largely gone unnoticed. They lived by themselves and survived mostly due to the ideological support of the larger Dagestani Salafi community. The number of their supporters had been declining rapidly before the outbreak of the war. Ninety-nine percent of the Chechen population adhered to Sufism, and the impact of that small group was negligible.[28]

The Salafist influence increased with the arrival in Chechnya in early 1995 of Sheikh Fatkhi, a Chechen from Jordan, and Emir Khattab, an Arab from Saudi Arabia. They were both veterans of the wars in Afghanistan and Tajikistan, where they allegedly waged *jihad* against Russians. The decisive factor in their move to Chechnya was probably Sheikh Fatkhi's ethnicity; he was a descendant of Chechens who migrated to the Ottoman Empire in the nineteenth century and settled in Jordan.

Sheikh Fatkhi and his partner Emir Khattab arrived in Chechnya

---

28. The chief Salafist ideologue was Akhmad Mataev, better known as Akhmad the One-Legged from the village of Bachi-Iurt. His views were closer to those of the Muslim Brotherhood than to Middle Eastern Salafists.

with a large sum of money. Along with Chechen Salafists they organized a military unit, which they identified as a *jamaat,* or assembly
of like-minded people. In the first Chechen war, that term was associated exclusively with Salafism. At that time, the treasury of the
general staff was empty. Most commando units were barely surviving,
their commanders begging for financial support. Next to the mendi-
cant rebels, members of the *jamaat* stood out by the quality of their
uniforms and by being well fed. They became known as "Snickers,"
because their commanders recommended that they eat Snickers and
Mars Bars to keep up their strength. It irritated the rebels, who could
not afford such treats and survived on food donated by the people.

The establishment of a military unit was not enough for the Salafists to have much influence in Chechnya at this stage. They needed
ties to the leadership of Ichkeria. This power was divided between
President Dudaev, located in western Chechnya, and his chief of
staff, Aslan Maskhadov, in the east. The divide between east and west
was the Argun River. The Salafists split themselves into two groups,
each trying to make contact either with Dudaev or Maskhadov. A
member of Dudaev's entourage, a onetime minister in Dudaev's
government, was a founder of the Salafist party, Movladi Udugov.[29]
The President never liked him. Udugov was unable to push Dudaev
to make decisions beneficial to the Salafists.

Among those hanging out in Maskhadov's waiting room was Islam
Khalimov, another founder of the Salafist party, who was trying to
ingratiate himself with the Chief of Staff. Maskhadov, however, was
a military man who had lived much of his life outside of Chechnya.
He was a Muslim, but he did not understand the intricacies of Salafist teaching. He considered everything that Khalimov whispered in
his ear burdensome. Thus, Maskhadov did not initially pay much
attention to the Salafist attempts at indoctrinating him.

Eventually, there was a rapprochement between Maskhadov and
the Salafists, but it did not happen over interpretations of Islam. It
came about in May 1995 in Vedeno, the last bastion of the general
staff before it relocated in the mountains. At this time the treasury

---

29. Among the earlier members of the Islamic Revival Party, founded in May
1987 in Grozny were Akhmad Mataev, Movladi Udugov, Isa Umarov, Islam
Khalimov, Supyan Abdullaev, Abdul-Malik Mezhidov, and Adam Deniev.

was empty. Khalimov came to Maskhadov carrying $175,000! He claimed that the money came from Turkish Islamic organizations to help Chechens fight the Russian army.[30] The contribution enabled Maskhadov to be financially independent from President Dudaev, who had limited resources. However, accepting that money compelled him to tolerate Khalimov's preaching on the adherence to pure Islam.

To what lengths would Maskhadov have gone to show his gratitude had it not been for his personal security guards, who came from parts of Chechnya where the influence of Sufism was unshakable? Khalimov's attempts to persuade them to take the Salafist path ended in outbursts. One day I saw a movie with Maskhadov's guards. It was an action film with more fighting than dialog, but the young guards watched it with great seriousness. Khalimov came into the room—apparently, he thought that by then he could give orders to Maskhadov's guards—and switching off the DVD player told us it was a sin to watch videos. The chief of Maskhadov's guard Il'ias Talkhadov called Khalimov a freak and said that if he ever again dared turn off a video he was watching, he would bury him in a place no man or dog would ever find. After that exchange, Khalimov never tried to teach the guards anything. Khalimov was not alone in trying to influence Maskhadov. Udugov and his brother, Isa Umarov, often tried to win Maskhadov over to their cause. Although Maskhadov did not succumb to the full influence of the Salafists, in gratitude for the money he had been given at a difficult time, he tried to stay on good terms with Khalimov.

The Salafist *jamaat* had grown rapidly and began to divide into branches in Argun, Khatun, Urus-Martan, Gudermes, Grozny, and many other places. The growth did not improve the *jamaats'* military achievements. The Salafist fighting units could not hold military positions because they avoided conventional battles. They only liked to make brief forays then retreat to their bases. Emir Khattab organized one battle, which took place near the village of Iarysh-Mardy on 16 April 1996. The fighting seriously degraded the military equipment of the 245th motorized rifle regiment and cost the lives of some seventy-five to two hundred Russian soldiers, according to various

---

30. Chechens were receiving support from the Turkish International Muslim Charity Organization, INN.

estimates. Other than that incident, Khattab was nowhere near any combat zone during the course of the war.

Maskhadov could not understand why the *jamaat* would not follow battle plans. The explanation lay in *jamaat* structure; its head could only be a Salafist. Sheikh Fatkhi was the Salafist leader in Chechnya; his orders could not be questioned. Therefore, the Salafists brought about a split among Chechen forces, those who recognized Dudaev and Maskhadov as commanders and those who obeyed Sheikh Fatkhi. After foreign volunteers from all over the Middle East came to Chechnya, the Salafists became recognizable by their physical appearance, that of classical Middle Eastern jihadists. I often heard people say that when the war was over we will deal with the Salafists. As Salafism spread, many underrated its vigor and capabilities. Salafists built their strength, and by the end of the conflict had become a real force.

The Russian media labeled everyone who came from the Middle East a mercenary. They also assumed that Chechens were paying those fighters to fight Russia. It may be hard to believe after years of Russian propaganda, but neither the Chechen government, general staff, nor individual commanders paid foreigners to fight their war. On the contrary, Salafists were paying Chechens who fought in their squads. They cannot, therefore, be labeled mercenaries.

The media often cited the number of foreign mercenaries in the thousands. It is unlikely their number exceeded a hundred at their peak. They were easy to identify because of physical differences with Chechens. Nonetheless, ordinary Russians thought that their army faced thousands of mercenaries. They also believed that snipers on the Chechen side came from the Baltic States and that they were often women. In the Russian popular imagination, Lithuanian women snipers ran over mountainous and wooded Chechnya wearing white tights. Films with themes of heroic soldiers breaking away from Chechen militants pictured foreign mercenaries and women-snipers in white tights. It is difficult to know how such myths originated.

The Explosion in October 1995

A powerful landmine was detonated on 6 October when a column of Russian Internal Forces, carrying General Anatoli Romanov, entered a tunnel near Minutka Square in Grozny. It was a huge explosion designed to kill dozens of people. The explosion happened in a confined space and it smashed the convoy to pieces. Romanov could not be found immediately among parts of human bodies scattered by the explosion. A belt with the general's buckle identified him.[31]

The assassination of the Russian general responsible for negotiations was a delicate moment for Aslan Maskhadov. He could not admit that fighters controlled by Chechen authorities were responsible; neither could he condemn the act, since Chechens saw any Russian general as an enemy who had come to destroy them. Whoever perpetrated the attack had not considered that Maskhadov was holding difficult negotiations and that there would be retaliations, most certainly against civilians. On that same day the bombing of the village of Roshni-Chu killed twenty-eight people and injured sixty. Twelve, mostly women, died in the shelling of Mesker-Iurt, and thirty were wounded. Throughout the week following the assassination, Russian troops called all their actions punishment for the attempt on their general's life.

It took effort by the OSCE to restore negotiations. After the Russians recognized that radical elements had carried out the explosion, they agreed to start over with Maskhadov. General Vasilko replaced Romanov as head of the Russian negotiators. Shortly after that, during the month of October, the OSCE delegation began experiencing problems: firing upon its mission and car accidents on deserted streets in Grozny. The Russians were trying to create an environment in which the delegation would be unable to fulfill its charge and have to leave the Republic.

International organizations became subject to pressure. The French humanitarian organization, Doctors without Borders, provided the only medical support for many Chechens living in the highlands. It worked in the rear guard of the Russian troops, helping Chechens with medicines. However, the fact that the doctors were able to move freely in any area of the Republic raised questions. The Russians supposed that if the organization had no problem with the fighters, it must have been helping them. Doctors without Borders did not engage in any activity that might damage their reputation as a humanitarian organization. They had no contact with the fighters and did not provide them with medicines, at least not directly. They worked with

31. Kulikov, A. *Tiazhelye Zvezdy.* M. 2002, p. 257.

existing hospitals or clinics. In the mountain areas, hospitals—often mobile—treated militants; this led to the Russians' accusation that the doctors were working directly with the rebels.

Paris to Chechnya by Car, March 1996

In February I was invited to Paris and tried to make the best of my visit by seeing interested parties and providing them with first-hand information. I had meetings at the Ministry of Foreign Affairs and the Ministry of Defense, held two workshops at the Ecole de Sciences Politiques, took part in a rally in support of Chechens, and spoke on several television channels. I made the acquaintance of several people who later became close friends: in particular, the philosopher André Glucksmann; the son of a minister of the North Caucasian Mountain Republic of the 1920s; and many other descendants of the old Caucasian diaspora in France.

During the return home, Il'ias Akhmadov was to travel with me after finishing his medical treatment. A chance meeting with him in Grozny in 1995 had led to his departure for France for treatment. The families of Sophie Shihab and Marie Bennigsen-Broxup, who by then were families to me as well, had arranged his stay. My arrival in Paris accelerated Akhmadov's decision to return to Chechnya. Marie Bennigsen offered to drive us back in a Land Rover that would be left as a gift to Maskhadov. She raised the funds needed for the car.

It was pure adventure. Marie and Il'ias drove back to Chechnya because I did not have a driving license; but not trusting Il'ias' driving skills, Marie did most of it. She was traveling with two Chechens who could be recognized and arrested as collaborators of Aslan Maskhadov, a potentially dangerous situation for her. Besides, it was risky for a foreigner to go to Chechnya without special permission from the Ministry of Foreign Affairs in Moscow.

We reached Kiev where my cousin Kharon decided to ride home with us, easing Marie's task since he was an excellent driver. Furthermore, she trusted him immediately, perhaps because his bandit look fitted her image of Chechens better than Il'ias and I, who came across as intellectuals.

Of the four, I was the only one with proper documents. Marie had a visa Rostov-Moscow; Kharon did not have a passport but had a driver's license; while Il'ias had an expired passport. We nevertheless rushed to Chechnya where a war was in full swing. In Ukraine nobody worried about our documents since we were in transit to Russia. Once there, the first customs post was near the city of Taganrog. Seeing a French passport, the customs officer was ecstatic; he explained to Marie how much he liked the novels of Alexandre Dumas and how much he had enjoyed the *Three Musketeers* movie. All his knowledge of France revolved around Dumas and the musketeers. Marie, however, had forgotten most of her Dumas. My attempts to break into the conversation to help her brought angry expressions to the customs officer's face. After a long exposition of his love for French literature, he finally let us go without asking for any documents or checking our luggage. Marie had shown him the car's registration and insurance, written in French, but no authorization to travel through Russia; he looked at the papers with a knowledgeable expression and said that everything was in order.

Once in Russia we were stopped at military checkpoints every forty to fifty miles; and each time Marie presented the French car documents, explaining that she was transiting through Russia to go to Azerbaijan. When we reached the Caucasus, from Rostov-on-Don to Mineralnye Vody, there were twenty-three checkpoints. We were detained three hours in the vicinity of Piatigorsk to verify the identity of the three Chechens; the officer manning the post bluntly explained that they were at war with the Chechens.

Only when we reached Grozny did someone think to ask us for our Russian papers. A shabby soldier with a snotty sleeve demanded to see our Russian documents and refused to listen to our explanation that the car was in transit through Russia. From other Chechens at the checkpoint, we learned that the Russians were angry because on 6 March Chechen fighters under the command of Ruslan Gelaev had entered Grozny and held it for three days, retreating the day before our arrival. The Russians did not believe that the rebels had just gone away; fearing an ambush, they were afraid to advance into Grozny. They did not know, of course, that Gelaev's incursion had been Maskhadov's dress rehearsal for a larger invasion, which occurred several months later. The soldier called his officer who, also angry with Chechens, told us we could not go through Grozny because all roads had been closed by Russian troops. The officer telephoned the Khankala military base and requested how to respond to travelers who wanted to cross the town. He received orders not to let anyone into Grozny.

The Chechens waiting at the checkpoint quietly turned their cars around and drove off. Running up to one of them, I asked if there was a road bypassing the city. They answered that there was one and that we should follow them over the hill; on the other side was the village of Maiakovski to the south of Grozny. Meanwhile, Il'ias Akhmadov, whose family lived in Grozny, had run into a neighbor who promised to take him home using a detour. Being so close to home, he decided to ignore prudence. Saying farewell to him, we rushed after the car that had disappeared along a sidetrack. It was getting late; and we needed to hurry if we wanted to reach my village before nightfall. As we turned onto the bypass road, we were unexpectedly overtaken by a thick fog and lost our way. When the fog dissipated, we found ourselves in front of a military post. Without betraying any emotion, Kharon turned the car around in front of the soldiers and slowly drove away. We all expected them to fire on us, but nothing happened. Shortly afterward, we stopped at a roadside cottage to ask for directions. The people there were horrified to learn that we had gone up to the Russian post and were surprised that the military had let us leave.

We were shown how to enter the highway that crosses Grozny from north to south, some twenty miles long. For several days, we had not listened to the radio or read newspapers and we had a poor understanding of what had occurred in Grozny. As we drove, we realized that we might have gotten into something way over our heads. We were moving through a ghost town. The streets and the highway, generally busy, were deserted. Here and there, we could see recently destroyed military equipment.

Stranger still, we did not come across a checkpoint until we arrived at Minutka Square, where we were stopped at a post manned by Interior Ministry forces. When the soldiers learned that Marie Bennigsen-Broxup was French, they began to joke that she was probably a spy. She told them something they could not have anticipated, that she was in Chechnya at the invitation of Anatoli Kulikov, Minister of Internal Affairs of the Russian Federation; and as proof she showed them his business card. She had met him in London during an event on Chechnya. They had had a friendly conversation during which he, a general himself, expressed his appreciation of her ancestor General Levin von Bennigsen (Russian hero of the Napoleonic wars), asserting that to this day he was respected in Russia. As they parted, he had given her his card. Stunned, the soldiers contacted the Khankala base; but no one there dared to contact Kulikov. They allowed us to go through and warned us that the army post a mile down the road were unconnected with them. At the army checkpoint Kulikov's card worked again; and the soldiers cautioned us that on the highway to Argun there was another post guarded by contract soldiers with whom they had no contact.

A feature of the Chechen war was the lack of communication between troops belonging to different ministries, Defense, Internal Affairs, and intelligence (FSK). Contact between the troops of the various entities had to go through the military bases, Khankala or Mozdok, even when, as in our case, they were only a few hundred yards from each other. The Chechen fighters made good use of this logistical peculiarity when planning their strategies. They knew that an assault on a checkpoint manned by soldiers of one ministry would not bring to the rescue soldiers serving at posts of different ministries located in the vicinity. On many occasions soldiers at one checkpoint sold weapons and ammunition to Chechens and asked them not to fire upon them but to attack positions run by other ministries!

We arrived home in Avtury at nightfall. There we realized that what we had done had been perilous. Few believed that we had crossed Grozny without incident. In the morning we left in search of Maskhadov. We found him with the Salafist brothers, Movladi Udugov and Isa Umarov, who, although they greeted us as guests, had tried to convince Maskhadov that we were spies of western intelligence services. But Maskhadov welcomed us; and with his guards we drove to the village of Gansolchu, where we spent the night in his home.

Goiskoe, April 1996

In April, Marie Bennigsen-Broxup came back to Chechnya with some French television journalists who wanted to make a documentary about Chechnya. We were asked to go to the village of Goiskoe, a few miles from the larger town of Urus-Martan. The village was preparing for battle. The Russians had ordered rebels to leave Goiskoe;

and when they refused issued an ultimatum that was to end shortly after our arrival.

Having passed unchecked through the lines of the pro-Russian Chechen militia, we found ourselves in the village where almost the entire population had been evacuated. Many evacuees left their houses to the militants. In the village we met with the commander in charge of defense Khusein Isabaev, his deputy Akhmed Zakaev, and his chief of staff Dolkhan Khozhaev. Because the deadline was approaching, there was an oppressive silence broken only by the mooing of cows and the cries of roosters.

The commander accompanied the reporters to the frontline, situated a few hundred meters from the Russian positions. I waited in the village. I did not like coming close to Russian troops; they were too unpredictable. Khusein Iskhanov, who accompanied us on this trip, went with the reporters and asked me to keep his machine gun. I do not like firearms and never use them. Conflicts should be resolved without weapons. He who kills does not win in the long run; he prevails only for a time. Only those who ponder how to avoid bloodshed can win.

I was standing in the center of the village with a gun in my hands and had the impression that the whole Russian army was eyeing me through their gunsights. At the same time I was ashamed to get down in the trenches dug around the perimeter of the village. There was one a few meters from me. I looked at the fighters lying in it and in an attempt to be derisive quipped, "Don't worry; if I stand here with a weapon in my hands, the Russians don't have a chance." However, they took my words seriously, and one of them responded, "So be it with the help of God."

Only fifteen minutes remained before the deadline when my party finally returned. I anxiously shouted that we did not need to die that day, that we would have another chance another day. Marie horrified me by wanting to stay; and I yelled in Chechen to Iskhanov not to allow anyone to stay behind. Thank God, the journalists agreed with me. The battle for the village lasted four days and entered Chechen history as another demonstration of popular resistance. The village was virtually erased from the earth, but the Russian army did not succeed in overrunning it. The fighters ultimately vacated the destroyed village, which for Russians was the most desirable outcome.

Historical Note

Chechens have maintained a sense of freedom by preserving through years of Soviet totalitarianism their traditions and culture. The honoring of elders, the cult of the woman-mother, the love of freedom, and the special Chechen code of honor are now subjects of intense study.

During the first military campaign, sympathies were noticeably with the Chechens. Politicians, journalists, or simple observers at times romanticized Chechens. They were described as positive, kind, and fearless— especially compared to the grimy Russian soldiers. The Russian army's brutality, particularly against civilians, only enhanced the favorable impression the world had of Chechens.

Chechens were seeking happiness through freedom; Russians, not having one or the other, did not want Chechens to attain them. Chechens defended their homes, families, and fatherland; Russians came to take away their right to protect them. Chechen decency clashed with the animosity of Russians, who did not realize that Chechens did not consider them enemies. Chechens did not understand why Russians from the Far East or Kaliningrad saw them as adversaries. The psychology of a Russian soldier, who wanted the whole world to be like him, with nothing to hope for in this life, was utterly inconceivable to Chechens.

Every Chechen knows from birth that he is a responsible member of society. Chechens are better aware of this concept than other peoples; they derive it from their extended sense of family. A Chechen family includes a large number of relatives, who in other cultures are called first cousin, second cousin, cousin by marriage, or in laws. A Chechen would not say that he's my first cousin; he always says that he's the son of my father's brother, making him dearer because of the mention of his father. A Chechen says my sister's son, instead of my nephew, making him closer in his system of values. To be a Chechen you must be born a Chechen. Chechens have preserved in their traditions and identity features long lost by other societies. This is why few understand them.

In April 1996, I was married. Amidst the horror of war people married, had children, died, and took care of their businesses. We did not have the procession of cars usual in Chechen weddings since we had to drive the distance between my bride's village of Shali and my village of Avtury before nightfall, when the Russians set up roadblocks. An air raid started in Shali just an hour before my party arrived for the wedding.

When we drove into town, people were coming out of hiding. There was no dancing at our wedding because people were in mourning for the dead and for those relatives or neighbors who had disappeared. It was an unusually modest Chechen wedding.

Yeltsin's Visit to Chechnya, May 1996

Boris Yeltsin had to visit Chechnya. Everyone expected him to come, but no one knew where or when. The President's appearance in Grozny, against the background of a destroyed city, could be counterproductive. His presence at one of the bases might raise suspicion that he was afraid to step outside Russian military protection.

The Russian government was in a quandary; no amount of propaganda could turn the military quagmire into a victory. It was imperative to abandon the military course for a political one. To begin that process, on 4 April the government unexpectedly announced a cessation of hostilities, an amnesty for rebels, except for those who had carried out the raids on Budennovsk and Kizliar-Pervomaiskoe, and a withdrawal of troops from "peaceful districts." The Russian government's concessions were illusory. The government intended to call elections for the Chechen Parliament and needed a period of tranquility. The Parliament, of course, would turn out to be controlled by Moscow. The Federal Minister for Nationalities announced the elections for the summer of 1996. The presidents of Tatarstan and Kazakhastan proclaimed their willingness to be intermediaries between Ichkerian leaders and Moscow.

Meanwhile, the local Moscow stooge Doku Zavgaev began a cat and mouse game. He proposed that each individual locality sign an agreement with him stipulating that, in exchange for peace, it would not allow fighters to remain. To those town or village heads who signed the accord, he pledged to provide the salaries for teachers and doctors and pensions for the elderly. To counteract Zavgaev's initiative, representatives of our government met with every local head. Those who refused to submit to the pro-Russian administration relinquished to us their official seals, symbols of Zavgaev's power.

Only the assassination of President Dzhokhar Dudaev of Ichkeria on 22 April near the village of Gekhi-chu allowed Boris Yeltsin to talk about progress in the negotiation process. The demise of their main political antagonist made it possible for the Russians to put up a bold front. After the assassination, the Federal government, for some unfathomable reason, decided that Chechens no longer intended to resist and suggested the creation of a delegation to negotiate with Moscow. On 27 May the delegation arrived at the Kremlin. Zelimkhan Iandarbiev, Acting President of Ichkeria, headed the negotiating party. According to the Russian plan, it had to look as if the emissaries were in Moscow thanks to the mediation of the Organization for Security and Cooperation in Europe.

The proceedings were broadcast. The Kremlin hall where negotiations were to take place had three doors. The pro-Moscow Chechens led by Doku Zavgaev came through one door; the Ichkerian delegation, headed by Iandarbiev, came through another door; and last, through yet a different door, entered Yeltsin as the master of the situation. This choreography implied that the conflict was between the Chechen factions and that the Russians were simply helping them solve their problems.

The Chechens had been unaware of this scenario until Yeltsin got to the head of the table. An angered Iandarbiev refused to sit down and negotiate with the Russian puppet, Zavgaev. The situation deteriorated until, at one point, Yeltsin yelled at Iandarbiev to sit down. He apparently supposed that having brought Chechen leaders to Moscow, he would be able to force them to make concessions. But the delegation refused to sit until Yeltsin left the head of the table and took the chair facing Iandarbiev, then occupied by Zavgaev, thus showing that the negotiations were not between independent Ichkeria and Doku Zavgaev, but between the Russian President and the Acting President of Ichkeria. The situation was so tense that security guards, fearing Chechen aggression, moved to protect Yeltsin.

The altercation was broadcast worldwide. In the end, the President of Russia took the seat facing Iandarbiev. Yeltsin asked Zavgaev to move down the table, reducing him to the role of an ordinary member of the Russian delegation, thus humiliating his protégé. It was a victory for Chechens. Another rite of independence was that, while waiting for the beginning of the proceedings, the Chechen delegation performed a Muslim prayer in the hallway of the Kremlin literally in front of Yeltsin's office, an unprecedented event.

The next day Yeltsin had his revenge. Without prior announcement, he suddenly appeared in Chechnya while the Chechen delegation remained hostage in Moscow. Yeltsin's plane flew to the military base in Mozdok, and he made the trip to Chechnya in a helicopter. The whole operation was orchestrated as a military exercise. According to an eyewitness, a flight of helicopters took off with no one knowing which one carried the President; and they flew at low altitude with machinegunners in position.

The occasion was intended to show the world that the President of Russia arrived in a peaceful republic. Yeltsin landed in an open field thirty miles north of Grozny. For us it was not difficult to understand the choice of location; it was in an area where there had been no battle since December 1994. Upon arrival, Yeltsin announced that Chechnya remained an integral part of Russia but would be given special rights. Speaking in front of the military, he declared that, by overthrowing the Dudaev regime, the Russian army had won. His speech was clearly not consistent with the statements that Moscow intended to seek a dialogue with Ichkeria.

Yeltsin's visit evoked Empress Catherine the Great's trip to the Crimea in 1787. Prince Potemkin had had sham villages built along Catherine's route through the northern Black Sea region only recently reclaimed from the Ottoman Empire. So it was with Yeltsin; grateful villagers, allegedly Chechens, welcomed the president. A few hours earlier, having learned that distinguished guests were flying in from Moscow, the Zavgaev administration gathered some of its members to greet the visitors. One of them later recalled that along with a female colleague, Russian by birth, dressed in the Chechen national holiday garb, they stood in the front row of the welcoming party. However, to Yeltsin's question, "Chechen, what do you want me to do?" he replied "peace," creating an embarrassing moment. Later, it transpired that a Russian woman dressed in national costume met the president because Chechen women working in the pro-Moscow administration refused to meet any high-ranking guest from Moscow.

A reception tent was set up in the field for Yeltsin to meet with "ordinary Chechens," who worked for the pro-Moscow administration. In a flamboyant demonstration of generosity, Yeltsin decreed the payment of old-age pensions, child benefits, and public sector wages. Considering his mission accomplished, he departed immediately, since there was speculation that if Shamil Basaev found out where Yeltsin had landed, he would not miss a chance to strike at him.

The Iandarbiev delegation, seeing in the news that Yeltsin was brib-ing people in Chechnya, took offense and that evening flew back to the North Caucasus to announce to the Ichkerian armed forces that the war continued because the Russians were just playing for time.

The Body Trade

Among the most unpleasant memories of the first Chechen war was the trafficking in dead bodies. Russian officers and soldiers learned that Chechens revered the dead. They would give up their fortune to recover the corpses of kinsmen arrested during house-to-house searches or detained at checkpoints.

A Chechen must be buried in the cemetery of his family's village. For this reason, there are few Chechen graves in Russia. Wherever a Chechen spent his or her life, after death the body must be returned home and buried with the members of his clan. The tradition is not religious; it makes no difference whether a Chechen dies in an Islamic country or not.[32]

Russian officers exploited the burial traditions by selling the dead bodies of Chechens to their relatives. After a long search for a missing family member, the possibility of having the body returned to the family was considered a godsend. Neither the prosecutor nor any other authority was able to stop this black market in corpses. The search by anxious relatives started in the military prisons. Russian officers involved in the trafficking, covering for each other, directed relatives to one location after another. When they could not find him alive, people then looked for a body. Families needed an intermediary to negotiate with the traffickers. Officers, themselves involved, seemed to be as helping people to find their dead, were in fact bargaining for the payment. The rate for the body of an ordinary Chechen not involved in fighting and victim of black marketers was about $3,000 US dollars. Few could pay that amount without the help of the ex-tended family, and often even clan members chipped in.

At the outset of the war, a relative of mine came back to Chechnya

---

32. If a Chechen dies in Saudi Arabia, his body cannot be brought home since Saudi laws do not allow the transport of bodies.

from Moscow to be with his family at that difficult time. Almost two meters tall, he was a handsome twenty-six year old, and like many of his peers engaged in bombings and attacks on Russian military units, without the approval of their parents. During a raid, he was wounded and taken prisoner. His family attempted to reach an agreement with the Russians. At first, it seemed to be working. His parents were asked to put down US $3,000 to get him released. They were requested to pay an additional $2,000, allegedly to prevent him from being shipped out of Chechnya. When it became clear that the whole deal was extortion, the negotiators admitted that my relative had died of injuries on the day after his arrest. To be told where he was buried, the family had to come up with another $2,000. He had been interred in the outskirts of the town of Shali, a few miles from our village, on the side of the road. We had passed his grave dozens of times, looking for him, hoping to find him alive. We were relieved when the body was finally buried in the family cemetery. There are thousands of Chechens who never found their sons, brothers, fathers, or husbands. For them, the horror of the war continues.

Historical Note

Russian archives held countless documents of crimes committed against Chechens during the colonization of the North Caucasus, crimes that were not just those of individual officers. In the course of my dissertation research, I was puzzled by the fact that Chechens attacked Cossack villages when they had lived peacefully together for centuries. The secret was revealed when I found a decree by Emperor Alexander II addressing the command of the Special Caucasus Corps and ordering it to put an end to the practice of beheading the mountain dwellers, scalping them, and hanging them on poles around Cossack villages.[33] Chechens, therefore, had to retrieve the skulls of their fellow tribesmen from Cossack villages. The practice was abolished only with the end of the war. Leo Tolstoy, who served in the war, noted that Cossack saddles were decorated with the scalps of slain highlanders.

A participant in the events of the time described the norms prevailing

---

33. GVIA RF, fund 13454, Op.8. Vatchagaev, M. *Chechnia v Kavkazskoi Voine XIX st.: Sobytiia i Sud'by.* Kiev, 2003, p. 293.

in the Russian army. "General [....] as usual ordered to sever the heads of the dead enemies and with these trophies went back to his Prochnyi Okop [his base]. A year later I met [him] in Stavropol. He was riding in an open sleigh and was followed by a fully covered one. 'Where are you going, your Excellency and what are you carrying? I am going on vacation, neighbor, and am bringing some resolved cases to Vel'iaminov.' With these words, he opened the sledge and I saw with disgust about fifty bare skulls. General Alexei Vel'iaminov dispatched them to the Academy of Sciences."

Vel'iaminov, Chief of Staff of the Caucasian Corps, liked collecting the bones of Chechen hands, and he sent them as "gifts" to the empire's scientific institutions. In 1854 a general was removed from his position by reason of insanity. For years he had massacred innocent Chechen civilians, getting, in his own words, great satisfaction at the sight of dead Chechen bodies. Chechens never mocked the dead. Most of the time it was Chechens who initiated negotiations for the exchange of bodies. They also considered it their duty to bury not only their own brethren but also their enemies.

Punishment meted out to Chechens by the Imperial government consisted of taking hostage the children of prominent families. This scheme was introduced in the late eighteenth century to ensure the loyalty of the families. It continued through the Caucasian War and persisted into the twentieth century. Because their parents violated cease fire conditions, many youngsters were taken to Russia as hostages, were killed, or sent to remote areas where most failed to adapt to the harsh conditions and died. Those who survived were educated in military schools to turn them into soldiers to fight against Chechens in future battles.

History shows no great difference between the policies of the tsarist regime during the North Caucasian colonization, Red Russia in the years of militant atheism, and the rule of Yeltsin's Russia.

Chapter 9

Military Victory

The Battle for Grozny, August 1996

In March Ruslan Gelaev's troops entered Grozny on Aslan Maskhadov's orders, held positions for three days, and withdrew without significant losses. This operation was a rehearsal for a larger battle. Maskhadov received important information from the maneuver: namely that Grozny remained the weak link in the Russian chain. He planned a new incursion, a decisive battle. For that confrontation, he intended to throw all Chechen forces into it.

Squad commanders were called to his temporary headquarters in Alleroi to discuss details of their potential involvement in a particular operation. Maskhadov requested details about fighting capacities. I attended some of the meetings to record what was said. Based on what I had heard at those meetings, I judged that most commanders provided figures ten to fifteen times more than their real capabilities. Maskhadov, trying not to show his irritation, repeatedly warned against inflating the strength of the units and explained that they would be assigned positions based on their size and would have to hold them without outside help. Only then did the commanders supply realistic figures; estimates dropped considerably.

Various sources gave different figures of the numbers of militants involved in the August attack. The number of troops Maskhadov actually deployed for his "operation *Jihad*" was 877. This total represented the sum of the reasonable figures supplied by commanders. Based on this, Maskhadov planned his operation and distributed sectors to each commando unit. Several days into the fight individual Chechens, realizing that this was a crucial battle, joined the squadrons.

Then the numbers of fighters grew rapidly. In March when Ruslan Gelaev entered Grozny, many, not knowing the operation was a trial run, came out to help liberate their city. After Gelaev retreated, those fighters were left to face the Russians. Many had to go into hiding, as they were easily identifiable.

Throughout May and June Maskhadov kept his preparations secret. Only the commanders and their adjutants knew that an operation was being planned. By July, however, it was increasingly difficult to hide that a large operation was in the making. On the eve of battle Maskhadov moved from Alleroi in the foothills to the large village of Tsatsan-Iurt located on the plain. There, he placed his command and control center in the house of a trusted friend.

In early August commanders received their orders, including the date to move toward Grozny, the number of fighters, their stations in the city, how to get there, and with whom to link once in position. Until the last moment radios were tuned to frequencies that could be intercepted by Russians. Therefore, the airwaves were flooded with information on alleged rebel movements in the mountains. As they entered Grozny, the commando units switched to a new frequency not immediately decipherable by the Russians. This allowed Maskhadov to give orders over the radio.

Radio communications were the responsibility of Ali Dimaev, a genius in that field. He had a team of his relatives to help him. Situated on the heights overlooking Grozny, their job was to ensure communication with Grozny. In those years Motorola radios worked through towers, and their range was short. Russians controlled all the hills around Grozny. Under their noses, Dimaev set up his telescopic tower and maintained connection with the fighters.

At dawn on 6 August, Chechen troops took their positions in Grozny. Most major commanders were present, except those who had been injured in previous battles.[34] The commandos' advance went unnoticed by the Russians; but the ratio of forces, one to twenty-two, was in favor of the Russians. Grozny was not the only target of operation *Jihad*, Argun and Gudermes were involved as well. However,

---

34. Among the major commanders were Ruslan Gelaev, Shamil Basaev, Vakh Arsanov, Doku Umarov, Khamzat Labazanov, Khunkerpasha Israpilov, Turpal-Ali Atgeriev, and Apti Batalov. Islam Khatuev was absent because of an injury.

fighting in those towns was aimed at preventing the Russian forces from rushing to the aid of Grozny. Taken by surprise, Federal forces in Gudermes simply fled. In Grozny a few Russian units (a staff group, part of the troops quartered within the city boundaries, and FSK squadrons) were able to hold the lines. Only a breakthrough of troops from the Khankala base, less than a mile from the capital, could aid the besieged Russian troops.

The Russian air power was useless. Chechen tactics scattered units in such a way that aircraft could not be used against them without also destroying the Russian forces. Chechens did not advance from the periphery of town to the center. They had taken up positions everywhere, at times moving from one place to another, but always staying close to the Russians. The Chechens were dispersed, and the Russians could not move troops without continuously stumbling onto Chechen units.

Since early morning of 6 August, Maskhadov was at his command center handing out orders and receiving information from his commando units. He did not seem nervous and joked with those with him. However, as he was walking back and forth, it was not difficult to understand the strain he was under. We followed developments in quiet but nervous anticipation, and we tried to figure out what was happening by watching Maskhadov's reactions.

Now and then, he would shout at one of his commanders who was trying to change his plan from the battlefield. I recall one of them calling to say that he needed help, and if he could not get any, he would be forced to move to a different position. Maskhadov reminded the commander that since he knew where he was going, had been aware of the risks, and had been willing to die for his country, why then was he changing his mind? After that no commander asked to alter Maskhadov's plan. Commanders knew that if they tried to change positions to save their squads, they could endanger others who were unaware of a change in disposition and who might find themselves encircled by Russians. Several hundred Chechens surrounded several thousand Russians. The Chechens' advantage was in knowing who was in front of them, how many they were, and what their potential escape routes were, while the Russians had no idea how many Chechens were attacking them.

On 10 August, Yeltsin proclaimed a day of mourning for the

Russian soldiers killed in Grozny, a foolish decision since fighting was still going on. The decree was never implemented. Casualties can only be guessed since traditionally the Russian army released several sets of figures. The lowest indicated more than two thousand soldiers wounded or killed. Unofficial data gave figures two and a half times higher, around 5,000 wounded or killed. Russian losses in military equipment were also heavy, up to two hundred armored cars destroyed and a few, including tanks, falling into Chechen hands. Chechen casualties were estimated at two-dozen, and those losses were impossible to hide since funerals were the affair of the whole Republic. The battle for Grozny was Aslan Maskhadov's victory over the Russian military establishment. He won it using the rules of warfare, and it was a testimony to his military talent.

The Khasaviurt Agreement, August 1996

Two weeks after the start of operation *Jihad*, the only Russian forces still resisting were the pro-Moscow Chechen police holding on in the area of the train station and the staff of the FSB building. Chechens did not give them a corridor to exit the city; they had no choice, therefore, but to fight.

The collapse of the Russian army forced the Kremlin to seek talks with the Chechens. General Alexander Lebed, Secretary of the Russian Security Council (appointed in June by the Russian president as his national security advisor) sought to contact Maskhadov. Lebed realized the enormity of the defeat in Grozny, and took responsibility for ending the bloodshed. He was not a diplomat and his tongue was harsh; but phone conversations with Chechen leaders convinced him that they had no intention of giving up their victory. His meeting with them was classified top secret; few even suspected that the Security Council Secretary intended to visit such a hellish place.

On 10 August, Lebed became the permanent representative in Chechnya of the President of the Russian Federation. There was still fierce fighting in Grozny when on 11 August he unexpectedly arrived in Chechnya to meet with Maskhadov and other Chechen leaders. Both parties agreed to reach an agreement within the next seven days after the cessation of hostilities and the withdrawal of Russian troops from Chechnya. On 14 August, Yeltsin signed a decree delegating the process of a settlement with Chechnya to the Security Council Secretary. Having obtained the necessary powers, on 15 August Lebed again arrived in Chechnya to consult with Zelimkhan Iandarbiev, Acting President of the Chechen Republic of Ichkeria.

On 22 August, Lebed, Maskhadov, Iandarbiev, and the Chechen Interior Minister signed a protocol "On joint activities for the initial phase of the implementation of the ceasefire agreement." It provided for a ceasefire, for withdrawal of the warring parties from Grozny, and the creation of a joint Russian-Chechen command to maintain order in the city. Aslanbek Ismailov was designated to take over the Chechen side of the joint command. Objections by the pro-Moscow government of Doku Zavgaev were ignored. On 28 August, Federal and Chechen troops left, and units of the joint command entered.

On 30 August, Russians and Chechens met in Khasaviurt in Dagestan to sign an agreement to end the war. Khasaviurt, with half its population Chechen and surrounded by several Chechen villages, could provide some degree of protection to Ichkeria's leaders in case they had to make an emergency exit. They could not be certain that the encounter would not turn into a trap. But the prevailing feeling was that the settlement ending the war had to be negotiated with an official representative of the Russian government who was authorized to make decisions without consulting the Kremlin.

The conference was held on the night of 30 August. The early hours of the meeting were essentially mutual recriminations. The Chechen demand that negotiations be based on international law became the main point of contention and brought an outcry from the Russians. Vladimir Lukin, a liberal politician and former Russian ambassador to the United States, shouted that there could be no solution to the problem on the basis of international law; in effect, that would mean recognition of Chechen independence. As Lebed was signing the document consenting to the Chechens request, Lukin, standing next to him angrily pleaded with him not to sign. After Lebed boldly ratified the document, Lukin, in a fit of rage, shouted at the Chechens, "You will not get away with it; we will come back to Chechnya!" He then ran out of the room, not to be a party to Russia's defeat. At the time, few people paid attention to his words.

On 31 August, the Chechens and Russians reached a consensus to end the hostilities. In the presence of the head of the OSCE Assistance

Group to Chechnya, they signed two documents: a Joint Statement affirming the commitment of both parties to finding a mutually acceptable formula for a political settlement and a declaration of the "Principles for Determining the Basis of Mutual Relations between the Russian Federation and the Chechen Republic" that identified a set of concrete obligations to serve as a basis for further negotiations.

After the Khasaviurt Agreement was signed on 3 September, Lebed and Lukin reported to a session of the Russian government presided over by the Prime Minister. After their reports the government approved the agreement. Lukin, all the while emphasized that the withdrawal of Russian troops from Chechnya should be accompanied by the disarmament of the Chechen military units, as specified in the agreement. That part of the resolution, however, was never implemented because Chechens were reluctant to comply and Moscow was too weak to compel them to do so.

The Khasaviurt Agreement was a sensation for Russians as well as Chechens. Many accused Lebed of treason. However, he, as a military man, had grasped the level of demoralization of the army and had saved it from destruction in Grozny. Many Chechens, who did not believe it possible to resist one of the most powerful armies of the world, were in shock. Others saw in it as a sign from above and took to religion. Skeptics suspected some hidden conspiracy.

For my part, the agreement remains a puzzle. It was signed with the involvement of the OSCE office in Chechnya.[35] The OSCE distributed worldwide an English translation of the agreement made without Chechen participation. There were discrepancies between the original and the translation. The Russian version stipulated that a final agreement on the status of Chechnya had to be reached "before" 31 December 2001 and not "after" as stated in the English version. The original text assumed that "the foundations of the mutual relations of Chechnya and Russia" could be settled at any time within five years[36] and not after a delay of five years as the OSCE mission announced to the international community. The result of the mistakes

---

35. The head of the OSCE in Chechnya was the Swiss diplomat Tim Guldimann.

36. Issues were de facto settled within five years with the signing of a peace treaty between the Russian Federation and the Chechen Republic of Ichkeria on 12 May 1997.

in the English translation was that Chechen authorities meeting with politicians and diplomats from around the world were told they had to wait until 2002 to begin discussing international recognition of Chechnya. Whether the English translation was a mistake or a deliberate deception remains an open question.

Russian ultra-patriots tried to have the agreement nullified. Ninety-three Duma deputies petitioned the Constitutional Court to declare it illegal. The court rejected the appeal and, confirming the legitimacy of the Khasaviurt Agreement, insisted on the need to comply with the signed decisions. Its judgment put an end to speculation that Lebed had exceeded his powers by signing the agreement with Maskhadov. The Khasaviurt Agreement was for Chechens an historic event. It was the first time Chechen officials had signed an accord with Russian authorities based on international law.

Maskhadov, half kidding, recalled how the Chechen delegation had extracted consent from the Russians on several issues. Lebed was a military man who could not stand long explanations. Maskhadov had noticed this during the long clarification of some point of international law made by the Chechen delegate Said-Khasan Abumuslivov. Lebed only wanted to hear summaries of all issues. Each time he would threaten not to allow something, Maskhadov would propose hearing the professional opinion of Abumuslimov. Lebed would listen for a while, then interrupt, accepting the Chechen requirements, and then request to move on. The scenario was repeated several times until one last time when Maskhadov offered to accept Abumuslimov's decision; and Lebed replied, "Give me to sign what you want...just do not give him the floor."

Historical Note

Russians had known that Chechens were warriors since the conquest of the region. In 1859 Prince Bariatinskii sent an army corps of 113,000 to Chechnya. The size of this force exceeded the population of Chechnya, which according to Russian sources numbered only slightly more than 100,000. Nowhere else in the Caucasus had Russia deployed an army with such a high ratio to the local population.

According to data gathered by a staff colonel, Russian casualties during the sixty years Caucasian War were estimated at 96,275. Russian losses in Chechnya were seven generals killed out of thirteen, who died during the entire war; 175 officers killed, 1,102 injured, and fifteen captured. The dead and wounded among enlisted men were 6,424 killed, 20,375 wounded, and 1,133 taken prisoner or missing. Russian losses in Chechnya totaled 29,224, including those taken prisoner or missing. Nearly one-third of officially confirmed Russian casualties occurred in Chechnya even though Chechnya's territory was not more than three percent of the Caucasus and Chechens did not constitute more than five percent of the Caucasian population. After its victory over Chechnya, Russia occupied the rest of the North Caucasus within five years.

My First Resignation, September 1996

After the Khasaviurt Agreement, a new chapter began in the history of Chechnya. The OSCE invited Aslan Maskhadov to a session of the Parliamentary Assembly of the Council of Europe (PACE) in Strasbourg. It was a unique opportunity to present to the international community his personal vision for Chechnya. The invitation meant international recognition of his authority. We had to harness the good will and burnish his image in the corridors of international political organizations.

To prevent the Russian government from creating difficulties, I decided to deceive them. OSCE members who like me believed that the trip must take place helped me. Through the intermediary of the OSCE office we booked tickets and hotel rooms in Moscow; we were doing everything possible to convince Russian authorities that Maskhadov was flying to Strasbourg via Moscow. Keeping him under surveillance was a priority for the Russian Security Council.

At the same time we worked out a different route: Maskhadov would fly to Strasbourg through Baku in Azerbaijan, and we would try to keep his departure as quiet as possible. Through the OSCE we ordered round-trip tickets Baku-Istanbul-Paris. We were counting on our friends in the Chechen community of Baku to help us arrange various aspects of the voyage, including its financing. Maskhadov's arrival in Strasbourg was expected; accommodations had been made for him and for Lebed, who were invited at the same time, and details of their speeches and meetings worked out. Everything was proceeding well and all technical issues were being settled.

However, my arrangements received a blow, and it did not come from the Russians. As we were ready to set the date for his departure, Maskhadov suddenly asked to see me. Not expecting anything special, I thought he wanted to discuss the trip. When I joined him, he asked his entourage to leave us alone. Next, he stunned me by asking, "Can you give me assurances that all will work out, and that the Russians will cause no harm to me personally?" I had not expected that question. I asked in return if he needed my guarantees and he replied that he did. Shocked, all I could say was, "Aslan, I'm not sure that anyone could give a guarantee but the Lord." He blurted out that Udugov, Umarov, and Khalimov had insinuated that I wanted to lure him into a trap and that I was an FSK collaborator planted a year ago to influence him!

The three founders of the Salafist party in Chechnya had decided to take control of Maskhadov, and to them I had a negative influence on him. I told Maskhadov that I would not let them harass him because of me, that I was leaving, and he would not see me again. He tried to say something, but I told him that I did not want any explanation. I also pointed out that he should bear in mind that they wanted to take away his triumph. I could not believe he could doubt my credibility. In contrast to all those around him, I was probably the only one who had never demanded anything from him.

I was prepared to expect any baseness from the Salafists. Hiding behind Islam, they do their dirty work; such is their way of life. One moment they smile and hug you and the next they are ready to betray you. They are afraid of those above them but attack those who show weakness. They envy others and invariably cause divisions. Having found new areas for their activities, they are presently busy in Syria and Iraq. Chechnya and the North Caucasus are not enough; they want to rule the Muslim *Ummah* (Community of Muslims).

Without warning, Maskhadov did not let his hosts know he would not come to Strasbourg. A number of politicians, led by Vladimir Lukin, protested Maskhadov's and Lebed's invitations. Consequently, Lebed politely declined to attend. Maskhadov lost an opportunity to become a politician with whom Europeans wished to work. Later, as President of Chechnya, he tried to reverse the situation, but no one in Europe was interested any longer. By then, Russia had created an image of him as an indecisive politician.

The Stampede of the Russian Army from Chechnya

After the Khasaviurt Agreement, the Russian army was in an ambiguous situation. It had lost the war, but it had to pretend to engage in post-war reconstruction alongside Chechens. Chechens de facto dominated the joint military command set up in Grozny. The role of the Russians was to diffuse tensions and reduce the Chechens' claims to realistic levels. Few reckoned with the Russian military posts, which often had to defend themselves against attacks from unarmed civilians or rebels, for whom the presence of the army served only as a source of weapons.

The military posts located in the mountains were brought to Grozny, most often to Khankala. Their departure was a shameful stampede. I was present in the village of Borzoi in Shatoi district when a rifle brigade left, followed by screaming and whistling villagers. It was interesting to watch children run after the departing tanks and raise their middle fingers at the departing soldiers. Other boys threw stones and no Russian dared even to bellow at the children. Still other youths wrote on walls along the road, "Pigs! Get out of Chechnya!" and similar slogans.

The presidential election campaign began, and interest in the Russian army waned. It looked as if the presence of its army in Chechnya was a problem only for Russia. In September, Chechen commanders walked into the Khankala military base and took away equipment; Russian officers sold everything they could. The Chechens were interested in weapons and other ordnance, and they took what little they had not captured during the fighting.

Once their security at Khankala was violated, the Russian army had to withdraw, not so much because of the agreement, but for their own preservation. On the morning of 21 December, Maskhadov sent his adjutant and Mumadi Saidaev to army headquarters in Khankala with a complaint. There was no sentry at the gate. At first, they thought discipline had broken down and that it could be dangerous. However, they soon discovered that the base was empty. Without warning the Chechen leadership discovered that the Russians had fled Chechnya. If invasion took the Russian army several weeks, it only took one or two nights for them to run away. When Russians talk about the withdrawal in 1996, they should clarify that it was a flight under the cover of darkness. When Iskhanov and Saidaev reported to Maskhadov that there were no more Russians in Chechnya, he asked, "No one at all?" It was a surprise to all Chechens.

Chapter 10

POST-WAR CHECHNYA

The Election Campaign of Aslan Maskhadov

The war was over, and many problems that had been in abeyance during the conflict resurfaced. Foremost was the issue of leadership. The death of the charismatic President Dudaev raised the question of a successor. Acting President Zelimkhan Iandarbiev did not want elections. He wished to turn Chechnya into an Islamic republic, a departure from Dudaev's attitude toward religion. Chechens consider themselves Muslims, but not many were ready to accept a state similar to those of Islamic countries. The Chechen vision of Islam differs from the Islam that Salafists were offering as an alternative to Sufism.

Nonetheless, the Acting President decided that what Chechens needed was the *shariaization* of Chechnya. In countries that had adopted a *Shariah* criminal code, the transfer from secular courts took years. Iandarbiev decided it could be done all at once. To our horror, we suddenly discovered that a translation of the criminal code of Sudan had been prepared for us. Philologist by profession and poet by vocation, Iandarbiev did not even bother to request a translation that would not offend his compatriots. Ianderbiev's goal of Islamization, although he was persuaded it was going to bring him victory in the election, clearly did not find support among the population.

He tried to persuade top commanders and politicians that there was no need for an election. He urged his fellow citizens to do away with the electoral system, leave the presidency to him, and start building a new form of government under his personal supervision. Most people took his performance for a joke; but it was not funny.

Later, in October, Iandarbiev decided to hold a convention

of military commanders. At the conference no one represented Maskhadov's position. The function of the caucus was to nominate a single candidate who would be the commanders' nominee for president; which of course would be Iandarbiev. When Maskhadov's adjutant learned the purpose of the convention, he appealed to the Naur battalion. It sent twenty of its fighters to support Maskhadov's candidacy. Iandarbiev's plan was foiled.

Seeing Maskhadov as his main competitor, Iandarbiev tried to have him relegated to a secondary position. He also laid the foundation for the future political conflict between Maskhadov and Basaev. After the Khasaviurt Agreement, the issue of an acting cabinet of ministers arose, which would address pressing issues before the election. The Acting President appointed Shamil Basaev and Ruslan Gelaev as his deputy prime ministers. This scheme sidelined Maskhadov.

The army general staff met frequently because many issues had to be solved, among them Grozny's joint military commandant, the exchange of prisoners of war, and the search for the missing. At one of those sessions the commander Mogamed Khambiev, future Minister of Defense under Maskhadov, admonished Basaev for accepting the post of Deputy Prime Minister. He also accused him of dividing military commanders into warring camps, which would let Iandarbiev remain President of Ichkeria—I am not sure Iandarbiev was ready yet to play that game against Maskhadov. Gelaev, absent from the meeting, was not included in the blame. Basaev was so outraged by the accusation that he tore up Iandarbiev's decree naming him deputy minister in front of everyone at the meeting, asserting that he was not interested in any post, and then left very much offended. After Basaev declined the position, Iandarbiev offered it to Maskhadov, who should have refused it, but did not. I think that from that moment Basaev and Maskhadov parted ways. Afterward, they met and made common decisions, but the relationship they had had during the war no longer existed.

Supporters of Zelimkhan Iandarbiev were former followers of Dudaev who considered that, as Dudaev's vice-president, he was his rightful successor. Those people were a minority. Most were frightened by Iandarbiev's scheme to introduce *Shariah* abruptly. At the time, Iandarbiev was the leader of two Caucasian movements: the Caucasus Confederation and the Organization of Islamic Unity of the Caucasus (OIUC). The purpose of those organizations was to liberate the Caucasus from Russian influence and to establish a North Caucasian confederation. The organizational structure of his devotees was the Chechen branch of Caucasus Confederation, which had an office and published a newspaper.[37] As the head of OIUC, Iandarbiev disputed the division of Muslims into Sufis and Salafists, arguing that inter-confessional differences were incited by Russian intelligence services.

At the end of October, Maskhadov announced his candidacy. Basaev and Iandarbiev were the other main contenders. Among other candidates were Zakaev and Udugov, who could not even count on their relatives' votes—as confirmed in the elections, but who were positioning themselves to bargain for nomination to the future cabinet. A dozen nominees completed the list. It is worth noting that Ruslan Khasbulatov was not among the candidates. The former speaker of the Russian Parliament expressed an interest in running, but his real ambition was to return to Russian politics. Maskhadov persuaded him to abandon the campaign by explaining that he could face danger in Chechnya. It was unlikely that he realized that he was one of the figures upon whom Chechens pinned the responsibility for starting the war.

Maskhadov chose Vakha Arsanov as his running mate. Arsanov, a native of the highlands, could be expected to bring the votes of the Shatoi and Itum-Kale districts, where Maskhadov's authority was not as strong as in Greater Chechnya, east of the river Argun. A member of the first independent Chechen parliament in 1991, Arsanov was not a stranger to politics. He had begun the war siding with Ruslan Gelaev, moved away from him, and became one of the major commanders; therefore, large numbers could be expected to rally around him. Some sources related that, together with some of his close friends, he could rely on two to three thousand soldiers. In Chechnya that was a great number.

The elected head of the central election commission was Saidulaev, a former army intelligence officer, a major in the Soviet Army, close to Maskhadov in his views. We welcomed his election; it gave us hope that the commission, whose members were mostly followers of

---

37. Also called Caucasus Confederation.

Basaev and Iandarbiev, would not be able to aid their candidate. To prevent any manipulation, commission members were requested to swear on the *Quran* that they would not engage in dishonest or illegal action on behalf of their nominee. No doubt the oath was a good idea, although not everyone considered it to be holy. I had a feeling, not based on any data, that some members considered themselves free from the oath when it came to the parliamentary election.

My Work as a Campaign Staffer

Commander Turpal-Ali Atgeriev, a friend of mine, was appointed Maskhadov's campaign manager. He asked me to be his executive director. I refused because I had not yet recovered from my distrust of Maskhadov. As I was driving home after talking to Atgeriev, a car forced me to stop. It was Batalov, commander of the Naur battalion, who already had rescued Maskhadov from Iandarbiev's machinations. He undertook to persuade me to join Maskhadov's campaign. After some argument, I agreed to go to campaign headquarters the following morning.

I knew that my participation in the campaign would again put Maskhadov under pressure from the Salafists. When I next visited his campaign headquarters, Maskhadov asked to speak to me in private. He did not mention the issue over which we had parted; as if the quarrel had never occurred, he asked for my help. Atgeriev was a military man, not a general manager; he did not have the experience or skills to win a political campaign. I had come prepared to turn him down, but he did not look like a victor and had doubts about running. I agreed to help on the condition that I would not be supervised or undermined, particularly by anyone from the team of his running mate. Alas, it was not that easy.

Just a week after I began working on the campaign, a man named Ruslan Kutaev, a politician, came to me to explain that he was taking control of the staff because he knew how to win elections. It was too much. I delivered an ultimatum to Maskhadov: It was either Kutaev or me. Maskhadov hesitated but a similar threat from Atgeriev forced him to choose us. Within the hour we forbade Kutaev to appear at headquarters under any pretext. After the election I saw him claiming to have directed the campaign staff and explaining how he won.

People actually had little doubt who led Maskhadov's campaign; thousands of activists across the republic worked for me. Few voters were even aware that the other candidates had headquarters. Moreover, the campaign treasury was at Atgeriev's disposal and was guarded twenty-four hours a day in our headquarters in Grozny.

Atgeriev and I managed to gain support for our candidate throughout the country. It was then that I met with Musa Nugaev who, as my assistant and my friend, later went with me to prison and into exile. For those who came to help, Maskhadov was the nominee best suited to get Chechnya out of the war. Next to the militant Basaev and the Islamic radical Iandarbiev, our nominee looked like a peacemaker. People wanted a president acceptable to Russia to maintain a dialogue. Russians would not tolerate the commander of the raid on Budennovsk. It was also difficult to imagine cooperation between Iandarbiev and the Kremlin.

Unfortunately, too many advisers flocked from all sides to advise Maskhadov. We knew that, fearing our disapproval, he secretly met and negotiated with people like the Salafist Khalimov or Kutaev. But the campaign staff did his organizational work. In every district of Chechnya, we set up staff offices; and no trace of other contenders existed. We arranged Maskhadov public appearances, at times several per day in different parts of Chechnya, wrote his speeches, and organized fund raising. We also had to correct mistakes made by Maskhadov's secret advisers. For example, bypassing us he agreed to make propaganda posters—they turned out to be good, but they were printed in Moscow. It allowed Basaev's staff to accuse us of accepting help from the Russians. We were forced to reveal our source, a Chechen who printed them at his publishing house in Moscow as a contribution to the Maskhadov campaign.

Much time was spent clarifying aspects of Maskhadov speeches for people who came to headquarters. Unfortunately, few of our visitors listened to our staff; they wanted to meet with Atgeriev or me. It annoyed me because I did not want our staff to believe that I thought myself above them or closer to the candidate. I had always stressed that we could only win as a team.

We made use of Chechen social structures, the clan and the Sufi orders. Maskhadov belonged to the large Alleroi clan, scattered across the Republic and present also in neighboring Ingushetia. We rallied elders of the clan in different villages. A few dozen Alleroi elders from the mountain districts once showed up unexpectedly at headquarters. I had to meet with them because Maskhadov and Atgeriev, another Alleroi member, were absent. They informed me that they had come to discuss things that members of other clans should not hear. Not being an Alleroi, I was going to leave the room when the oldest man in the group called me back. I sat down, thinking that they had decided I could hear the secrets of their clan. They again began by saying that this conversation should remain between Allerois! I again headed for the door; and once more the leader yelled at me. I explained that I belonged to the Tsikaroi clan. Seeing astonishment on their faces, I realized that because I worked for Maskhadov, with the Alleroi Atgeriev, and was friendly with many Allerois (most of Maskhadov's guards), they assumed I was one of them.

They told me that I was more one of them than many born Alleroi and they had nothing to hide from me. There was no secret except that they demanded that Allerois campaigning for Maskhadov throughout the country be official members of the campaign staff. I convinced them that Allerois should help but not in an official capacity. We were working for the election of the President of Chechnya; we should not be accused of trying to elect an Alleroi. My suggestion was adopted unanimously, and the elders assured me that they would help.

Learning about the incident, Maskhadov's Alleroi bodyguards made fun of me. The clan factor was relevant in the election. Other contenders did not, it seemed, take advantage of this element. They believed demagogues who claimed that the clan no longer had any weight. The clan had lost some importance, but people still considered it when making crucial decisions. When Maskhadov's nominee for Vice-President heard the story, he rebuked me. His clan belonged to the union of Cheberloi, as was mine. He did not like it that I was on Maskhadov's team. Our relationship, he thought, should have brought me to his side, but I did not know Arsanov and considered myself closer to Maskhadov's views. Arsanov never forgave me.

Besides the clan, the Sufi orders were the other feature of Chechen identity we tried to engage. Three-dozen Sufi orders exist in contemporary Chechnya, split between the Naqshbandiand Qadiri. The naqshbandi is divided into twenty-two orders, and the Qadiri into six orders. Orders vary widely in terms of followers, between a few hundred to tens of thousands, and they are not evenly distributed geographically.

Ali Mitaev was a popular Qadiri sheikh of the early twentieth century. The Ali Mitaev order is one of the largest in present-day Chechnya. There are villages in the Shali and Gudermes districts where the whole population belongs to that order. When Shamil Basaev mentioned that his grandfather had been a close companion of Ali Mitaev in his campaign rallies, I knew he was appealing to the disciples of the Ali Mitaev order for their votes. Potentially, there were tens of thousands of followers of that order in the Republic. We could not let his ploy go uncontested.

Maskhadov did not even know the difference between Sufi orders. With advisors like the Salafist Islam Khalimov, for whom the mention of Sufi orders was like the cross to the devil, it was not difficult to understand that I had a lot to teach him. In my attempt to play the Sufi card, I was helped by a special circumstance, which I think changed much in this campaign. A man came to headquarters to tell me that Shamil Mitaev, visiting from Moscow, wanted to see me. Shamil was the grandson of the founder of the order and was believed to be its spiritual leader at that time. His grandmother was a relative of mine; his feelings for her encompassed all her relatives in the Tsikaroi clan. He was interested in everything that was happening in Chechnya, and he was well informed. I had the impression that he was making plans to leave Moscow and return to Chechnya. I suggested that the period of anarchy we were in might not be the best time to make plans. He liked that I did not try to convince him of anything and that in some cases my outlook was more conservative than his.

I asked Mitaev if it was true that he ordered his disciples to vote for Basaev. It made him laugh. He assured me that he had not, although he knew that Basaev was talking about his grandfather at rallies. Without his knowledge, people close to him had spread the word about the vote, believing it was his wish. I asked if he would deny the rumor and speak in support of Maskhadov, but he would not support anyone—although he had sympathy for Maskhadov. I then told him that Maskhadov would like to meet him, knowing full well that he was unaware of Mitaev's very existence; but I had few days to fix the problem. If successful, I could engineer a change of support among disciples of the Sufi order from Basaev to Maskhadov.

I met with Maskhadov to explain that it would be good if we

could get tens of thousands of votes in one fell swoop. I had to explain to him the specifics of the Sufi orders, and I must say he took seriously everything about the election and trusted me. The next day I invited Shamil Mitaev to meet with Maskhadov at a relative's house for evening tea. But Mitaev responded that he did not want to meet! I had to rethink the format of the meeting and invite him to the home of my relative (the head of my Tsikaroi clan), whom he knew and respected, for the Sufi reading of the *Mavliud* (the hymn dedicated to Prophet Muhammad). Mitaev could not refuse. Of course, I brought Maskhadov to the *Mavliud*. After the reading the topic of the election inevitably came up. Shamil Mitaev did not say anything, but Maskhadov described his vision for Chechnya.

I knew that those who accompanied Shamil Mitaev would communicate to members of the order that their spiritual leader had met with Maskhadov. Within two days, when I returned to my village, I had many visits from people who wanted details of the meeting between their sheikh and Maskhadov. I replied that the encounter had taken place, but that I did not know what passed between them. The more mysterious the get-together, the more convinced they were that I knew a great deal. I was sure we had scored points over Basaev. In the end, that turned out to be true.

Victory in the Election and My Second Resignation, January 1997

As the elections scheduled for January 27 approached, the race became increasingly acrimonious. Initial promises to run clean campaigns were forgotten. Basaev expected his fame to carry him to victory. So confident was he in his success that he promised that in the event of defeat he would abandon politics for beekeeping. Iandarbiev accused all the candidates of engaging in an unpatriotic struggle for power, since the civic thing to do would be to keep him as president. Zakaev's campaign consisted in bargaining his votes for a position in any future government. Udugov understood that, except for his security guards and the relatives of his three wives, hardly anyone would vote for him, not even his fellow Salafists—for whom the election was unlawful in the context of *Shariah* law. Almost the entire population disliked both his manner of advertising and his impudence. The role of his staff was to keep him in the news by any means and to engage in a flurry of activity to give the appearance of popular support.

Maskhadov's predicament was to change his reputation as the head of the war party. Furthermore, Moscow's evident preference for his candidacy created additional problems. To appear to have dealings with Russia when the war was not yet finished would be disastrous. We, his staff, had to deny that he had any contact with Russia and to intimate that Moscow's approval was probably a strategy to harm his candidacy. Basaev was Maskhadov's only serious challenger; from polls taken in every village, we knew that the other contestants were negligible. Maskhadov, influenced by the Salafist Khalimov, believed that Iandarbiev and Udugov were his main rivals.

The OSCE was the guarantor of fair elections. It advised the organizers and did everything in its power to prevent fraud and interference by Moscow. Election observers came from the European Council, European Parliament, OSCE, and several European and Russian human rights organizations. People flocked to Chechnya to witness an historic event.

The morning of January 27 began with massive queues at polling stations. The OSCE had provided all of the stations with phosphorescent ink to track voters. In the presence of international organizations and representatives of the candidates, double voting was impossible. All day long, our workers reported various technical problems—some person did not find his name on the lists or another was trying to act as an independent observer—but no fraud. The only weak moment was the delivery of ballot boxes to the Central Election Commission in Grozny. There was no guarantee that the boxes would not be tampered with during transport. To assuage our concerns, the OSCE proposed to pass on to the commission, by radio (telephone lines were destroyed in the war) and in the presence of observers, the number of ballots in each box.

Election Day was a day of celebration. I had not seen such enthusiasm since 1991. People believed that they were forging their destiny. The OSCE had estimated half of the population voting; no one had expected the entire nation to turn out. By 8:00 p.m. lines at polling stations had not diminished, and the voting hours were extended to 10:00 p.m. The OSCE considered it unsafe to prolong the hours beyond that time, and polling stations closed at 10:00 p.m., despite people still waiting to vote.

By 2:00 a.m. we received information that Maskhadov was leading. I drove to the Election Commission, where angry Basaev representatives met me shouting, "This is your doing; this is your fault." It turned out that their candidate did not carry any locality in the Shali and Gudermes districts, which accounted for a third of all votes. I let an incredulous Atgeriev know that he could safely inform Maskhadov of his victory. I had never doubted his success; the issue for me was its size; I had calculated that he should defeat his main opponent by thirty percent. By 8:00 a.m., Maskhadov was winning with a margin that exceeded my most optimistic expectations.

Journalists from the leading world news agencies packed Maskhadov's house, expecting the official announcement. He waited for the OSCE's confirmation of his victory to be sure that the outcome could not be reversed. He received 59.3 percent of the votes, 228,000 more than he needed to win. Basaev got 23.5 percent, and Iandarbiev was soundly defeated with only 10 percent. The remaining contenders, including Udugov and Zakaev, received less than one percent each. At 9:00 a.m. I introduced Maskhadov to journalists as the new President of Ichkeria. From that moment onward, people who wanted some role in his administration began lining up in front of his house. A week later Maskhadov moved to the presidential residence, which had been stripped of furniture, carpets, door handles, even light bulbs by Iandarbiev's people.

Every day I went to the residence to transmit news reports around the world and to get Maskhadov to speak on one world network or another. One morning everyone turned away from me, ashamed to look me in the eyes. My friend, Il'ias Talkhadov, still head of Maskhadov's security, told me that a protégé of the vice president, Kazbek Khadzhiev, had been appointed press secretary and that Atgeriev, in protest, refused the position offered him.

Yielding to outside pressure, Maskhadov once again failed to protect me; this time, I bore it better. I refused to go to him, turned, and walked out. It would not change anything to put him in an awkward position; and, after all, I had not worked on his campaign in order to get a post. I had an intense dislike of the other candidates, and I felt I had a responsibility to my country. Most difficult to face was people's disbelief that Atgeriev and I, who were the authors of Maskhadov's victory, did not figure in the new government. I had no idea then that Maskhadov would betray me two more times.

Before I departed for my village, Atgeriev asked me to meet him at our headquarters in Grozny. It would be a shame to disband the good team we had gathered to get Maskhadov elected. We resolved to recast the organization we had created for the presidential campaign into a political party. After all, thousands of people had believed in us and worked with us. If Maskhadov would have nothing to do with me, he never stopped seeing Atgeriev and was aware of our intentions. He continued, unofficially and discreetly, to finance our staff.

The Stolen Victory

The beginning of Maskhadov's presidency was fraught with problems. According to the Constitution of Chechnya the positions of President and Prime Minister were combined. Anyone quoted as "prime minister" in Maskhadov's government was, in fact, Deputy Prime Minister. For a short period in 1998, Shamil Basaev was appointed Acting Prime Minister because he promised to turn around the republic's destroyed economy. In the time allotted to him, Bassev had no success; the figures clearly showed a continuous decline.

On February 16, a decree set up a thirty member Presidential Council with advisory powers. Chaired by Maskhadov, it consisted of powerful field commanders, representatives from the Parliament and the Administration of Spiritual Affairs, including the *Mufti* Ahmed Hadji Kadyrov and state and economic leaders.[38] From February to May, the council appointed the ministerial cabinet, ministers and heads of departments. During the confirmation process, candidates answered questions about their religious practices. After the cabinet was chosen, the general department of human resources under the president filled the remaining positions.

When the cabinet of ministers was announced, I realized that I had completely underestimated the impact of the Salafists on Maskhadov. If the appointment of Akhmad Zakaev (not a Salafist) as Minister of Culture was not a surprise and was welcomed—after all, he was

---

38. Among the commanders were Arsanov, Basaev, Ghelaev, Zakaev; among the state and economic leaders were Biibulatov, former Finance Minister, and Iarikhanov, former President of Southern Oil Company.

an actor—the nomination of Salafists to three important ministerial posts was a bolt from the blue.

Movladi Udugov received the Ministry of Foreign Affairs, although neither his intellect, his popularity, nor his rank among Salafists warranted such a position. He is falsely credited with winning the propaganda war against Russia, which in fact was due to the collective work of dozens of independent Chechen journalists—none of whom had any relationship with Udugov. Foreign journalists who had met Udugov did no more than mention his name occasionally. Russian journalists, however, sympathizing with the Chechens (and much of the Russian press did sympathize with them) routinely alluded to him in their articles. The buildup of Udugov as a Chechen Goebbels was an unfortunate mistake helped along by the Russian media, which portrayed him as someone unusual.

Maskhadov offered a second ministerial position to Islam Khalimov, who was appointed Deputy Prime Minister in charge of social issues. Later in the second Maskhadov government, Khalimov would receive the Ministry of Internal Affairs (MVD), which he immediately reorganized into a Ministry of *Shariah* State Security, thus transforming the secular police into a religious one.

Khalimov's deputy was another Salafist.[39] A last ministerial post, the Ministry of Education, was assigned to an active member of the Salafist party Abdul-Valid Khusainov. A Salafist, Shamsudin Batukaev, was named head of the *Shariah* court; and another, Abdul-Malik Mezhidov, leader of a new structure, the *Shariah* guard.[40] Finally, the nomination of a last Salafist, Arbi Baraev, who was also a notorious gangster, as Deputy Minister of Defense caused confusion among the population.

It looked as if Maskhadov and the liberals had lost the election, and the Salafists had won it. People accused Maskhadov of being too weak or not tough enough to pursue his own policies. I do not agree; Maskhadov was a soldier, capable of being tenacious in matters of principles. His biggest fear at the time was that Chechnya would follow the path of Afghanistan and Tajikistan after the departure

---

39. Supyan Abdullaev, together with Khalimov and Udugov, was a founder of the Islamic Revival Party in 1987.

40. Mezhidov was a founder of the Islamic Revival Party.

of Russian troops and slide into civil war. He was afraid of spilling more Chechen blood. The operation in Gekhi in September 1994, where Chechens fought Chechens on political issues, was always on his mind; and he never forgave himself for failing to prevent it. The Salafists were no longer the two-dozen they were before the war; they were new people willing to kill other Chechens to see their party win. By offering them posts, Maskhadov wanted to involve them in the reconstruction of the state. In fact, he tried to create a coalition government by offering positions to all leading politicians: to Iandarbiev, who refused because he would not accept anything lower than the presidency, to Basaev, Gelaev, and others.

Maskhadov's adversaries interpreted his strategy as weakness. I remember about a month after the election I was going to a funeral when a jeep driven by Shamil Basaev intercepted my car. He offered me a ride to the funeral. On the way, he inquired if I was pleased with recent political developments, since I was responsible for many of them. I asked him what he meant; and he replied, the election results. I told him I was glad that we had outperformed our rivals and that our campaign was transparent and fair, which could not be said about his. After listening to me, he said, "In a war-ravaged country, your efforts brought a gutless man to power. Take my word for it, in no time he will give everything away." Such was the mistaken belief of many who did not know him well. Shamil Basaev was humiliated by his defeat; he did not leave politics for beekeeping as he had promised; instead, he joined the opposition and engaged in personal attacks on Maskhadov.

By extending a hand to his opponents, Maskhadov thought to neutralize them; that by accepting important governmental posts they would be obliged to implement his policies. For a while, this tactic gave him breathing room by weakening the opposition. However, as they became stronger, the Salafists—who did not recognize a secular state but only their emir's laws and orders—became conceited; they imagined that they could demand Maskhadov's removal and the establishment of their own leader.

Furthermore, by inviting the opposition into the government and forsaking his campaign team, I believe Maskhadov not only weakened his party but also made the republic vulnerable. People elected him believing he could avoid conflict with Russia. And here he was, inviting Salafists into the government who wanted a break with Russia and with whom Russia refused to have a dialogue.

The Parliament of Chechnya

In January the people elected the parliament to complement the president. According to the constitution, the Chechen Parliament was an important body[41] that amended the constitution, ratified laws, and monitored the executive branch. It confirmed the appointment of members of the cabinet ministers, the constitutional court, the Supreme Court, the court of arbitration, and district judges. It nominated the attorney general, his deputies, and district prosecutors, members of the investigative committee and of the national bank. It set election dates, held referendums, approved the state budget, and endorsed international treaties.

In the first round, less than half of the sixty-three deputies were selected. There were a few political parties in Chechnya—the Salafists had one, Basaev had one, as did a few others—but Maskhadov did not have a party to back him. Most contenders running for parliament were not members of a party but were defined according to their sympathies for a particular presidential candidate. The number of contestants was large, and the race was fierce. The second round on February 15 chose only thirty-two deputies, less than the quorum needed for the parliament to conduct business. It was a surprise. In Maskhadov's headquarters we had our nominees, but our participation in the parliamentary competition was limited to photographing them with Maskhadov, confirming their like-mindedness and future cooperation. We thought it would be enough. The vast majority of the elected representatives were indeed supporters of Maskhadov.

Because of the lack of a quorum, at the beginning of March the Election Commission reviewed its decisions and confirmed eleven more winners. That decision was a political expediency: the republic could not afford more campaigning and its new parliament could

---

41. According to the Chechen Constitution, based on the Constitution of Lithuania, the parliament was the main ruling body; the office of the president was mostly representative. In 1992, Dudaev was able to engineer a constitutional change making the president the main decision-making figure, by combining the office of president and prime minister.

not get to work since forty-two representatives were required. It was, however, a questionable decision and, as many of the eleven deputies were not supporters of Maskhadov, one that made me doubt (after the fact) the Commission's integrity, even if all its members took an oath on the *Quran*.[42] On March 10, the old pre-war parliament convened and ratified the mandates of the forty-three deputies. On March 13, it transferred its functions to the new legislative body. Major parliamentary committees were set up by May: foreign relations, defense and security, media and press, and social affairs and health.[43]

A former field commander Ruslan Alikhadzhiev, supporter of Maskhadov, became speaker; and a former lawyer, Selim Beshaev, deputy speaker. The only competitor of Alikhadzhiev was a close friend of Basaev. Maskhadov's adjutant also became a deputy. He and his competent and well-spoken staff member, a friend of mine from university,[44] kept our new party well informed abouts developments, allowing us to control situations.

Many sources falsely allege that two factions dominated the Parliament, those of Ruslan Kutaev and Movladi Udugov. They are misinformed. Maskhadov's party controlled it with thirty deputies; Basaev could claim the loyalty of four or five representatives; and several MPs were undecided, most eventually joining the Maskhadov camp. Kutaev had one man in the parliament and Udugov had none. The false allegation seems to have originated in a report on post-election Chechnya given to the Russian Parliament by the Secretary of the Russian Security Council, Ivan Rybkin.

Unfortunately, the Chechen parliament never became a body working closely with the president. The government was too poor to pay salaries, and deputies began seeking outside funds. Nonetheless, it remained the guardian of the Republic and its constitution, defending them against encroachment by those who wanted to change the system.

---

42. During the counting of the votes in the February election, members of the commission let us know that two commissioners were trying to get one candidate elected.

43. Their respective chairmen were Akh"iad Idigov, Abubakar Magomadov, Ramzan Akhmadov, and Satsita Gairbekova.

44. Eventually, Ruslan Azimov, who also spoke English, became Deputy Foreign Minister during Il'as Akhmadov's tenure.

Chapter 11

EARLY POLITICAL STRUGGLE

Maskhadov First Political Victory, May 1997

The Chechen victory in the war had to be consolidated by a treaty with the Russian Federation. On February 19, the government created a commission headed by Udugov to negotiate a treaty.[45] It was empowered to settle the full range of issues arising in the relationship between two sovereign states. Contracts concluded between Russian and Chechen enterprises and organizations could not come into force without approval of the agreement. Through informal channels and personal contacts, members of the commission tried to find politically influential people in Moscow who would advance their claim for independence; while at the same time Russian politicians were looking for ways to pressure the pro-independence Chechen leaders to give up sovereignty.

On May 12 in the Kremlin, Boris Yeltsin and Aslan Maskhadov signed an "Armistice and Principles of Inter-Relations between the Russian Federation and the Chechen Republic of Ichkeria." Acknowledging centuries of conflict, Yeltsin stressed that it "puts an end to 400 years of war and opposition." He stayed clear from any hint that Chechnya was a subject of the Russian Federation. Connections between the parties, the protocol stipulated, would be settled "in accordance with the generally recognized principles and norms

---

45. The commission included: Akhmed Zakaev; a former president of the Chechen oil company, Khozh-Akhmed Iarikhanov; Interior Minister, Kazbek Makhashev; and presidential adviser Said-Khasan Abumuslimov.

of international law."[46] In the history of relations between the two countries, it was the first document of its kind.

The signature of the Russian Head of State on an official document carrying the full name of Chechen Republic of Ichkeria was interpreted as Russia's acquiescence to Chechen independence. Legal acceptance would require the approval of a future peace treaty by the Duma. There was a feeling among some members of the new political elite that we had proclaimed our independence and did not need Russia's recognition. This ridiculous presumption prevented many things from being achieved during the years of independence.

On the same day, Prime Minister Chernomyrdin and Maskhadov signed an agreement of economic cooperation that would pave the way for a potential economic treaty between the two countries. The document provided, in particular, for the immediate restoration of critical Chechen infrastructure, payment of pensions and social benefits, and the release of all forcibly detained persons. Shortly afterwards, the Russian Ministry of Fuel and Energy and the Chechen Southern Oil Company came to an agreement to rebuild the energy facilities destroyed during the war.

The armistice was a huge political victory for Aslan Maskhadov. Russia's acknowledgment that it had waged war upon Chechens on and off for four centuries and its acceptance of international law as a basis for future relations were historical developments undreamed of a few years earlier. All politicians should have celebrated its signing as a triumph of the Chechen people. Instead, almost all of Maskhadov's opponents downplayed the event.

Russia and Chechnya after the Armistice

Despite his explosive temperament, Boris Yeltsin always followed his team's advice. In the case of the armistice, his *eminence grise* was Boris Berezovski, who was trying to get his hands on all former Soviet pipelines. As Deputy Secretary of the Russian Security Council, he

---

46. Because in the armistice text Russia refused to refer to the Khasaviurt Agreement, which made reference to international law, the Chechen side insisted that it should be specified that future relationships between them be in accordance with the principles of international law.

was as powerful as its Secretary, Rybkin, without the accountability.

On April 4, Rybkin reported on the situation in Chechnya to the Duma. He began by confirming the overwhelming participation in the presidential elections and Maskhadov's victory and expressed regrets for the appointment of Shamil Basaev as First Deputy Prime Minister, as it might complicate relations. Since 1991, he stressed, Chechen politicians had considered their republic an independent state, its independence enshrined in their constitution and not negotiable. Notwithstanding that reality, Rybkin suggested that Chechnya's change of status should be settled within the framework of the Russian Federation's laws and, to that effect, accords limited in scope should be reached before any full-fledged peace treaty could be agreed upon. Pressing issues, such as airports, borders control, or economic concerns, could serve as starting points for compromise.

The armistice signed in May was a product of Rybkin's recommendations. Despite the agreement's historical moment, it was believed that it was only a first step toward a peace treaty. Specific agreements, in particular in the economic and military spheres, could divert Chechen focus away from independence toward questions of common interests with Russia. Chechens, however, were interested in a treaty that would be a first step toward international recognition of Ichkeria.

By August, Chechens and Russians exchanged tentative suggestions for a treaty between the two countries. Differences between the proposals exposed the widely differing visions of Chechnya's status. The Chechen document's main concern was independence. The name Chechen Republic of Ichkeria at the top of its text underlined that it was a new entity distinct from the Chechen Republic listed in the Russian Constitution as an autonomous republic of the Russian Federation. The Chechen proposal offered mutual recognition as sovereign states, subjects of international law, and requested that Russia sponsor Ichkeria's membership into the United Nations. It also invited cooperation in defining the material and moral damage inflicted by the war on the Chechen State and its people.

The Russian proposal avoided the words independence and international law and never mentioned the United Nations. It did not speak of war damage, but simply earmarked money for specific projects. Its main concern was the delegation of power: the proposal stressed that the Chechen State had full authority on its territory, including conducting foreign trade, with the exception of the powers delegated to the Russian Federation. As the Russian Constitution gave the same powers to all its autonomous republics, the document demonstrated that Russia continued to view Ichkeria as a subject, not a sovereign state.

Therefore, relations between Moscow and Grozny had made limited progress since 1991. Moscow would not accept Chechnya's breaking away from the Federation. And it was not, as most analysts erroneously claimed, because of oil. Chechen oil accounted for less than one percent of all Russian deposits. It was only of importance to Chechens, because it could replenish their treasury. However, Russia feared a domino effect! Tatarstan and Bashkortostan, in the Volga region, and the Republic of Tuva, on the Mongolian border and annexed only in 1944, showed signs of separatist sentiments. Chechnya's departure could open a Pandora's Box.

Most Russians were not ready to accept Chechen independence. Nationalists perceived its loss as a sign of the continuing weakening of the country that had begun with the collapse of the Soviet Union. No Charles De Gaulle arose to solve the Chechen problem once and for all by cutting it loose.

The visit of Maskhadov to Moscow on August 18, therefore, was predestined to fail, even though he believed he could persuade the Russian President of the necessity of recognizing Chechen independence in a face-to-face discussion. The miracle did not happen, even if Boris Yeltsin left a slight hope that such could be the outcome after protracted negotiations.

During that same meeting with Yeltsin, Maskhadov asked for an explanation of the resources earmarked for reconstruction of Chechenya. The Chechen government was promised 120 billion rubles (approximately $20 million), part of which had not been disbursed—whereas some members of the Russian government referred to an amount six times higher, about 800 billion rubles ($120 millions). It turned out that the Prime Minister had not yet considered approving any such amount.

New Elections and a New Party, May-August 1997

Turpan-Ali Atgeriev and I had a new project. Elections for the mayor of Grozny were announced. The acting mayor was Lechi Dudaev, a nephew of the assassinated president. I did not know Lechi personally, although people had good things to say about him; for me he was only a candidate in a campaign. The excitement of the presidential election had not fully disappeared. I had to prove to myself that our team could win the mayoral race, that what happened in January was not due to chance but was the result of effective methods and techniques which could be repeated.

Turpan-Ali Atgeriev decided to run for mayor of Grozny. Unlike with Maskhadov, I was completely at ease with him. He had what I did not have: boundless courage and a certain childish ability to believe in action that he thought would strengthen the state. He was four years younger than I and did everything four times faster.

Atgeriev was from the village of Alleroi and was a member of the Alleroi clan. After high school he worked in construction and graduated from the law department of the Bykovski State Farm College in the Volgograd region. In 1992, he fought in Abkhazia with North Caucasian volunteers under the command of Shamil Basaev. Upon his return, he worked in the Ministry of Internal Affairs, and in 1994 he was promoted to sergeant in the 21st Company of Grozny Traffic Police. His involvement in the armed conflict in Abkhazia, he explained as following the lead of his fellow villagers. He had stayed there only three months; he thought he went to help Muslims persecuted by Christians, but he claimed, he never came across any Muslim Abkhazians.[47]

Atgeriev was, needless to say, involved in the Chechen War. He commanded the Novogroznenski regiment that was active in east Chechnya and in other military units and, at times, was in charge of sections of the front. He participated in the defense of Grozny, Argun, Gudermes, Alleroi and other towns. After the capture of Argun and Gudermes by Federation forces, he moved north and, while there, joined Raduev's raid on Kizliar military airfield. After the bungled raid, he led a breakthrough from the village of Pervomaiskoe. Because of his participation in the raid, he was put on the Russian wanted list and charged with banditry, hostage taking, and terrorism (Articles 77, 126, and 213-3 of the Russian Criminal Code). This, however, did not limit his movements across the North and South

---

47. Abkhazians are nominally Muslims. The conflict in Abkhazia was purely ethnic, Abkhazians against Georgians. Religion played a minimal role.

Caucasus. Later he headed the counter-intelligence department of the Chechen army and was promoted to brigadier general after the war. He was wounded twice and received the Orders of Hero of the Nation and Honor of the Nation, the highest award of the republic. He was a praise-worthy head of Maskhadov's presidential campaign, immediately becoming its moving spirit. With such a background, he was the ideal candidate for mayor.

Elections were set for May 31. Our staff, inherited from the presidential election unlike those of our opponents, was outstanding and we had a widespread network of workers. Every day we met with Grozny's residents to explain our program and listen to suggestions. There were several candidates, but Atgeriev's only serious competitor was the acting mayor, Lechi Dudaev. The Election Commission favored Lechi. Several times, its members approached us trying to convince us to withdraw in favor of Dudaev as a tribute to the assassinated President. We even heard of secret meetings, purportedly trying to find a way to persuade Turpan-Ali to give up, so as to honor the uncle, but he refused to give way to the nephew. I had no doubt that we would win; it was just a question of by what margin.

On Election Day our observers were at all the polling stations. At the outset it became obvious that there would be disruptions and that the Election Commission was responsible for them. Under various pretexts a number of polling stations did not open because there was no chairman, no ballots, or both. In all the stations that were operating, our candidate turned out to be the favorite, his lead overwhelming. In the end, although Atgeriev received more than 44 percent of the votes at polling stations considered pro-Dudaev, he was obliged to concede that the elections were troubled. The Commission recognized that Atgeriev had won but, because of the numerous election violations, invalidated the results. Re-elections never took place, and Dudaev remained in his post. For the sake of stability, Maskhadov decided to take Turpan-Ali into his government. The position of mayor of Grozny was not worth damaging his political ties with those who considered themselves close to the first president.

Shortly after the election Maskhadov asked to be invited to our headquarters to meet with the staff. We had reformed the organization that we had created for the presidential election into a political party. It was liberal and democratic, but also traditionalist in the sense that it defended Chechen customs and observances. People from all walks of life—cultural, educational, and political intelligentsia—identified with its values. Our party was pro-Maskhadov and was designed to help him resist the influence of Salafists and others like them. We named our party the Chechen Islamic State Party. The term Islamic was introduced to spike the guns of the Salafists and to show that the traditions and customs of the Chechen people were fully compatible with the Islamic understanding of state and society. We chose Maskhadov's first visit to our headquarters after his election to announce the creation of the party.

I had not met Maskhadov since January. The encounter was tense. Staff members resented that he had insisted on new mayoral elections. He felt uncomfortable with those who fought for him but whom, in the end, he had sacrificed for the sake of political stability. I alone felt at ease. I was glad that I did not need anything from him; that I was able to prove to myself that with such a team we could win any election; and that hundreds and thousands of people came to me, asking for clarification of a particular action of the president because they trusted me. Of all those attending the meeting, I was the most free of the president.

Everyone, from Atgeriev down to the staff workers from the villages expressed their disappointment with Maskhadov for being the only politician embarrassed in front of his team. Using Afghanistan and Tajikistan as examples, he defended himself, explaining that he viewed his main task as trying to avoid the deepening of internal conflicts.

Concluding the session, I suggested to Maskhadov that, should he appoint our party workers to government positions, he would be able to accomplish whatever he planned easier and faster. He liked my idea of a "reserve cadre" and promised to consider it; and meanwhile he would start with Atgeriev, whom he appointed Vice Prime Minister. I do not know if we made a step towards reconciliation, but we were not enemies. The situation in the country was delicate and our president needed help.

Boris Berezovsky, Money, and Oil

The Kremlin *eminence grise* Boris Berezovsky played a disastrous role in relations between Russia and Chechnya.[48] On 17 October 1996, the Russian president forced the resignation of Alexander Lebed (architect of the Khasaviurt Accord) from his positions of Secretary of the Russian Security Council and National Security Advisor. In his place, the spineless Ivan Rybkin was appointed—a man whose character was opposite that of Lebed. Within two weeks, a presidential decree named Berezovsky as deputy secretary of the Security Council. For many politicians and experts the presidential Chief of Staff Anatoli Chubais was responsible for this assignment. Berezovsky held this position for thirteen months and was eventually fired by Chubais. Rybkin, ill at ease among the stars of politics, went everywhere accompanied by his deputy. It was not difficult to guess who made the decisions.

In early 1997, Berezovsky and his boss arrived in Grozny to meet with the newly elected president. Rybkin had barely finished his speech congratulating Maskhadov for his victory when his deputy asked to speak to Maskhadov in private. According to Maskhadov, Berezovsky offered to assume the cost of restoring the oil industry in exchange for control of the republic's pipelines.[49] The oil fields in Tatarstan and Siberia, developed in the 1970s, made Chechnya's reserves insignificant. But Chechnya's role in oil processing and transport remained relevant. In the vicinity of Grozny there were three refineries capable of processing up to 20 million tons a year. Several pipelines crossed the Republic from Azerbaijan and Astrakhan, through Grozny, to the terminals of the Black Sea port of Novorossiisk. Thus, conveying oil through Chechnya could bring in huge revenues.

The Chechen government, in Berezovsky's words, should be grateful for his offer to rebuild the processing plants and should show its appreciation by relinquishing the control of its pipelines to him. He would ensure that a large part of Kazakh oil would flow through Grozny, providing employment in its refineries. He also promised to share a portion of his profit from oil transport to local communities,

---

48. Berezovsky made his fortune in the 1990s when Russia went through the privatization of state properties, gaining control of various assets. In 1997 his wealth was estimated at US $3 billions.

49. He also offered to repair a chemical and a gas processing plant and two dozen small associated businesses to his offer.

but refused to quote a percentage. For Ichkeria, however, the pipelines were much more than a source of potential revenues; they were political leverage in its negotiations with Russia.

Maskhadov refused Berezovsky's offer, thus acquiring a powerful enemy. Forever after, Berezovsky made no secret of his desire to harm Maskhadov. He flirted with the anti-Maskhadov forces, and his role was disruptive. He subsidized various projects of the opposition, including a modern television center for the Salafist party; $2 million to Basaev for the reconstruction of the important Chiri-Iurt cement plant (the largest in the North Caucasus and controlled by Basaev), which could bring huge revenues; and several million dollars to Udugov for the Islamic radicals' attack on Dagestan, which would trigger the second Chechen war. When the Deputy Secretary of the Security Council went on television to boast that he would pay any amount for the release of Russians held captive by Chechens, he inspired a spate of kidnappings, encouraging criminals to search for victims. Later, at the beginning of the second Chechen campaign, Berezovsky was closely associated with Vladimir Putin, then Secretary of the Security Council, whom he claimed to have brought to power. He may indeed have engineered Putin's rise on a wave of anti-Chechen hysteria.

Chapter 12

CRIMINALITY, SALAFISTS, AND
INTERNATIONAL RELATIONS

Kidnapping in Chechnya

Nowadays, world opinion of Chechens, in contrast to what it was during the first war, is thoroughly negative. One issue that sullied our reputation was the wave of kidnappings that took place between 1996 and 1999. It is a painful subject for a Chechen. The complexity of the historical moment, mainly the absence of a full-fledged state, could explain the appearance of socially negative extremes. But there was more to it. Chechnya was cut off from all other countries; no beneficial influence had ever come from the United States, Europe, or even the Middle East. Its only relationship had been with Russia and its military culture.

The behavior of the Russian army during the war made some Chechens deviate from traditional values. They rationalized their acts by the deeds of their enemy, and they adopted its methods. The military leadership was also to blame for not curbing the early isolated incidences of violence—on the presumption they would disappear after the end of the war, and moral principles would return.

The rapid growth of Salafism, with its repudiation of traditions and conventions, had a role in the emergence of sociopathic behavior. In fact, it can be argued that the combination of Russian and Salafist affects on society led to the destruction of Chechen ethic.

During the war, the Russian army had engaged in the business of selling dead bodies to relatives. Various groups of people were drawn into this dark trade: the imams in mosques; the heads of settlements, who were trying to redeem the bodies of Chechens from Russian commanders; and middlemen looking for missing persons and negotiating the release of bodies on behalf of families. The quest was a protracted affair—inquiring at official and unofficial prisons, hunting for contacts, bargaining prices, following payment procedures, and receiving delivery of the remains. Furthermore, these tasks could multiply, because it was often a mystery which military entity had arrested the missing person in the first place. There were so many possibilities: the army, the Ministry of Internal Affairs, the FSB, military intelligence, or the prosecutor's office. The search had to start anew with each unit. In time this commerce involved hundreds of Chechens acting as go-betweens. Society despised them, but could not do without them. Using them, however, financed this illegal and unprincipled industry.

In a devastated country, criminals had quickly realized that they could make money from people who had come to help, journalists and workers of humanitarian organizations. Some of the same people involved in the cadaver traffic were implicated in the rash of kidnappings. More difficult to explain is why some honorable members of society became involved in this business; rumors had it that even some government officials engaged in it.

Certain abductions obviously had purely commercial aims; others had political or religious motivations. Nonetheless, they all had something in common: their blatant politicization. This trafficking hurt Maskhadov, showing up his inability to control the situation. Without any doubt, it harmed Chechen prestige, a result that could profit only Russia. In the same vein, it may be that a few Russian politicians contracted some kidnappings. So many captives, for example, were released after Berezovsky's intervention—always accompanied by a great show in the media—that suspicion arose that he had ordered the hostage takings himself. The seizure of the prominent Russian journalist Elena Masuk, well known for her pro-Chechen war reporting, was a famous case. Her disappearance in May was a shock for all Chechens and for all who helped them. Freed within a week, after Berezovsky paid her ransom, she immediately turned against the Chechens. The result was a victory for Russian propaganda: it could claim, "Look, those who aid Chechens eventually become their victims."

Journalists were the preferred victims. Their kidnapping and release almost always resembled the Masuk case, the hostages liberated after Berezovsky's interference.[50] Members of humanitarian organizations were less prized captives than journalists, their value on the trade market being less. Nonetheless, many of these seizures of nongovernment organization (NGO) workers dealt irreparable political damage by changing forever the way the international community viewed Chechens.[51] The worst crime, a kidnapping turned deadly, was perpetrated against six workers of the International Committee of the Red Cross, shot in the hospital of Novye Atagi in December 1996.

Some hijackings took place in Dagestan; but these were attributed, without much proof, to Chechens since the hijackers had told their victims that they were Chechen. Many of the hostage takings that occurred in border areas could possibly be ascribed to criminal elements from Dagestan, Ingushetia, or Ossetia. The detainees were often released outside of Chechnya. Abductions, it seemed, was a problem not only in Chechnya but also in the entire North Caucasus.

Kidnappings with religious motivations also occurred, as in the example of two Orthodox priests captured in the Urus-Martan district. Religion also may be the reason for the gruesome murder of three British and one New Zealand engineers employed by the UK company Granger Telecom, who were beheaded in December 1998 and left near the Ingush border. Their execution was believed to be the handiwork of Salafists, followers of the Deputy Minister of Defense. That episode also had a political implication since it damaged Maskhadov's image by showing his inability to control such religious groups.

---

50. To name only a few, the following were taken hostages: Roman Perevezentsev and Viachesl Tibelius, two journalists of the Russian television station ORT in January 1997; an Italian journalist Mauro Galligani of the weekly magazine *Panorama* in February 1997 in Grozny; three employees of Radio Russia, Nikolai Mamulashvili, Iuri Arkhipov, Lev Zel'tser; ITAR-TASS correspondent Nikolai Zagnoiko in March 1997 in Grozny; ITAR-TASS correspondent Said Isaev in March 1999 in Grozny; ITAR-TASS photojournalist Vladimir Iatsina in July 1999; and French photo-journalist Brice Fleutiaux in October 1999.

51. Among the best known cases were the abductions of members of the Italian humanitarian organization *Intersos*, taken in September 1996; two British citizens, Kamil Carr and John James, abducted in July 1997 in Grozny; and several Hungarian employees of the humanitarian mission, Action by Churches Together, seized in October 1998 also in Grozny.

Training Camps of Amir Khattab

An unfortunate event, and one that also injured Chechnya's reputation, was the transfer of two children's summer camps, damaged in the war, to foreign Salafists. Many foreign fighters did not leave after the end of the war. On the contrary, they acquired a base to spread their ideas not only in Chechnya, which was of no importance to them, but throughout the entire North Caucasus and beyond. For local Salafists, they provided contacts with like-minded communities abroad, primarily in Turkey and the Middle East; and they taught them clandestine action.

When they first arrived, foreigners were careful to avoid involvement in the Republic's political affairs. Then, their leader Amir Khattab became close with Shamil Basaev. His ties to Basaev protected him and his group from squabbles with the local population, which, for the most part, did not approve of Salafists who rejected Chechen beliefs and traditions, first of all Sufism. It was Basaev who, as deputy prime minister after the war, allocated the two children's camps to their use.[52]

Once settled, the Salafists launched activities to spread their ideas. The Republic was transitioning from civil to *Shariah* courts, but did not have enough staff versed in *Shariah* law to serve them. Finding an opening, Khattab offered accelerated courses of law at his camps. In Arab countries mastering the law takes seven years; Khattab's teaching lasted a few months. Together with Islamic law, apprentices received a more practical education: how to lay mines and neutralize them or how to construct bombs from materials at hand. In this way, Khattab's graduates became his followers, and he and his group widened their influence.

Khattab's training center began fairly rapidly to draw youth, attracted to Salafism, from the entire North Caucasus and beyond: Uzbekistan, Tajikistan, Kyrgyzstan, and Kazakhstan. Instruction could last from three to nine months; but the basic components were always Islamic law, mines and weapons, and leadership and the organization of underground cells. The number of people who

---

52. The children summer camps were called Gagarine and Mountain Air. They were located in Avtury even though most souces on Khattab described them as being in Serzhen-Iurt. Avtury and Serzhen-Iurt are separated only by a stream.

passed through the camps is difficult to pinpoint, as there was no documentation; but a fair guess would be more than a thousand. The impact of this training, however, could grow exponentially if each trainee returned home and set up his own cell or *Jamaat* and taught his own recruits. The camps would become a source of major problems for Russia. Young trainees returning to their respective North Caucasian republics formed local underground *Jamaat*, which later became active against Russia.

Thus, with the silent consent of Chechen authorities, a terrorist site developed in Chechnya. To disband it by force would have meant open war with Basaev. Maskhadov did not want to risk a civil war.

Press Secretary to the President

From the moment Atgeriev joined the government, I knew that he would attempt to recruit me. To prevent this from happening, I announced that I intended to pursue a post-graduate degree (Doctor of Sciences) in Moscow.[53] I even flew there to enroll in a program at the Institute of Oriental Studies of the Russian Academy of Sciences. The head of the Middle East Department, an acclaimed Arabist, agreed to be my academic consultant, a definite honor.

While in Moscow, I realized that history was closer to my heart than politics. I felt a new lease on life; libraries and archives always acted magically upon me. There I could forget everything and, with my mind at peace, enthusiastically immerse myself in my research. Working on my Ph.D., I followed a schedule that all my friends knew: Mondays, Tuesdays, and Wednesdays I spent at the Military History Archive; Thursdays and Fridays at the Archive of Ancient Acts; and Saturdays and Sundays at the Lenin Library. I was looking forward to this new routine. Before I could engross myself into history, however, problems had to be resolved, in particular how to settle in Moscow

---

53. Candidate of Sciences degree (earned after obtaining a PhD) is the highest academic qualification a scholar can achieve. It is awarded for original research and significant contribution to the field. To qualify, candidates must write a professorial thesis, reviewed by and defended before an academic committee. The level of scholarship has to be considerably higher than that required for a PhD thesis and must be accomplished independently. In the US it would be the equivalent of tenure.

as a married man. A long distance relationship was not realistic, not least the financial cost of maintaining two households. I returned to Chechnya eager to work out details.

Back home, I found insurrection in our new party. Some members, the careerists, blamed me for not being forceful enough in promoting their interests. They wanted me removed as chairman and replaced by someone more assertive. There was some truth in their criticism. Maskhadov had consented to use the party as a pool for government employees, but I did not intend to put him in an awkward position by constantly pressuring him to arrange work for or replace his existing employees by our affiliates. I called an emergency meeting. Organizers of the *putsch* against me hoped that I would smile and step aside. But having decided to renew my studies in Moscow and having been accepted in a doctoral program, I decided to tell, frankly and even harshly, what I thought about the Republic, its leaders, the party, and, of course, individual careerists. In the end, of all those present, only four sided against me. I was vindicated, although it was a triumph for which I did not care much at the time.

This event and my intention to leave for Moscow made Atgeriev scramble to find me a government position. In early January 1998, Maskhadov called me in and offered me the post of press secretary. To say that I was surprised would be a lie, but this offer jarred upon my feelings. Furthermore, his present press secretary, an intelligent and educated man, was perfectly competent; and I was pleased with him. The only fault I could find in him was his lack of confidence, since he was affiliated with the vice president. Tactfully, I told Maskhadov that I did not want a job and that he should not feel guilty for having dispensed with me after his election. He explained that at the time he had had to go along with the vice president, who categorically opposed my appointment as press secretary.

At this point I realized that there must be a cooling in relations between Maskhadov and his vice president. I was not sure that I wanted to make enemies of Arsanov and his team by accepting the position. To my surprise, Maskhadov began to pressure me; and I realized that, even in the event of my refusal, he had decided to dismiss his present press secretary. I told him that I needed twenty-four hours to think it over. Accompanying me to the door, he said he expected a positive response. Outside, his guards met me with hugs and shouts of approval that only cooled off when I informed them that I had not yet accepted the job. All my attempts at justifying myself made no sense to them. I had barely reached party headquarters when an outraged Atgeriev, with equally infuriated Il'ias Tolkhadov and Akhmed Avdorkhanov, arrived to berate me. From what they disclosed, I understood that divergences of opinion between the president and his vice president were deeper than I had grasped from my conversation with Maskhadov. By lunchtime, the headquarters filled with party members and government employees who wanted to hear why I had not yet agreed to take on the press secretary job; they considered my rationale unacceptable.

The next morning I returned to Maskhadov to tell him that I did not want to be a scapegoat for competing teams and, to accept the position, I needed assurances that I would be independent. Therefore, I required a status shielding me from attacks. Maskhadov offered me the post of first assistant to the president, responsible only to him. I suggested that he let me establish an analytical department, to which he consented. By lunchtime we were still discussing the country's affairs, with Maskhadov giving me his position on many issues, when his chief of staff[54] brought the decree ratifying my appointment for his signature. Maskhadov amended the text, naming me First Assistant and Head of the Analytical Group of the President. Seeing the chief of staff's reaction, I guessed that he would never be one of my supporters, an insight that was confirmed later.

After leaving Maskhadov, I went to the press office. Alas, neither Maskhadov nor his head of administration bothered to warn Press Secretary Kazbek Khadzhiev that he had been dismissed and that I had been named in his place. I had no choice but to inform him myself; and I will never forget the expression on the faces of him or his subordinates. I asked everyone, including Khadzhiev, to stay on and continue to work for my service. Kazbek understandably refused, and most of his team left in support of its sacked boss. Some took valuable hardware as partial payment of their wages, and I had to see that it was returned.

After taking responsibility for the office, I found it inefficiently run; there were two sets of cameramen, one working with the

_____

54. Vakhit Murdashev.

president, and the other with the vice president. It took me a while to make Maskhadov and Arsanov understand that I would decide who filmed them. Surprisingly, there was a television station as a branch of the press department, which meant that the amount of work increased drastically. The hardest part of the job, however, was maneuvering between the two presidential teams, and I consider my greatest achievement the avoidance of major conflicts.

To raise the status of the department, I moved it to the Presidential Palace and then succeeded in assembling a core of young and enterprising people who, having no steady wages, worked selflessly with me. None was a professional, but all were keen apprentices. The Analytical Group quickly became the envy of every senior official, including the chief of staff. One of Maskhadov's trusted donors, a Moscow businessman, gave us invaluable assistance.[55] He supplied the unit with priceless assets, computers and the necessary software, and at times provided staff members with small monetary aid permitting them to survive in an economy with ninety percent unemployment.

As press secretary to the president, I often appeared on television. The opposition blamed me for all of Maskhadov's decrees and orders and decided that their problems were connected with me. Opposition rallies were frequent morning occurrences in the center of Grozny. They were made-to-order, the same participants brought in for each occasion by buses from east Chechnya. A journalist told me one morning that I was anathematized at these events as a U.S. agent after I accompanied Maskhadov on a trip to the United States. I became interested and asked a friend to record and film the gatherings. Listening to the recording, we heard, "Let's start our meeting and curse Mairbek Vatchagaev who sold himself to the U.S.", and saw that all those present raised their hands and invited the All Mighty to chastise me. Later, I was blamed as a Mossad agent and an MI5 agent. Earlier on, of course, I had been stigmatized as a Russian agent.

Maskhadov's Journeys Abroad

Maskhadov went on several official visits abroad; and, to give him

---

55. Olkhazur Abdulkerimov began his career as a lawyer then moved into business. He was one of the richest businessman of the Chechen diaspora.

credit, he did relatively well. Those he spoke to responded well to his soldier's integrity, modesty, sincerity, and charm. His first foreign trip was to Moscow in May 1997. It resulted in the signing of an armistice, for which he could take personal credit. In a private interview he was able to convince the Russian president that it was time to lay the foundation to end a conflict that had existed between our peoples for centuries, and that only the president could make that happen. His second trip to Moscow in August 1997, however, proved less successful. The Russian authorities did their best to prevent Yeltsin from signing a peace treaty recognizing Chechnya's independence.

The same month President of Georgia Eduard Shevardnadze received Maskhadov in Tbilisi. The encounter was crucial; Georgia, an internationally recognized sovereign state, was (and is) the one country, besides Russia, bordering on Chechnya. The Russian Federation surrounded Chechnya on three sides; and, to the south, across the Main Caucasian Ridge, was Georgia and the way to the rest of the world. In Soviet times, nothing even resembling a road crossed the mountains. Inhabitants of these regions, however, preserved the memory of thoroughfares having existed in the past, before Russian colonization. The Tsarist authorities had maintained only three corridors (for easier control) leading from the North to the South Caucasus: the Georgian Military Highway, the Sukhumi Highway, and a coastal road along the Caspian Sea, all by-passing Chechnya, rendering impassable the two-dozen pathways across the main ridge that had historically joined the North Caucasus to Georgia.

Maskhadov came to Sheverdnadze with a proposal to rebuild one of those ancient roads, one that remained a narrow track large enough for a horse, or at best a cart, and this not everywhere, leading along the Argun River from the Chechen village of Itum-Kale to the Georgian village of Shatili. The Georgian president, not particularly concerned with Russia's reaction, gave his consent. Nonetheless, he took every opportunity to say publicly that strengthening relations between Georgia and the peoples of the North Caucasus could be good for Russia. It is strange to recall that Mikhail Saakashvili, in those days the majority leader in the Georgian Parliament, was responsible for the failure of this project stating, "This perplexing formation that is the Chechen Republic of Ichkeria may be responsible for a worsening of our relations with Russia."

For us, it was vitally important to establish trust and confidence with Georgia; it implied the possibility of strong relations for the future, but it was not an easy task to accomplish. Many Georgians believed that they had lost the 1992 war with Abkhazia because of Chechen participation, including that of Basaev and Gelaev, on the Abkhazian side. The proportion of Chechens in the conflict did not exceed that of other North Caucasians, but the myth of Chechen invincibility played against us. Maskhadov had to convince the Georgians that most Chechens were not happy about the participation of a handful of their countrymen in that war. Only then could he suggest turning the page and moving on for the sake of future generations.

Twice Maskhadov journeyed to London, in October 1997 and March 1998; I was with him the second time. They were not official visits. The Chechen government knew from the outset that, to avoid offending Moscow, no member of the British government would receive Maskhadov. British authorities, however, did not oppose his visits and were obviously interested. The Chechen politician and businessman Khozh-Ahmed Nukhaev sponsored both trips. The purpose was to raise European awareness of Chechnya, present the Chechen president to the European public, and negotiate business projects. Nukhaev and Lord Alister McAlpine of the Conservative Party discussed oil projects.[56] A third of the British Parliament, both the House of Lords and House of Commons, came to a reception organized by the Chechen delegation. Even skeptics came to have a look at Maskhadov, the man who had brought the Russian army to its knees, and vigorously applauded his speech.

Margaret Thatcher came to dine with Maskhadov. The evening did not begin well; Mrs. Thatcher's principle interest was the fate of British nationals missing in Chechnya. No matter what topic Maskhadov introduced, she invariably concluded by saying, "You have to admit, Mr. President, the citizens of Great Britain must be found." On my advice, he oriented the conversation toward the subject of war; only then did the "Iron Lady" become attentive, interested, and supportive. She recalled that, after learning of Russian troops' entry into Chechnya,

---

56. McAlpine, businessman, politician, and writer. He was an advisor to Margaret Thatcher, and was briefly involved in the movement by some British conservatives to help Chechnya, especially its oil industry.

she had requested her assistant to fetch a map and magnifying glass to locate the Republic on the map. As the war unfolded, she could not comprehend how such a small place, not much bigger than a dot on the map, could resist and outmaneuver the mighty Soviet army. The war allowed the West to understand, she claimed, that there was no Red Army any longer; and that, along with the Soviet Union, the army had passed into history. Saying goodbye, she turned to Maskhadov with a smile and said, "Your country is so small, I am sure you can find them [the missing British nationals], Mr. President."

Maskhadov also journeyed twice to the United States, first in November 1997 and then in August 1998. I was with him the second time. In August 1998, Maskhadov was invited to Washington to participate in the International Islamic Unity Conference, held under the auspices of the Islamic Supreme Council of America. As the trip took place shortly after the Salafist rising against the government that shook Chechnya in July, Maskhadov was often questioned on that issue.

Several embarrassing moments occurred during our U.S. trip. First was the provocative announcement by Minister of Foreign Affairs Udugov, while the delegation was still in transit in Istanbul, that Maskhadov was to meet President Bill Clinton—even though Udugov knew that no meeting with Clinton was planned or expected. Another awkward situation transpired when the organizers ran out of money and were rescued by the former Chairman of the National Bank, Nazhmutdin Uvaisaev, who accompanied us on the trip. On arrival in the United States, Maskhadov's security team did not want to part with their weapons and had to be reassured that Maskhadov would be under the protection of a special unit of the FBI tasked with the security of high-ranking visiting officials and that the weapons would be returned to them upon their departure. Finally, as we were settling in at the hotel, someone knocked on the door and was chased away by one of the guards, who did not speak English, or even Russian. It turned out to be the venerated Cypriot Sheikh Nizam al Daghestani, who funded our visit to the United States!

American Muslims greeted Maskhadov as a hero, as the man who led the *jihad* against the Russians and won. The conference could not start because people wanted to touch him and talk to him; we had to pull him forcibly from the crowd to sit him at the presiding table. Participants in the conference from all over the world tried to establish contact with Maskhadov. Among them was the president of an Islamic Development Bank in South Africa, who offered to open a branch of the company in Chechnya. We construed his proposal as a stroke of good luck, especially as he made it clear that Russian *desiderata* would have no influence on him.

We received an unexpected invitation to meet Secretary of Agriculture Dan Glickman. Glickman talked with Maskhadov for a few minutes then withdrew and let his staff discuss ways his department could come to Chechnya's assistance. We were totally unprepared for the encounter and did not even know what could be requested. I had to inquire from our hosts what kind of help they provide to developing countries, and then translated to Maskhadov that they were offering us grain. But we had no idea what quantities we could request and, once again, I asked about how much they apportioned to countries in need. Before I had time to translate that Pakistan had been allocated 20,000 tons and tell Maskhadov to ask for the same amount, he blurted out a shocking figure. He was able to get out of a delicate situation by saying that Chechnya needed 100,000 tons to restore its destroyed economy but that 20,000 tons would help greatly that year. The staff assured us that such an amount would not be difficult for the United States to procure, and asked us to name the closest port where the grain could be shipped. We were surprised to be offered aid similar to that given to Pakistan, but were informed that 20,000 tons was the usual amount dispatched around the world to countries in difficulties. Deeply thankful, we wanted the grain as quickly as possible; it would revive our mills.

The agreement signed with the Secretary of Agriculture was the first accord contracted with a cabinet member of the United States government. Unfortunately, by early 1999 the shipment had not yet arrived, and by then the quantity to be delivered had fallen to 5,000 tons. Worse, when dispatched, the grain was sent to Russia and never made it to Chechnya because of a blunder of the Chechen government.

Unexpected also was the invitation to meet with an assistant Secretary of State at the State Department—generally unofficial visits are held at a different location—despite the Russian Embassy's careful tracking of our delegation's every move. In Washington, Maskhadov also ratified a document permitting the opening of a branch of the Islamic Development Bank in Grozny, whose charter capital would be financed by the biggest banking system of the Islamic world, Al-Baker. Maskhadov warned the representatives of Al-Baker that Russia in all probability would oppose the project and try its best to make them abandon it. They replied that Russia's wishes would be a minor consideration since their sacred duty was to give Chechnya an access to international financial markets independent of Russia. Washington may have had a hand in this scheme. Altogether, Maskhadov's visit to the United States was a success; most important, he may have achieved a breakthrough in Chechnya's international isolation.

To sustain Chechnya's international exposure, Maskhadov traveled to numerous countries, generally informally. He visited Azerbaijan to congratulate Geidar Aliev on his President's Day and stopped numerous times in Turkey in transit. Turkey's government was careful not to offend Moscow but could not deny that they were attracted by the region's potential. Many Turkish politicians, in one-on-one conversations with Maskhadov, acknowledged their North Caucasian roots, Turkey having admitted hundreds of thousands of North Caucasian immigrants in the nineteenth and twentieth centuries. During his first *Hajj*, Maskhadov met with King Fahd, who tried to touch his feet in a sign of respect for a man who had fought and won a *Jihad* against the Russians and who claimed to be glad and honored to receive such a guest. Maskhadov also journeyed to Malaysia, Indonesia, and Poland. Therefore, despite Russia's attempts to blockade Chechnya from the outside world, Maskhadov, step by step, widened its international network.

The Visit of Sheikh Nazim

A deputation led by Sheikh Nazim al-Dagestani came to Grozny after Maskhadov's return from America. Respected and influential in the Muslim world, he could have been immensely helpful to Ichkeria.

For each international guest, we devised a program of activity tailored to his area of expertise: religious, economic, or political. Believing Sheikh Nazim would not be interested in economic or political discussions, I arranged a trip for him to several holy places. I was mistaken. When on the second day the sheikh discovered that he was going to be driven to more Sufi tombs, he lost his temper. He was not concerned about the dead, he claimed; he cared about the living and for economic development; and he desired to be included in all of the economic and financial conversations, in particular, those with the representatives of the Islamic Development Bank, who came to negotiate the opening of the bank's branch. Sheikh Nazim's contribution to these talks was valuable. Knowing the difficult state of the Republic's finances, the bankers offered interest-free loans to start the company. Having credit within the Malaysian Islamic community, the sheikh was later instrumental in arranging the visit of the deputy speaker of the Malaysian Parliament to Grozny. During his stay, the speaker, ignoring Moscow's possible reaction, openly proposed various kinds of assistance.

Given time, Maskhadov's international missions, in particular in the Muslim world, may have borne fruit. All came to an end in 1999 with the beginning of the second Chechen war. Possibly, Maskhadov's incremental successes may have played a role in prompting Moscow into a second war.

Chapter 13

SHARIATIZATION
OF ICHKERIA

Shariah Courts

A development of considerable importance in the life of the Republic was the reintroduction of the *Shariah* religious courts. The Bolsheviks had banned them in 1925. Nevertheless, the *Shariah,* and even more the *adat* (common) law, continued, if secretly, to regulate conflicts within Chechen society. Petty quarrels, brawls, insults, and other minor incidents were rarely taken to Soviet courts. It was distasteful to do so, and they were dealt with internally by each community on the basis of *Shariah* or *adat,* as they always had been.

The Salafist opposition, allied with Basaev, demanded the establishment of Islamic law. Maskhadov's decision to initiate a return to at least some elements of *Shariah* was a political maneuver to counter them. For most Chechens, who had heard much about religious courts within their family circles, their reappearance in 1998 was not a complete novelty. On the one hand, people were afraid of them; on the other, regrettably, they tended to idealize them as an incorruptible system in which judges could not be bribed, and unfair decisions could not be made.

Religious courts took over in a big way. Their first decision was a death sentence for a man and woman for adultery, to be carried out publicly on one of Grozny's central squares. This act of savagery and cruelty was executed in front of children and women; and as no one had any experience in conducting such executions, it was butchery. Sadly, I discovered that there was a category of persons who wanted public punishments, demanding prior announcement of them so they could be present. What I viewed as a barbaric event, some considered a spectacle.

Flogging, for drunkenness and other minor transgressions, was another verdict pronounced by the courts. One of the earliest victims was the former *Mufti*, who had fled the country at the beginning of the war without declaring *Jihad* against the Russians; he was arrested and sentenced upon his return. Television broadcast those ghastly ordeals. Among the victims I recognized some familiar faces of journalists who by their work had done much for the Chechen cause.

Judges, most of them graduates from Khattab's courses, defended public chastisements—not even forbidding children to see them—maintaining that the vivid example would make people afraid to violate the law. I did not believe that Chechens had ceased to have extramarital affairs, but rather that justice had become a parody. Anyone could be suspected of infidelity; simply talking to a fellow student, colleague, or former classmate of the opposite sex could be enough. And the *Shariah* police took bribes to keep quiet.

The young judges, knowing nothing of Islamic law, discredited it, and everything associated with it, in the eyes of the population. Khattab's teaching was only an introduction to the *Shariah*. During the few months they were taught in his camps, these pseudo-judges could learn little of it. Very quickly, they began adjudicating on the basis of their sympathies and became mired in corruption. The courts, which Chechens had supposed could only be impartial and morally upright, were sullied as they openly engaged in extortion. To rectify this appalling situation, the government hired back the staff from the Soviet judicial system, people who knew how to conduct an investigation or to pass sentence based on precedents. The Supreme *Shariah* Court employed an advisor, Bek Mezhidov, a jurist who had made his career in Soviet times, but had also spearheaded the Chechen revolution in the early 1990s.

Judges of the Supreme *Shariah* Court were supposed to be theologians, but none had a degree in *Shariah* law. Furthermore, there was high turnover among them. Burdened by the responsibilities to both society and the Almighty, all of them resigned after less than a year. One judge, whom Maskhadov had not been able to persuade to stay on, when asked his reason for quitting, replied succinctly, "I'm afraid of God," meaning that much of what he did had no bearing on the *Shariah*.

The damage Khattab's young pseudo-judges did to the standing of the *Shariah* courts was immense. Russia would not have succeeded any better had it attempted to vilify them. Moscow proceeded to stigmatize the entire Chechen people by broadcasting to the whole world the mistakes these judges made. There was no need to invent anything; it just had to report what was taking place. And the world agreed with Russia: Chechen society needed a radical shakeup.

The Fundamentalist Uprising, July 1998

By the summer of 1998, local Salafists, who believed they had become a force to reckon with, were dissatisfied with the positions they occupied in Maskhadov's government. They wanted more. They were quarrelsome, and they appeared to be moving toward open conflict with the authorities.

After the unexpected death of their spiritual leader Sheikh Fathi in 1997, Chechen Salafists elected another Jordanian of Chechen descent, Abdurakhman al-Shishani, to replace him. Born and raised in the city of Azraq in Jordan, he was fluent in Arabic and Chechen, and he was young and ambitious. His election surprised his family and the entire Jordanian Chechen community since he did not have even a high school education, let alone a spiritual one.

Sheikh Fathi had refrained from clashes with the authorities. The new leader began by declaring his rejection of all power except the power of the God, a pronouncement testifying to his low level of education and his lack of understanding of the situation. He and his group assumed that they could successfully oppose the authorities. They had no doubt about the weakness of Maskhadov's government and thought that the weakness of the government had forced him to compromise with them. Their only goal was the overthrow of the government and the establishment of an Islamic state, as they understood it.

Despite their apparent uniformity, Salafists were not a homogeneous group. Their talk of one Islamic community *(Ummah)* hid strong divisions between leaders, all of them fancying themselves caliph of the future Islamic state. They were united only in their hatred of the government. Had they been able to seize power, they soon would have been at each other's throats.

The Salafists' presence in the Republic's power structures—judicial, internal affairs, and defense—generated severe tensions. Some of them, while verbally proclaiming the supremacy of the law of God, did not bother to comply with it. My press service received several audio and video recordings of *Shariah* guardsmen shamelessly carousing. However, they were not averse to blackmailing people for the same behavior. At their prompting a witch-hunt began in Grozny against dating couples. These *Shariah*-lovers could spend hours hiding in bushes or trees to take pictures of youngsters engaging in "immoral" behavior, and then extort pay-offs for their silence. They would stop cars and demand that their occupants disclose their relationship. Chechens, who had never heard of such rules, were overwhelmed and began expressing their anger against the government, and Maskhadov personally, for having empowered the Salafists.

The followers of *Shariah* interfered in most aspects of life. They even prohibited the celebration of the New Year, considering it a Christian holy day, and forbade both public and private celebrations. Their meddling discredited everything connected with Islam. The Salafists did more to harm the reputation of the *Shariah* law than the long years of Soviet anti-religious policy. In this climate, people tried to show their rejection of the new laws. They hung Christmas tree branches on their cars to show that they would celebrate the New Year. Those who never drank took to drinking or pretended to do so while sitting in their cars downtown. Singing was a crime, so they loudly played pop singers. The more the Salafists tightened the screws, the more protest they elicited. Conflicts between those who supported *Shariah* and those who did not increasingly flared in various parts of the Republic.

Salafists deceived themselves in the belief that they had the strength to oppose Masakhdov. They made an alliance with Shamil Basaev, whom they elected head of their Congress in Chechnya and Dagestan. They needed a leader with a name, and Basaev wanted a following that would permit him to compete with Masakhdov. In fact, the Salafists had agreed to an association with Basaev less for his achievements than to a request of Amir Khattab, who, thanks to Basaev's protection, could quietly train men for guerrilla warfare in his camps.

In early May a clash erupted between Maskhadov's security and

Shariah followers when the latter tried to punish Maskhadov's guards for drinking alcohol. Maskhadov's friends and foes alike knew that his people never drank. A week later Atgeriev, Chairman of the Cabinet of Ministers, was stopped under the same pretext; and a vicious fight broke out when the Salafists declared they had no president called Maskhadov. Their president was God and His emir on earth was Abdurakhman al-Shishani. No one was safe from harassment, not even Basaev's men. It looked like the emir was pushing his adherents toward a confrontation with the authorities.

Such a situation could not last long. At some point there would be a clash involving firearms. It happened on July 14th in Gudermes. Emir al-Shishani had his quarters there as did Commander Sulim Iamadaev, a strong anti-Salafist. Their paths were bound to cross in that settlement of no more than 40,000 souls.

After lunch on that day a group of *Shariah* supporters, looking for action, stumbled upon four of Iamadaev's men, who blocked their path and challenged them. Instead of turning back to take a different road, the Salafists decided to stand their ground and called in reinforcements. Only after several dozen of their supporters joined them did they attack Iamadaev's group and had no difficulty in overpowering them. As soon as he heard that his people had been disarmed and beaten, Iamadaev sent for his troops and ordered Gudermes surrounded.

The Salafists had no intention of leaving the town: using the radio, they summoned their forces from around the country to come to their assistance. The news spread rapidly; and individuals willing to fight the followers of *Shariah* also converged upon Gudermes from various directions and in great numbers. Meanwhile, Iamadaev began hunting Salafist supporters in the town. It was the beginning of the civil war that Maskhadov had dreaded. He tried to persuade the commander to stop but to no avail; the beast was out and would not be recalled.

Maskhadov then tried to contact Emir al-Shishani. I was with him, as were other members of his government, during that tense period when he was attempting to stop the carnage. Using the radio frequency utilized only by Salafists, Maskhadov's radio operator established a liaison; but whoever was on the line refused to honor the president's request. Maskhadov took the microphone, introduced himself, and explained that he needed to talk urgently to

Emir Abdurakhman. Persons on the other end laughed and replied that there was no President Maskhadov, nor was there an Ichkeria or Chechnya; they took orders only from their emir, who did not wish to talk at present. Maskhadov did not lose his temper over the insults and kept insisting he be connected with someone in power, the emir or a field commander; but they continued to mock and abuse him. After hours of effort, he finally declared angrily, "I tried to save you, but you do not want help."

Salafists were confident their forces would easily crush Iamadaev's soldiers and those few who would join them. This was a tactical error. The news that a commander in Gudermes had decided to deal once and for all with the Salafists spread like wildfire and was greeted with resounding approval from most of the population. I asked Atgeriev to broadcast an appeal for calm. It was a mistake. Atgeriev, who recently had been the focus of attacks of *Shariah* followers, appealed to Chechens not to rush to Gudermes because the government was able to deal with the situation. However, he made the mistake of concluding that the dispute was between Sufis and ungodly Salafists and not the concern of the Republic as a whole. It was the last straw. Sufis began converging *en masse* upon Gudermes to defend Sufism against Salafists. Maskhadov had to deploy thousands of National Guardsmen along the roads connecting the city to other localities to stop the tens of thousands of *murids* (Sufi disciples) wanting Salafist's blood.

Maskhadov scolded me for letting Atgeriev speak to the media; I did not try to explain that we had not expected such an eventuality. Shamil Basaev arrived at the presidential residence shortly after the broadcast and, in front of a large group, complained, not about what was occurring in Gudermes, but rather that the fight was described as a contest between Sufis and Salafists. Aslanbek Ismailov, who Maskhadov had designated military commander in charge of the situation, exploded in anger. He blamed Basaev for what was happening; it was his flirtation with the Salafists, the military parades in Khattab's camp, and his acceptance of the presidency of the Salafists's Congress of Chechnya and Dagestan that led to this disaster. He was, shouted Ismailov, responsible for every death occurring that day. Turning to Maskhadov, he asked to be relieved of his command because he wanted to go to Gudermes to take part in the destruction of Salafists. Without a word, Basaev left the room; but in the doorway he stumbled upon a friend of his who told him reproachfully, "I hope you are going to Gudermes to kill those Salafist dogs."

Meanwhile, in the audio room, the radio was tuned to the Gudermes frequency, and we were able to follow what was going on in town. Iamadaev was in control from the start. He kept repeating that he did not need reinforcements; the only help he was willing to accept was that of preventing Salafists from slipping out of town. He was hunting for them all over the city—to kill them all.

The following day, Salafists at last admitted that without Maskhadov's assistance they would be massacred. Their radiomen begged to talk to him but were put through only after they spelled out his full name and title. Maskhadov had not slept for two days and was in constant communication with his forces. In late afternoon, when it was confirmed that the Salafists had been defeated, and it was just a question of hunting them down, Vice President Arsanov with Shamil Basaev came to see Maskhadov to plead the Salafist cause. They did not try to justify them; they begged him to let the stragglers leave Gudermes alive.

To give himself time to make a desicion, Maskhadov ordered me to announce a truce on the radio. An irate Iamadaev thought that I had taken it upon myself to call for a ceasefire; but, realizing I was not in a position to take such a decision, he calmed down. He asked me to tell Maskhadov in private that he needed "only three hours to find their hiding places and that of their leader; only three hours to deal with them once and for all." I went to Maskhadov and gave him the message; he had a split second to make a desicion and chose a truce. I contacted Iamadaev again and instructed him to stop all military action. The command was announced on all radio frequencies at once, and I heard a shout from the Salafi channel that they would immediately obey the presidential order.

Arsanov and Basaev proceeded to Gudermes to escort the survivors out of town. They were taken to Urus-Martan, which in a short period of time became a Salafi bastion from which they spilled forth their hatred of Maskhadov. The president's truce had saved them from certain death at the hands of Iamadaev but plunged the republic into further chaos.

Maskhadov appeared on national television and strongly criticized all supporters of Salafism: The revolt was a devious stab in the back of the young state, vulnerable after the devastating war with Russia. He described all those who took up arms against their government at such a crucial moment as people without honor or dignity. Moreover, he enjoined all foreigners who had taken part in the uprising to leave the territory of Chechnya immediately. The injunction mostly concerned Emir Abudrakhaman. Russian media claimed that the order also applied to Khattab, but it did not. I personally read the ruling on television, and Khattab was not implicated. He had not supported the mutiny, and Maskhadov knew it. In protest, Islam Khalimov resigned with his entire team of Salafists from the Ministry of *Shariah* State Security (formerly Internal Affairs) and was replaced by a supporter of the president

Just a few days after the coup (July 20th), a presidential decree disbanded the *Shariah* Guard and the units of the *Shariah* Regiment, both nests of the Salafits. Furthermore, if members of those units were apprehended on the street with weapons, they would be disarmed; and, if they resisted, they would be eliminated on the spot. Two members of the Supreme *Shariah* Court who had spoken in support of the Salafists were fired; and two preachers (Jordanian Chechens), accused of hate speech and incitement to violence, were expelled. The latter sentence, however, was not implemented because the men had no documents, either Jordanian or Russian; if ejected they would find themselves in Russia where they would undoubtedly be arrested. Maskhadov did not want this to happen. Emir Abdurakhman agreed to leave, but asked for time to plan his departure to avoid falling into Russian hands.

On July 22nd the Republic's supreme commander banned the activities of private television and radio stations in Grozny. The measure was aimed at the Salafist broadcasting media, known as *Caucasus,* run by Udugov and functioning thanks to the help of Berezovsky and the Russian channel ORT. Udugov pretended it did not concern him personally and was in no hurry to quit his position as Foreign Minister. Nonetheless, everybody understood that the government would be re*shuff*led and that those tied to Salafists in any way would be asked to resign. The first was Shamil Basaev, who by then was in open conflict with the president. The Gudermes affair had damaged the opposition but had not destroyed it. Many of the subsequent developments were a continuation of that event.

The battle in Gudermes had a number of implications. Salafists became conscious that they were a very small minority. Many young people left their ranks, suggesting that they had joined not because of ideology but for the opportunity to earn money. Maskhadov was able to distinguish friends from foes, and he never forgave the mediating role played by the vice president. The population gave Maskhadov a vote of confidence, and opposition commanders such as Basaev realized that they had no chance of winning against him in an armed conflict. They switched to different tactics: in particular, they tried to remove him through legal channels using the *Shariah* courts.

An attempt on Maskhadov's life was another act of the armed opposition. On July 23rd a huge blast exploded in Grozny on the road where Maskhadov's house stood. In that situation we had to tread carefully, and we decided with Maskhadov to play a double game. On behalf of the president, I announced that the explosion was probably the work of foreign secret services, implying they were Russians. He, for his part, declared that he had no doubt the attack was organized by Zelimkhan Iandarbiev, his former competitor in the presidential election and, by then, a Salafist himself. The Supreme *Shariah* Court subpoenaed Iandarbiev and other Salafist supporters to give evidence in the assassination attempt and let it be known that those who refused to comply would be brought to court by force. Iandarbiev presented himself but refused to plead guilty and expressed a willingness to take an oath on the *Quran*. At the same time *Mufti* Kadyrov summoned a Muslim congress in Grozny, with *Ulemas* (religious scholars) from other North Caucasian republics in attendance, which issued a strong condemnation of Salafism as a radical trend, contrary to Chechen culture and behavior. The situation was very tense, and the threat of another massacre of Salafists was in the air. Responding to that danger, the leading pro-Salafist opposition commanders,[57] including Basaev, expressed their solidarity with the president. All discord should have ended, and the situation should have been ideal to start rebuilding. Instead, open conflict broke out between Basaev and Maskhadov.

---

57. Those included Shamil Basaev; Arbi Baraev, Deputy Minister of Defense; the Akhmadov brothers (Ramzan, Uvais, and Rizvan), leaders of the Urus-Martan Salafists; and Abdul Malik Mezhidov, Head of the Shariah Guard.

Shamil Basaev against Aslan Maskhadov

In September a group of commanders represented by Shamil Basaev, Salman Raduev and Khunkerpasha Israpilov brought an impeachment suit against the president for incompetence, violation of the constitution, unwillingness to adopt *Shariah* law, and a lack of transparency over the management of a charitable fund administered by his wife Kusama.

That Basaev was a party to the suit did not come as a surprise. Neither was the fact that he managed to enlist Raduev. To most Chechens, Raduev seemed unstable, even if harmless: he liked to wear medals of his own design; he called himself commander of a non-existent army of Dudaev; and he refused to accept Dudaev's death. He claimed to know that Dudaev (his father-in-law) had survived the Russian rockets on that fateful day over two years earlier, and that he was about to return to Chechnya, the date of his return being continuously postponed. With this last assertion, he was able to draw the attention of a number of people, former supporters of the assassinated president.

The presence of Israpilov, whom Maskhadov considered a supporter, among his adversaries was unwelcome. He had underestimated Israpilov's ambition. Israpilov, who viewed himself as an outstanding military commander at least as good as Basaev, if not better, resented not having a cabinet position. Instead, Maskhadov had created for him and his soldiers a special structure, the Police Special Force. The job, however, did not have ministerial rank. Basaev was able to play up the offense to enlist Israpilov.

The three commanders were willing to withdraw their suit if Maskhadov disbanded the parliament and announced early presidential elections. Maskhadov could not accept their conditions. To divide his opposition he instituted criminal proceedings against Salman Raduev, who a few months earlier had failed to appear when subpoenaed in the murder case of Lechi Khultygov, Head of the Bureau of Investigation,[58] who had been killed during a raid of Raduev's followers on the television center in Grozny. The Supreme *Shariah* Court sentenced Salman to four years in prison for his role in the

---

58. The Chechen equivalent of the FBI.

attack. The president proceeded to demote Raduev to private and deprive him of all awards and titles. The procedures against Salman startled Basaev, who began daily rallies supporting him, which were also occasions to call for the president's resignation. Shortly after, Ruslan Gelaev added his voice against Maskhadov, accusing him of dividing the nation along clan and geographic lines—and so did Ianderbiev, who felt offended by being accused of involvement in the assassination attempt on the president. By year's end Maskhadov was at odds with many of his former companions in arms.

Maskhadov wanted to get out of this dramatic situation. I suggested showing his opponents the strength of his popular support, using the Sufi orders. To that end, I suggested inviting a different Sufi order every day to meet with the president and to talk to him about its traditions and philosophy. Maskhadov was skeptical of my scheme; but after getting to know the various orders, listening to them, and speaking to them day after day, his enthusiasm grew. The Sufis, who had been offended by Maskhadov's earlier lack of attention, were glad to get acquainted with him. Each order left with the impression that they had made a special impression on the president.

After Maskhadov had met all the Sufi orders, I decided to take the risk of organizing a rally supporting him in Grozny. I chose December 17th. The public meeting was to be more than simply large; it had to give the president a resounding vote of confidence. I turned to our party activists to make that day a historic one.

On 17 December a feeling of anticipation hovered in the air. I sat in my office afraid the gathering would be a failure and watching various channels on the Internet discuss the rally's progress. Then the worldwide media—Reuters, the BBC, France-Press, etc.—began giving figures. After the Russian Interfax reported 50,000 to 70,000 people present, I ran to the meeting square to see for myself. The assembly was impressive, especially when compared with the twenty or so people of Basaev's daily support for Raduev. It was time to bring Maskhadov out. He could not believe that we had managed to draw so many people. When he heard the figures given by the world news agencies, he ordered his guards to take him to the rally. The crowd greeted him as a long-awaited idol, chanting, "Lead the assault on the opposition" and "Onward to Urus-Martan [the Salafist stronghold]." Maskhadov asked people not to take independent action but to let him and his government deal with the opposition. People were tired of lawlessness and universal unemployment; they wanted change and, on that cold and drizzly day, they came to the capital to support their president, who represented that change.

Maskhadov was like a recharged battery. The public had expressed approval and encouragement for his policies. He became conscious that the opposition was no more than a handful of commanders making power plays. Nonetheless, the rally angered his opponents, who petitioned the court for a speedy decision in their suit against the president.

The "Trial" of Aslan Maskhadov

During the last day of testimony in the case of Basaev and company versus Maskhadov, there was an incident involving my persona. In the heat of an angry indictment, I asked Maskhadov why he had not intervened when he heard the charges against me. He responded that he had long ceased to listen and react to such accusations, and that he knew no commander or politician who had not been blamed for having links with the Russian special services. This was true: there were rumors that Shamil Basaev was working for Russian military intelligence; that former Acting President Zelimkhan Iandarbiev had been an agent of the KGB; or that the Salafist leader Movladi Udugov was actually an atheist and a drug addict long ago recruited by the KGB. With many questions and few answers about many issues, the people turned to conspiracy theories.

The trial distressed Maskhadov. He viewed the actions of his former companions in arms as a heinous personal betrayal. The verdict of the court was intended to calm passions. It did not find the president in violation of the constitution. Nonetheless, it found him guilty of some transgressions, such as appointing persons who had collaborated with the pro-Russian administration to senior positions. This breach concerned only six members of Maskhadov's entourage, assistants or heads of departments, and one cabinet member. The court also instructed the president to relieve his wife of her duties as chairman of the charitable fund, since the *Quran* and *Shariah* allegedly barred women from leadership positions.

Maskhadov accepted the verdict. I announced on the evening news that the president intended to implement the court's decisions. He immediately signed a decree abolishing his wife's foundation and created a commission to examine its records. His wife Kusama was the sacrifice to be paid in exchange for a light court judgment.

The dissolution of the parliament and the introduction of the full *Shariah* rule were central to Basaev's tactics. The court did not act upon these issues and never mentioned them in its decision. Maskhadov was willing to introduce some aspects of Islamic law, but a full *Shariah* system would not only abolish his position, but also be the end of the Republic of Ichkeria and its democratic constitution. It would usher in a new form of government without a presidency.

Maskhadov was humiliated by the whole process and decided to take revenge by using Basaev's rules. In early January 1999, three generals, Atgeriev, Khambiev, and Batalov, all members of his cabinet,[59] filed a libel suit against Basaev, accusing him of numerous public insults upon the president. The generals' statement addressed to the judge raised suspicions regarding some of Basaev's actions, both during the war and in peacetime, suggesting that he conspired with the Russian secret services.

---

59. T.A. Atgeriev was a brigadier general and Deputy Prime Minister; M. Khambiev was a major general and Minister of Defense; and A Batalov was a brigadier general and Head of the Presidential Administration.

Chapter 14

STORM CLOUDS GATHERING

Maskhadov and the Parliament, Spring 1999

In the tug of war between the president and the opposition, the Parliament played an important role, even if inconspicuously. Chechnya's drift towards Islamization meant the eventual elimination of the Parliament as a legislative body. Despite the fact that its members displayed a full range of political opinions, it resisted any change to the system. It saved the president from all attempts to restrict his power. Therefore, it is all the more interesting to watch the workings of the Parliament's evolution from unequivocal support for Maskhadov in 1997 and 1998 to its readiness in 1999 to discuss Maskhadov's removal for encroaching on the tenets of the constitution.

The Parliament counted few experienced politicians, but it had lawyers, historians, economists, and other educated professionals. Maskhadov's choice for speaker was Ruslan Alikhadzhiev. Maskhadov wanted not just an ally, but also someone who owed him a debt. Alikhadzhiev was a professional soldier who had served in the Soviet Army in the tank corps. He was not a warlord who commanded a following permitting him to act as an independent politician. However, he turned out to be a disappointment to Maskhadov.[60] Alikhadzhiev

---

60. Before Maskhadov announced his pick, there had been a push to reelect the chairman of the former pre-war Parliament, Akh"ad Idigov. The president's main ally in the legislative chamber remained his former adjutant Khusein Iskhanov. Thanks to him, we mostly managed to nip problems in the bud and work out conflicts without exposing them to the public. Khusein was liked and respected, and his fellow MPs sought his advice.

quickly understood that Maskhadov needed him more than he needed Maskhadov so he tried to play an independent role.

After the Gudermes affair and the increase in his support, Maskhadov once again did a *volte-face*. Instead of striking a blow to the opposition, as the public demanded and as I and others thought imperative, he turned against his allies; his first victim was the Parliament.

The Parliament was debating a project submitted by the Supreme *Shariah* Court. The Court was under the influence of Salafists. The project proposed reforming the government by creating a new body, a supreme religious council or *shura*. At stake was the very essence of the State of Ichkeria: should it be a civil state ruled by a civil law or an Islamic state ruled by the Islamic law. The Supreme *Shariah* Court had issued a ruling in December suspending the legislative function of the Parliament, presumably to be given to the religious council.[61] On 30 December, the Parliament vetoed the ruling, supported in its action by the *Mufti* of the Republic, Akhmad-haji Kadyrov, an opponent of Salafism. The chairman of the Court[62] threatened the deputies with punishment in the next world. They, however, were more concerned by what would happen in this world should they cave in.

On 2 January 1999, in the presence of the *Mufti*, the Parliament and the *Shariah* Court met in session to hear a legislative initiative submitted by the Court. It proposed changing the Parliament's designation to the Arabic *majlis* (gathering or council),[63] and creating an Islamic council, or *shura* (consultation),[64] as an independent body to which members (presumably Salafists) would be selected by the *shura* itself. The MPs saw those changes as unconstitutional. After much debate and consultation with influential theologians and representatives of the *Mufti*, the deputies put forward a proposal of their own for an Islamic council. In essence, it would replace the former parliamentary

---

61. Ruling: «On the suspension of the legislative activity of the parliament» and «On the release from his position of the Speaker of the Parliament of Ichkeria, Ruslan Alikhadzhiev.»

62. Bekkhan Khasukhanov.

63. *Majlis* (Arabic) the term can refer to a legislative assembly.

64. *Shura* (Arabic): consultation. *Majlis al-Shura* is an advisory or consultative council.

committee on religious affairs. This parliamentary *shura*, like the one proposed by the court, could have non-parliamentary members, such as religious scholars *(Ulama)* selected by the deputies. In the court version the *shura* would be a constitutional body, and in the parliamentary version it would be a committee of the Parliament.

Leery of encroachment on his prerogatives and anticipating problems, Maskhadov stepped in and announced that the *shura* would be an advisory body to the president and that he would select its members. Most MPs, already angered by his lack of support in their battle with the court, saw his move as a compromise with the opposition. For the first time, they opposed Maskhadov. As the president was reshuffling his ministerial cabinet, Parliament refused to confirm seven out of thirteen nominees. They rejected those they saw as sharing Maskhadov's anti-Parliament attitude.[65] On behalf of the president, I had to announce on television that the same names would be re-submitted and that the Parliament should not delay ratification. Maskhadov's statement clearly was not a gesture of peace. For the second time, the MPs rejected his candidates. Maskhadov then chose to bypass the parliamentary confirmation process, thus violating the constitution.

The crisis between Parliament and the president reached a climax in February, when Maskhadov decreed rule by *Shariah* law. Maskhadov never spoke about suspending the Parliament, but his decree announcing steps to be undertaken to reach Islamic rule, left no role for it. In response, the MPs swore to uphold the Parliament as the legislative body and a symbol of democracy. The constitution, they argued, gave enough prominence to Islam; article 4 proclaimed it as the State religion and article 95 approved the *Shariah* courts for legal procedures. The President's efforts to substitute an unconstitutional religious *shura* for the Parliament would only lead to Islamic law replacing the constitution, undermining the foundations of power and legitimacy of the Parliament. The deputies pronounced that the decree on full *Shariah* was unlawful, and they demanded a halt to its implementation. The attempt to sideline the Parliament "was illegal and could have unpredictable consequences."

---

65. They were Minister for the Economy, Isa Bisaev; Finance, S.I. Kurbanov; Health, Umar Khambiev; Housing and Public Utilities, Ali Osmaev; and Culture, Information, and Press, Akhmed. Zakaev.

From then on, relations between the legislative and the executive function resembled a psychological war in which democratic forces could only lose. Somewhat hastily the Parliament elected a new Chairman of the Constitutional Court,[66] whose most pressing responsibility would be deciding on the constitutionality of the president's decree on full *Shariah*. On 22 February, the deputies vetoed another presidential decree naming Salman Albakov as Attorney General; according to the constitution, the appointment and dismissal of attorneys general was the prerogative of the Parliament. Instead of Albakov, they debated reinstating the attorney general suspended in August 1998 at Maskhadov's demand for indecision in the arrest of the instigators of the Gudermes rebellion.

In that difficult situation the deputies decided to seek out allies, even among the opposition. The opposition was not homogeneous. It gave the deputies a chance to find supporters among the various opposition groups. Therefore, on 15 February the Parliament created a commission headed by the Minister of Foreign Affairs and Chairman of the Committee on Foreign Policy, Akhyad Idigov, to look for ways out of the political crisis. The commission held a series of meetings with Basaev, Arsanov, and Udugov. Then the commission proposed a round table to bring together leaders of political movements, commanders, and MPs for discussion. In March, the Parliament issued an appeal to all political and social leaders in which it noted that it "fully endorsed the course of building an Islamic state, but would not permit the removal of the Chechen people [represented by the Parliament] from participation in that important process."

At the same time, individual members began raising the issue of impeachment. Shamil Basaev vigorously supported this position, and not surprising that those calling for impeachment were Basaev sympathizers. The vast majority of the deputies, however, were not ready to go that far. All understood that it would only deepen political, religious, and social radicalism.

In April the Speaker of the Parliament talked of reaching an understanding with the president; he even spoke of a settlement of the conflict between them. However, he spoke too soon; after he and Maskhadov agreed to commence work on a new constitution based

---

66. Umar Denliev.

on Islamic law, prominent MPs, including Maskhadov former adjutant, opposed the policy. Eventually, deputies had to accept a reform of the Parliament along *Shariah* lines. Because most MPs had been elected because of their support for the president and because of the Parliament's lack of resources, they had been unable to develop an independent role or an independent following. In their conflict with Maskhadov, they did not have popular support.

After the Parliament consented to reform itself, the Supreme *Shariah* Court rescinded its earlier ruling suspending the Parliament's legislative functions. It then issued a judgment giving the president ten days to submit amendments to bring the constitution in line with Islamic law and the Parliament two monthsto vote upon them.

Shariah Rule

The move to *Shariah* rule was a gamble. Neither the president nor the Parliament denied the need to live by the laws of Islam. The issue was how to make religious law an organic part of society and avoid imposing it upon a reluctant population. The opposition insisted that *Shariah* law should be introduced at once, in full, and without reservation. Everybody else believed that launching it that way would lead to chaos. Having no expert on religious law, the courts would be farmed out to young inexperienced people.

During the *Hajj* to Mecca in 1997, Maskhadov met with the Sudanese president, who expressed surprise upon learning that Chechnya had adopted the *Shariah* criminal code prepared by the *Ulama* of his country. Sudan was cautious in switching to religious rule, he explained, and Chechnya should be doubly so because of the long Soviet era during which religion was banned. He recommended that the country not rush into it but make incremental changes—otherwise the population might not accept it.

The opposition, however, was not interested in people's welfare. Their goal was to overthrow Maskhadov. Religious rule, they reasoned, would deprive him of his constitutional framework. He could then be removed. The leader of an Islamic state should have a thorough knowledge of Islam. In the field of theology, Maskhadov understood very little since his life had been service with the army far from home. Vice President Arsanov, whose relationship with the president had deteriorated to the extent that they no longer spoke to each other, endorsed full *Shariah* law; and in December 1998 he openly advocated the dissolution of Parliament to remove the last bastion of the constitution.

Every day Maskhadov was getting closer to accepting the opposition's demands. For those who did not know him, it could have seemed that he wanted to remain in control. However, he did not desire power; he considered it a burden and constantly had to convince himself that if he left politics there would be war between the commanders, who were unlikely ever to agree to sit at the same table, so different were their views on authority and the situation in the Republic.

At last he agreed to suspend Parliament and form a new structure, the *shura*. I was required to read the presidential decree announcing full *Shariah* rule on the evening news.[67] The decree imposed the new law and ordered all government institutions to be brought in line with its norms. It also stipulated that the reform of the government, along a specially developed program, would begin with the signing of the decree but that the oversight of implementation remained the prerogative of the president.

The opposition should have been satisfied, but it was not. It criticized the president's initiative as a ploy to become head of the Islamic state. Everyone understood that the opposition's flirtation with *Shariah* law was nothing more than a ploy to remove the president from office; the only one who refused to recognize it was Maskhadov.

Members of Parliament looked upon me as a traitor after my broadcast announcing the introduction of full religious rule. They probably believed that I could influence the situation. In fact, my authority was limited to the press service, which protected me from involvement in political disputes. I never gave Maskhadov advice and only answered questions when asked. A few days later on 8 February I had to perform another objectionable task: reading the presidential decree setting up an Islamic council.[68] In Maskhadov's vision such an assembly would replace the Parliament, be more representative of all political forces, and be chaired by the president.

---

67. Decree number 39: "On the introduction of full Shariah rule on the territory of the Chechen Republic of Ichkeria."

68. Decree number 46, "On the *Shariah* Constitution."

At a specially convened press conference Maskhadov revealed that because of the country's move to full *Shariah* law, the Parliament would lose its legislative function and have only a supervisory role. The republic's legislative body must be an Islamic council *(shura)* assembling the most influential religious leaders and warlords. A new Basic Law, developed along *Shariah* norms, would replace the secular constitution in force since March 1992. Religious precepts would regulate all aspects of life from government to pre-school education.

A special commission headed by Minister of Culture Zakaev was instructed to draft the Basic Law, coordinate with the Council of *Ulema* of the Republic, and submit it for approval to a National Congress, convened for the occasion. A committee chaired by Atgeriev was to prepare and organize the National Congress. Until the new religious constitution was adopted, the former secular constitution would remain in effect but would be amended to meet *Shariah* requirements.

The first meeting of the *shura* took place on 9 February at the concert hall, its members selected by Maskhadov. As its first task it confirmed the power of the president. Zakaev then announced the makeup of the commission that would be writing the new Basic Law: it included famous theologians, warlords, politicians, and members of parliament. By late February it had developed a model, based on the constitutions of Iran and Pakistan, and was ready to submit it to Parliament.

The purpose of all of Maskhadov's political decisions was to forestall the opposition's insistence on the "defense of Islam" and *Shariah* rule and to combat his foes' popular Islamic slogans. Caught in a chronic tight spot, Maskhadov was still trying to save the presidency as the only guaranty against bloodshed.

Clearly, Maskhadov's adversaries had not anticipated his moves and found themselves briefly stymied. They welcomed the president's initiative but declined to join his Islamic council *(shura)*; among those who refused to participate were Basaev, Iandarbiev, Gelaev and the vice president. The composition of the council, carefully chosen by Maskhadov, included not only his supporters, who supported his policies, but also his challengers, whom he hoped to involve in the process. Thus, people for whom the *shura* was created refused to join. Furthermore, they formed their own opposition *shura*. Maskhadov was left confronting an antagonistic parallel institution, able to counteract his actions and to split the Republic apart.

Chechnya plunged into a constitutional crisis. Wanting to introduce full *Shariah*, the country was left without a secular or a religious constitution but with two *shura* and a defiant Parliament. Obviously, the course planned by Maskhadov and his secret advisors to neutralize the opposition had gone astray. Since some of his confidential councilors had been on the side of the Russians during the war, we were left to speculate whether they had not wished for just such a chaotic scenario.

Another Resignation, July 1999

I began looking for a reason to resign. Any hint from Maskhadov that I had done anything wrong would have given me an excuse to tender my resignation. Alas, he said nothing. Finally, I hit on a pretext. Maskhadov refused to take the Salafists' threats against me seriously. I was told they had raised the price on my head to 100,000 US dollars. I joked they should give me the money, and I would go to their lair to collect it.

I cared somewhat about what happened to me, but mostly I did not want those around me to be hurt. Maskhadov still did not react. Then, I openly asked him to provide me with a weapon and to arm those close to me, so that if we were attacked we would not go down without firing a shot. Everyone who had dealt with me knew that I never carry firearms on principle: guns having a habit of going off. All Chechen males carried arms; a fact I strongly opposed. I worried that because of their hot tempers they would tend to resolve disputes with guns instead of through dialogue.

Maskhadov unexpectedly replied without explanation that there was a shortage of guns and he could not accede to my request. In a republic crammed with arms, where every shepherd had an arsenal at his disposal, his refusal to provide my entourage and me with weapons was shocking and upsetting. I went to see Apti Batalov, Head of the Presidential Administration, with whom I was on friendly terms and to whom I could talk openly. I summed up my dealings with Maskhadov and told him I wanted to resign effective immediately. Batalov tried to dissuade me from acting so impulsively and said he could find me a machine gun. But that evening I wrote a letter asking to be released from my duties and noting my wish to pursue my post-doctoral work in Moscow.

Later, Batalov told me he went to the president straightway and asked him to speak to me, to which Maskhadov replied that he did not dare to do so since Vatchagaev was looking for an excuse to leave and would jump on any of his remarks as a motive to resign. Finally they decided that Batalov and Atgeriev, both of whom I respected greatly and whose opinions I valued, would try to change my mind. But this time, I did not let myself to be convinced.

The very next day, the news of my resignation had spread. The worst moment was when Il'ias Talkhadov and Akhmad Avdorkhanov came to see me together. The former was commander of the Presidential Guard and the latter commander of his bodyguards. They could not fathom why the president could not find me a gun for protection. They thought the real reason behind my resignation was financial difficulties. The fact was that, during my entire time as press secretary, I had received payment only three times and always in kind: first, a sack of sugar; second, a bag of rice; and last, a sack of flour. Talkhadov and Avdorkhanov made me an offer: if I stayed, they would chip in for my monthly salary. I was touched. I had not realized that since 1995 we had become so close that they would readily divert some of their own meager resources for my wages. I had to explain the real reason for my resignation: that I felt let down by Maskhadov. They got angry and asked me to give them a day to talk to the president. It was hard to disappoint them, but I decided not to give in. Otherwise, one day at some crossroads in Grozny, Salafists would fire on my car and that would be the end.

My office was soon crowded with people and delegations coming to inquire whether rumors of my departure were real and if I was leaving because of enemy intrigues. Among my visitors was the minister in charge of the petrol sector. Having received assurances that I was giving up the press service, he made me a tempting proposal that I might combine my studies in Moscow with the position of general representative of the Republic in the Russian Federation. I was aware that the last spokesperson had been removed and that the government was looking to replace him. It was not an interesting job, but the minister lured me with the promise of finding me a private flat and paying my wages. It was a spectacular offer as I had not yet figured out how to earn a living and do research.[69] I thought about it and accepted the post. I did not ask for the job, but I could be useful to Chechnya while working on my post-doc.

On 13 July, a presidential decree released me from my duties as press secretary and appointed Said-Selim Abdulmuslimov in my place. Another followed immediately naming me envoy of Ichkeria to Russia.[70] I was elated!

My work as Chechnya's Envoy in Moscow

The situation in the Republic was increasingly tense, but even more worrisome were signs that Moscow was radically changing its attitude towards Chechnya. The influence of FSB Director Vladimir Putin was being felt everywhere. I left for Moscow on July 22nd. My departure for the capital was hastened by an incident. A few days earlier on 16 July, Turpal-Ali Atgeriev, First Deputy Prime Minister, one of the most senior persons in the Maskhadov government, was apprehended at Vnukovo Airport in Moscow as he was flying back to Grozny after an unofficial visit to Moscow. Still in Grozny, but already acting as the ambassador to Russia, I announced his arrest on the news, stating that he was in Moscow on business, meeting high-ranking representatives of the Russian Federation. I also pointed out that his detention was a provocation on the part of the Russian secret services against Chechen authorities and against Maskhadov personally. In fact, I did not know why he was in Moscow. After all, the Russians wanted him for being a participant in the Kizliar-Pervomaiskoe raid in January 1996; and any police officer could take him into custody at any moment. I knew he expected financial help from Chechens living in Moscow, but there had been no talk of his flying there.

Sergei Stepashin, briefly the prime minister, using his authority, and to his own detriment, ordered Atgeriev's release and permitted him to return home. The Russian media denounced Stepashin's decision as a blow to Russia's prestige and a retreat from principles.

---

69. During the five months of my stay in Moscow, the minister never paid my salary and he did not find me an apartment. Once, he brought me a cake and another time offered me a cup of coffee.

70. Respectively decree numbers 231 and 232.

Upon my arrival in Moscow, I announced that my main mission as general representative of Ichkeria would be to disseminate the facts about the situation in Chechnya and break the information blockade imposed by the Russian press. Another task I had set for myself was the defense of the rights of Chechens living in Russia, who were harassed and discriminated against on the basis of their ethnicity. At the time the capital was in the grip of an anti-Chechen hysteria incited by television and newspapers and its streets were unsafe for Chechens.

Chechnya did not unilaterally set up my new position. The Russian prime minister and the Chechen president had agreed upon and signed a document regulating the exchange of diplomats between their two countries. Russia had an envoy in Grozny, and Chechnya had one in Moscow. Our spacious offices were located on Denezhny Lane very near the Russian Ministry of Foreign Affairs on the third floor of a multi-story building also housing diplomats from other regions of the Russian Federation. The building was guarded and maintained by the Office of the Russian Presidential Administration, which also paid for our rent, telephone, and other services.

My predecessor had had a staff of ninety-eight. On my first day I announced that the embassy would keep a workforce of only eleven employees and that the rest would have to find employment elsewhere. Most of those carrying identity cards designating them as embassy staff were, in fact, bodyguards of Chechen businessmen, who because of their affiliation with the embassy had the right to bear arms. The identity cards were also sought-after because they opened many doors. My first week was occupied in interviewing the cardholders all of whom tried to convince me that they had obtained their cards directly from Maskhadov. I was able to reduce the labor force to nine members.

The position of envoy came with an apartment, the size of which clearly showed that officials of the Russian Presidential Administration did not deny themselves much. The living space—1,399 square feet with a terrace of 355 square feet—was very large by Russian standards, and the furniture came from the best shops. But there was a drawback; anyone entering the building had to go through police control then through an FSB checkpoint. In addition, the residence had its own security, and its guards patrolled the floors every hour.

I immediately tried to contact the office of the Russian Presidential Administration, as it was clear that the fate of Chechnya was decided in the bowels of that organization. Unfortunately for us, in August Vladimir Putin replaced Stepashin as prime minister. The new prime minister was a surly man with the permanent expression of someone carrying a grudge; few people knew him or what he stood for. The fact that under his management the FSB was preparing the second invasion of Chechnya became clear only later. The decision to go to war preceded the Salafist raid into Dagestan, the excuse for opening hostilities.

Personal acquaintances helped me gain an interview with the Minister for Nationalities, Viacheslav Mikhailov, and a protégé of Vladimir Putin. While I was in his office, I was able to glance at a document that gave a clue about the nagging worry about another invasion of Chechnya. During our conversation Mikhailov's "white telephone" rang. Only a small circle of people from the presidential administration had the right to use such a phone. Apologizing, he stood up to take the call. From his demeanor, I could tell that whoever was on the other end of the line was someone he feared. He remained standing at attention and listening, tense and intent, to what was said to him. He instinctively turned his back to me, perhaps to prevent me from eavesdropping.

With nothing to do, my eyes wandered and stopped on a pile of papers on the minister's desk. The file on the top of the pile was stamped in red ink, "For official use only," and "Return after reading and signing." I had to try to find out more. The document, consisting of a few pages, was a resolution of the Security Council dated December 1998. Following a report made by the then FSB director Vladimir Putin in view of a possible outbreak of hostilities against the Chechen Republic, the council determined to initiate a full-scale ideological preparation of the country and the international community. Of the resolution's twenty-seven points, I could steal a look at only a few that specified ways to promote biased information about Chechnya and Chechens or induce foreigners to write negatively about them, all the while believing they acted on their own.

Thus, in the winter of 1998, a year before the outbreak of the second Chechen war and over a year before any provocative Islamic fundamentalist raid into the territory of the Russian Federation, Moscow began a psychological anti-Chechen campaign in preparation for a potential renewal of aggression. The Russian government did not forgive the defeat of its army by a handful of Chechens, and they wanted revenge. I had no time to read the entire paper before the minister hung up the phone, but considering there was another man in the room who watched me in horror, I was lucky to have read as much as I did. I could hardly wait for the end of the interview so eager was I to notify Maskhadov. I reported to Batalov and, only much later learned of Maskhadov reaction. He did not believe my story and thought I was spreading disinformation. Had I known his reaction, I would have resigned and would have saved myself from future imprisonment.

A few days after my meeting with the Minister for Nationalities, an elderly woman came to my office to speak to me. I never refused to listen to people; it was part of my job. Surprisingly, she asked to talk in the street. Once outside, she turned on a small radio at high volume and quietly began to explain that she wanted to disclose to me some information about Chechnya and what might happen there in the near future. At first I thought she was a dotty old lady out to save the world from alien invasions. But her first words got my undivided attention. She worked, she said, at the State Duma, not as a deputy but as a secretary of one of its numerous committees and, although it was high time for her to retire, her employers kept her because she was reliable and dedicated.

The day before there had been an unusual gathering of her committee, not of the full membership, but of a small group. The purpose of the meeting was to review an army plan for an invasion of Chechnya. The preparation detailed what military units would be used and how and from where they would launch the assault. That secret strategy was not discussed in the full committee because of the possibility of a leak. She left a copy of the report in our main office, on the desk of our secretary. I gave her my word that no one would ever know she was my informer. She smiled and replied that although I was still young, I should not be so naïve: "they" would discover everything quickly. I thanked her profusely but could not resist asking why she had taken the risk of notifying me. I never forgot her sad eyes as she looked at me and replied in pure Chechen, "I do care about the fate of my people, even though I have lived all my life without my people." I was shocked. She must have been one of those thousands of

Chechen children who lost their parents during the mass deportation and ended up in orphanages or were given Russian names and placed into Russian families to be made into Russians.

I heartily thanked her again, ran back to the office to secure the papers before anyone could find out about them, and dispatched my deputy, Musa Nugayev, to Chechnya to deliver them into Batalov's hands. I thought that I had learned something vitally important to my homeland. Maskhadov, on the other hand, believed the plan to be an FSB hoax. He was confident that Russia, after 1996, would not dare invade again. It might bomb or fire from afar, but not send the army. Later, when the Russian troops entered Chechnya, the plan was confirmed point by point. Chechens knew the military units, their numbers, and where they would attack, but they never acted upon the information. Once the Russian assault began, it was too late.

From Moscow, and with what I had discovered, I had no doubt that the Russian government was stepping up its aggression against Chechnya. My work in those days consisted mainly in conducting numerous daily briefings for journalists, in which I tried to offset the Kremlin's negative statements about the Chechen Republic.

Then, on 8 and 13 September, bombs exploded in two apartment buildings in Moscow.[71] In those terrorist acts, 224 ordinary people were killed and more than 700 wounded. Immediately the authorities accused Chechens as the perpetrators. The Mayor of Moscow, Iuri Luzhkov, arriving at the sites of the horrible destruction, declared in front of national and international media that, "the Chechen stamp is obvious." Many people, even today, are unaware that Russian courts failed to prove Chechen involvement either as masterminds or perpetrators of the blasts. But in those days Chechens were harassed across Russia, and particularly in Moscow where tens of thousands of them lived and worked. Any sympathy that had existed for Chechens evaporated just before the second attack on Chechnya.

In Moscow, Chechens were arrested by the thousands. I, as representative of the Chechen government, did not have the time to protest all of the arrests. Between September 1999 and June 2000, over 5,000 Chechens admitted, after being beaten and tortured, being implicated in the bombings! In the Butyrska prison alone, about

---

71. Respectively on Gur'anov Street and the Kashir Highway.

3,000 confessed to the crime. None stood trial for the explosions; but many received sentences ranging from six months to several years in prison for felonies they had not committed, mostly charged with possession of weapons or drugs. Again, it is an undisputable fact that no Chechen was ever convicted in a court of law for those explosions.

When the Russian army invaded Chechnya in October 1999, journalists continuously begged me for news. For dozens of Russian and foreign journalists, I was able to organize trips to Chechnya so they could see for themselves what was happening. Twice, sometimes three times a week, I would arrange for my deputy Musa Nugaev to accompany journalists to Ingushetia, North Ossetia, or Dagestan, and from those locations secretly to Chechnya, bypassing checkpoints set up by Russian troops. They were met at the border by Chechens, most often Batalov's people, and taken to Grozny. Because hundreds of foreign journalists were able to send footage of what was happening in the republic, Russians were unable to control information about their actions.

I contacted Maskhadov and asked for permission to close the representation office. While the war was going on in Chechnya, it seemed morally wrong for me to remain in Moscow to conduct briefings from a building belonging to the Russian government. But he refused my request and ordered me to continue my activities from a private apartment if my office was closed by the Russian administration.

The soldiers standing guard in front of my apartment building invariably wondered aloud, when I returned home at night, what a Chechen was doing in Moscow while Russians were fighting in Chechnya. Twice on the Russian First Channel, a commentator asked why the Chechen envoy was allowed to continue his activities against Russia from Moscow. I expected to be seized at any moment. Naively, I assumed that I would be expelled. On 21 October, I was arrested and taken to the Butyrka Prison, where I would spend nine long months; but this was another story.

The Radicals' Raid in Dagestan, August 1999

Everyone in Chechnya expected that radicals, followers of Salafism, would one day raid neighboring Dagestan. Every night the Salafist television station controlled by Movladi Udugov preached the spread of true Islam to Dagestan. It must be remembered that Islam had penetrated into Dagestan in the Eighth Century from the city of Derbent. Muslim cemeteries in that city have tombs dating back to that century, among them several graves of *Sahabah* (companions of the Prophet Muhammad). Sufi Islam dominated in Dagestan as in Chechnya, an intolerable situation for Salafists who rejected Sufism. They longed to proclaim an Islamic republic, impose *Shariah* law and eradicate Sufism.

The chief ideologist of the Salafi movement in the North Caucasus was Sheikh Bagaudin Kebedov, imam of the city mosque of Kiziliurt in Dagestan. Kebedov was an ethnic Khvarshi, a group numbering a few thousand people residing in mountain villages along the Andi River near the borders of Chechnya and Georgia. He was born in 1945 in the village of Vedeno in Chechnya, son of Dagestani residents resettled on Chechen land after the deportation of 1944. An authority in theology, he did not possess the art of eloquence and showed poorly in public debates with Sufis. For his Salafi followers, however, he exuded a sacred aura.

In the fall of 1998, Kebedov decided to move from Dagestan to Chechnya and settle in Urus-Martan, an unexpected decision when a small section of Dagestan[72] had by then announced it would live according to the precepts of the *Shariah*. Obviously, he thought that Chechnya's secession from Russia was real and that his relocation there could protect him from any unpleasant consequences resulting from provocations by his devotees. He explained his choice by claiming that Chechnya was a Muslim country whereas Russian Dagestan was mired in disbeliefs. He compared his move to a small *Hijra*, analogous to the *Hijra* of Prophet Muhammad from Mecca to Medina. Chechen Salafists, left leaderless after the Gudermes debacle, had acquired a spiritual head.

Once in Urus-Martan, Kebedov and his party began a two-pronged action. They rolled out a large-scale campaign to discredit the Chechen government that was sheltering them. Several members of the Dagestan intelligentsia[73] resettled with the spiritual leader provided

---

72. The Kadar Zone south of Buinakhsk district, specifically the villages of Karamakhi, Chabanmakhi, and Kadare.

73. Among them the poet Adallo Aliev and the writer Magomed Tagiev, both popular in Dagestan.

skillful assistance. They also prepared a march on Dagestan to force it to rebel against Moscow. Circumstances in Chechnya, with the never-ending disputes between the government and the opposition, kept Emir Bagaudin in the news. The opposition wanted to lend a hand to the emir in his Dagestan adventure.

To me, a raid on Dagestan was absurd. People of Dagestan did not want to leave the Russian Federation. On the contrary, they could not understand the Chechen aspiration for independence, which had cost so many lives and turned Grozny into rubble. Had a majority of people in Dagestan declared their desire to live by the *Shariah*, we could have deluded ourselves into believing that we were rescuing our neighbors. But it was only the inhabitants of three villages out of three thousand. How could we be so blind? Chechens were spellbound by the desire to free Dagestan. It was almost as if Russian intelligence services, using deception and the manipulation of data, planted the idea among Salafi leaders. Otherwise, how could a sober person of sound mind expect Dagestan to rise against Moscow?

Most Russian historians and political scientists described the raid into Dagestan in the summer of 1999 as an incursion of Salafists. The reality was more complex. The raid included peoples of differing beliefs, both Salafists and Sufis; of differing social backgrounds, from intellectuals to ordinary men from mountain villages; and different leaders, who in normal times barely communicated with each other. The units of commanders Gelaev and Umarov considered themselves squarely in the Sufi camp. Shamil Basaev, invariably portrayed as a Salafist by Russian analysts, may have revised many of his beliefs for political reasons; but he was not a Salafist. He was proud of his ancestors, all of whom were close to Sufi sheikhs.

More than once, I asked Basaev's friends to explain his support of Kebedov and his participation in the attack on Dagestan. His comrades, and Basaev himself, always claimed that his aim was solely to divert Russia's attention from Chechnya, to focus it on Dagestan and, thus, forestall a Russian invasion of Chechnya. Whether or not Basaev made an honest mistake, his goal misfired: the foray into Dagestan speeded up the assault upon Chechnya. In an interview from prison with *Nezavisimaia Gazeta*, I stated that the raid was the pre-condition Russians needed to march into Chechnya. There is a saying among Chechens that Basaev went to war in Dagestan to bring it back to Chechnya.

Shortly before my move to Moscow, I had chatted with a young and well-educated acquaintance, Nasrudin Mintaev, a deputy in the parliament, whom I admired for his erudition. As he prepared to leave, he added, "farewell; it is unlikely we'll see each other again." I thought he was referring to my departure for Moscow, but he told me that he was preparing to march on Dagestan. I was stunned. I could not imagine him swallowing the Salafi bait. We went on talking, and it turned out that Doku Umarov, his commander in the first war challenged his former fighters to follow him to Dagestan if they considered themselves men. How casual and criminal it was to play upon mountaineers' pride! All my attempts to dissuade him from going failed. "How can I look into my wife's eyes if I am a coward!" he asked. In a moment that turned out to be prophetic, I retorted that decent people would die in this adventure and those who had incited the action would continue living. My friend was killed by an artillery shell in one of the first battles near the village of Botlikh. He had never been a Salafist.

During the month of July, men from Kebedov's party gathered on the border between Chechnya and Dagestan. Their number in early August amounted to a few hundred people. Russians, monitoring the crowd, chose to send a force of a hundred police officers to the area. At that point, only ethnic Dagestanis under the command of their Emir Bagaudin intended to move into Dagestan. No Chechen joined them.

On 1 August, Dagestani units began crossing the border into Dagestan in the Tsumadin district. Small clashes took place between militants and local police, and on 5 August, Russians sent the 102nd Brigade of Interior Ministry forces to close the border. On 7 August, however, a second squad penetrated into the Botlikh district.

On 6 August, Dagestani militants issued documents proclaiming the overthrow of the Dagestan republican government to be replaced by an Islamic state and the substitution of an Islamic *shura* for the state council. With the proclamation of an Islamic state, Bagaudin Kebedov apparently considered himself to be the new head of state.

Ten days after the beginning of the operation, the leaders of the newly announced Dagestan *shura* asked Basaev and his opposition *shura* for help. Here lies the major discrepancy with Russia's version of events. According to Russian sources, Shamil Basaev's forces together with Emir Khattab's foreign fighters had entered Dagestan on

1 August. They asserted that Chechens invaded Dagestan when in reality it was Dagestan Salafists headed by Kebedov who marched into Dagestan and only later asked Basaev for assistance.

At a press conference in Groznyi on 10 August, before Basaev got involved, Maskhadov was able to affirm that no Chechen took part in the incursion. In Moscow, I issued a news release denying Chechnya's role in the raid and trying to imply that, as Dagestani attacked Dagestan, the conflict was an internal affair of the Russian Federation.

On 11 August, the Dagestan *shura* elected Shamil Basaev and Emir Khattab commander in chiefs of the combined Dagestani, Chechen, and foreign fighters. Vladimir Putin, on 12 August, threatened retaliation against Chechnya. The following day, on behalf of the Chechen president, I issued an official protest and exhorted the two heads of state to meet urgently. In Chechnya a state of emergency was declared on 15 August, and reservists were called up. On 16 August, speaking to a large rally in Grozny, Maskhadov condemned Chechens taking part in the attack and demanded their immediate return.

On 18 August, realizing there was no support among the population, Chechen commanders in Dagestan called a meeting with Basaev and demanded explanations. Basaev encouraged them to pledge their continued support in the fight for the release of Dagestan from the "infidels." He failed. After a week in Dagestan, Baraev led his men out, conceding that nobody in Dagestan was going to rebel against the Russian Federation. All other Chechen units followed suit signaling the collapse of Kebedov / Basaev / Khatab's plan to overthrow the Dagestan government. Neither did Basaev find any backing among the Chechen population; people resented his interference in the affairs of another country and showed their discontent.

Grozny emphatically denied any involvement in the raid but this did not satisfy the Russian government. It insisted that Chechen authorities must disavow the Islamists by consenting to a joint Russian-Chechen military action to wipe them out. The Chechen government could not accept collaboration with the Russian army against its own citizens.

Russian media misinformed its public. Again and again it broadcast the same news, alleging that Maskhadov refused to disown the Islamists and condemn their actions. The news blocked all Maskhadov's denouncements of Basaev and the Islamists. I managed to contact several members of the Dagestan leadership to assure them that the Chechen government was not involved in the attack. But it was to no avail.

On 3 September, unable to meet with the Russian prime minister, I sent him an open letter through the press in which I protested the Kremlin's threats against Chechnya and the numerous detentions of Chechens in Moscow. I hinted that such policies were the result of the decision by the Security Council of December 1998 (kept secret) to promote biased information about Chechens. However, I concluded my missive on the positive note that under the leadership of Vladimir Putin "Russia will find the courage and wisdom to abandon the policy of discrimination of the Chechen people and solve its disagreements with the Republic of Ichkeria at the negotiating table."

Again, all was in vain.

Putin shunned Chechen state officials. At the same time all media reported him welcoming opposition members. Once again, former leaders were redeemed from oblivion to be established as bona fide players on the political scene. I objected to the Russian government's meetings with such former politicians as Doku Zavgaev; Amin Os-maev (former head of the puppet parliament set up during the war) who could not hide his surprise to be received in the Kremlin; the former mayor of Grozny, who declared his willingness to serve the glory of Russia in Chechnya; or prominent businessman Malik Said-ulaev, who consented to head a mysterious temporary government.

On 7 September, Prime Minister Putin talked publicly about the need to abandon any guilt for the Chechen war and urged the can-celation of the Khasaviurt Agreement. The next day a State Duma deputy, ethnic Chechen General Ibragim Suleimenov, told reporters that Maskhadov was deposed by Basaev's troops. It was a red her-ring; but it implied that extremists had taken over in Grozny and that Russia's intervention was necessary to reestablish order. Russian aviation bombed Chechnya's mountain districts, which were not the areas where Islamists were in large numbers.[74] Three weeks were left prior to the full-scale beginning of the war.

On the wave of the war, Vladimir Putin was hailed as a hero who saved Russia from an Islamic threat. He was the long awaited idol of those who had not accepted the collapse the Soviet Union and thought

---

74. Few Salafists lived in thebombed Nozhai-Iurt district.

the Red Army could restore its past glory. The Russian army wanted revenge for their shameful loss in the war. It had drawn conclusions from its defeat and the second time came well prepared.

CONCLUSIONS

Three short years after the end of the first conflict, Chechnya again plunged into war. The Russian army came to kill the very idea of an independent Chechnya and any hope of peaceful coexistence with Russia. The army wanted revenge and for that it needed a lot of blood.

I often heard Chechens say that Russia is responsible for the disastrous outcome of those years. Yes, of course Russia is to blame; it is hard to disagree, but are we beyond reproach? We made numerous mistakes, even if most of them were committed under hard pressure from the Russian Federation. But do we have the right to refer to Russian culpability and not draw conclusions from our errors?

From 1991 to 1999, Chechnya and Russia engaged in a power play during which many people died and neither country took into account the human cost of its policies.

Our victory in the war of 1994-1996 allowed us to misjudge Russia's weakness. Chechens sincerely believed that, even if Russia wanted another war, its army would never again try to occupy their land, and that shelling and bombing would be done from neighboring republics.

Chechens underestimated Russia's desire for revenge. We thought an agreement with Russia was possible, while Russia only played for time.

The Salafists were not perceived as a threat to the sovereignty of Chechnya because we believed that, if needed, at any moment we could deal with them.

Battle commanders were engaged in a tug of war with the president. They claimed to be spokesmen of the people, whereas they defended their own interests, which at times conflicted with what the population expected. People became isolated from political developments. This was the tragedy of the young republic. The removal of ordinary Chechens from decision-making was the main failure of the young republic.

Chechnya entered the second war fragmented and weak as never before. Its only source of support in the new conflict would be the Chechen people. And it was the Chechen people who bore the brunt of the new tragedy.

Short Biographies of People Involved in the First Chechen-Russian War

Abdulkhadzhiev, Aslanbek (known as Big Aslanbek): native of the village of Germenchuk. Close associate of Shamil Basaev. Commanded a battalion in the war in Abkhazia in 1992 and took part in the raid on Budennovsk in 1995. He became chief executive officer of the *Chechenkontrakt* complex in 1997. Killed during the second war in 2002.

Abdurakhman al-Shishani: ethnic Chechen, native of Azraq (Jordan), leader of Chechen Salafists from 1998–2001. He directed the confrontation between Salafist and pro-democracy forces in Gudermes in July 1998. Killed during the second Chechen campaign.

Abumuslimov, Said-Khasan: native of Argun. Ph.D. in economics. Prominent politician and historian, he was an active participant in the formation of Ichkeria. After the death of President Dudaev, acting president Zelimkhan Iandarbiev appointed him vice-president.

Aidamirov, Abuzar: native of the village of Meskety. Well-known writer, his works were a classic of Chechen literature. Some of his arrangements of folk poetry became the anthem of independent Chechnya. Later, he condemned the resistance to Russia. Died in 2005.

Akbulatov, Aslanbek: native of the village of Shatoi. Taught at the Leningrad State University. Appointed overseer of President Dudaev's staff in December 1991.

Akhmadov, Daud: native of the village of Borzoi. Taught at the Grozny Oil Institute. He supported Chechen independence in the fall of 1991 and became an assistant to President Dudaev and member of his inner circle in 1992. Maskhadov appointed him Minister of Industry in 1997.

Akhmadov, Khusein: native of the village of Dzhalka. Historian and philologist. A leader of the Chechen revolution, he served as deputy chairman of the executive committee of the All-National Congress of the Chechen People and speaker of the first parliament of independent Chechnya. Favored limiting the rights of the president. Resigned in May 1993 and withdrew from politics.

Akhmadov, Ramzan, Rizvan, Uvais, and several other brothers: leaders of the Salafists of Urus-Martan. Accused of numerous crimes against Russians and Chechens who did not share their views. Four brothers were killed in the second war. Uvais emigrated.

Albakov, Sultan: former employee of the Supreme Court of Chechen-Ingush Autonomous Soviet Socialist Republic. He was Minister of Internal Affairs under President Dudaev and Attorney General in 1998.

Alikhadzhiev, Ruslan: native of Shali. He was field commander in the war and Speaker of the Parliament from 1997–2000. Detained by Russian troops in 2001 and subsequently went missing.

Alsabekov, Mukhamed-Khusein-haji: born in 1958. President (Rector) of the Islamic University in Alma-Ata (Kazakhstan) in 1990, he became advisor to President Dudaev in 1991. He was chosen *Mufti* of the Republic of Chechnya in 1993, from which position he was dismissed in 1995 for his reluctance to declare *Jihad* on Russia.

Ampukaev, Ramzan: native of the village of Duba-Iurt. He organized protest rallies against independence in the early 1990s and imigrated to Poland during the armed conflict. After the war, he supported Chechen independence but sided again with its opponents during the second military campaign.

Arsamikov, Isa: native of Urus-Martan. Prominent politician of the early independence movement, he was member of the executive committee of the All-National Congress of the Chechen People, member of the executive committee of the *Vainakh* Democratic Party and of the Assembly of the Mountain People of the Caucasus, and founder of the socio-political newspaper, *Bart* (Concord). Killed by opposition forces in Grozny in 1993.

Arsanov, Akhmad: son of the prominent Sufi sheikh, Bagautdin Arsanov. He was deputy for Chechnya in the Russian Parliament from 1990–1993 and representative of the Russian president in the Chechen-Ingush Republic for the short period of October–November 1991.

Arsanov, Il'ias-haji: native of the village of Shalazhi, son of the prominent Sufi sheikh, Deni Arsanov (father of Sheikh Bagautdin Arsanov). He refused to recognize the independence of Chechnya and supported the pro-Russian opposition to Dudaev. He was arrested after the war but was released on Maskhadov's orders; afterward he moved to Ingushetia where he died in 2002.

Arsanov, Vakha: born in 1950. Prominent military commander with the rank of major general. He was an active participant in the independence movement from 1991, supporter of President Dudaev, and member of the first parliament of independent Chechnya. In the war, he fought first with Ruslan Gelaev; commanded his own unit in 1995; and was in charge of the Northwest front in 1996. Elected Vice-President in 1997. Killed in the second military campaign.

Arsanukaev, Abu: native of the village of Starye Atagi. He was head of President Dudaev's security unit and of his bodyguards with the rank of brigadier general from 1992–1994. Did not play a role during the war or the inter-war years. Sided with the Russians in the second military conflict and became an activist of the United Russia Party.

Arsanukaev, Il'ias: native of the village of Starye Atagi, brother of Abu Arsanukaev. Chaired the defense committee of the All-National Congress of the Chechen People. Under President Dudaev, he commanded the National Guards and was the officer in charge of recruitment and logistics. At the beginning of the war, was accused of handing over military bases to Russian troops. Did not play a role in politics after the conflict and emigrated in 2000.

Aslakhanov, Aslanbek: native of the village of Novye Atagi. Major general of the Russian police, he played a role in both Chechen and Russian politics. He supported Dudaev in 1991 and opposed the Russian invasion in 1994. During the fierce battles of the second war in 2000, he stood for election in the Russian Parliament as representative from Chechnya and became an adviser to President Putin on issues relating to the North Caucasus.

Atgeriev, Turpal-Ali: native of the village of Alleroi. Active participant in the independence movement from the early 1990s, he became a respected commander of the Chechen resistance. Took part in the war in Abkhazia in 1992 and in the raid on Kizliar-Pervomaiskoe in 1996. He managed Maskhadov's presidential campaign after the war. He was arrested at the outbreak of the second war in 2000 and convicted of terrorism in Russian court. Killed in prison in 2002, according to his family.

Aushev Ruslan: ethnic Ingush, born in Grozny. Was elected President of Ingushetia (1993), he maintained close contacts with the Chechen leadership and tried to prevent the Russian invasion; he encouraged negotiations between Maskhadov and the Russians. For his conciliatory attitude towards Chechnya, he was forced to resign as President of Ingushetia at the beginning of the second Chechen campaign.

Avdorkhanov, Akhmad: native of the village of Alleroi. Close associate of Aslan Maskhadov. Commanded the president's bodyguards at the beginning of the second military campaign. He was a well-known and popular leader of the resistance from 2002–2005. Allegedly poisoned by Russian secret services in September 2005.

Avturkhanov, Umar: born in 1946. Professional policeman. He joined the opposition to President Dudaev in December 1991; chosen chairman of the pro-Russian Provisional Council in December 1993 and chairman of the Committee of National Consent (pro-Russian government set up after Russian troops entered Chechnya) in March 1995, from which position he was relieved in May 1995. He was Deputy Director of the Tax Enforcement Agency of the Russian Federation in 1995 and 1996.

Baraev, Arbi: head of the Alkhankali Salafists, was one of the most obnoxious Salafi politicians in the postwar period. Served as Deputy Minister of Defense from 1997–mid 1998, afterward in fierce opposition to Maskhadov and his government. Suspected of having attempted to kill the president by blowing up his house.

Basaev, Shamil: prominent commander. Led the detachment of Chechen volunteers in Abkhazia in 1992 and the raid on Budennovsk in the summer of 1995. He headed the *Marsho* Party in 1996-1997, was a candidate in the presidential election in 1997, and First Deputy Prime Minister in Maskhadov government from 1997 –1998. He was the principal figure in the opposition to Maskhadov, a leader of North Caucasian Salafists and of the Salafist Congress of Chechnya and Dagestan (1998–1999), and an organizer of the *Jihadists'* invasion in Dagestan in the summer of 1999. During the second military campaign, he created a network of Islamic military groups or *Jamaat* across the North Caucasus and was vice president in 2005. Killed in Ali-Iurt in Ingushetia in July 2006.

Batalov, Apti: native of the village of Varandoi. He commanded the Naur battalion during the armed conflict. After the war, he directed the National Security Service and headed the presidential administration in 1998.

Batukaev, Shamsudin: native of the village of Prigorodnoe. Religious and social activist. He chaired the Supreme *Shariah* Court in 1997–1998. In the second campaign, he represented Doku Umarov abroad.

Beloev, Balaudi: native of the village of Borzoi. Social and military leader. Elected to the parliament in 1997.

Beno, Shamil: ethnic Chechen native of Jordan. Social activist, analyst, and businessman. He was Minister of Foreign Affairs in 1991–1992 and later served on numerous social committees and associations. He joined the opposition to President Dudaev in 1995 and became member of the pro-Russian Chechen Committee of National Consent in March 1995.

Bisultanov, Khodzh-Ahmed: engineer by training. He headed the Union to Promote Perestroika in 1988 (later reorganized into the People's Front of the Chechen-Ingush Republic). He retired from the revolutionary movement to accept a ministerial position in the government of Doku Zavgaev in 1989.

Bugaev, Abdulla: native of Tolstoi Iurt. Taught in the history department of the University of Grozny from 1978 to 1993. Elected to the Supreme Soviet of the Chechen-Ingush Republic in 1990 where he advocated unity with Russia. He was deputy, then first deputy, to Doku Zavgaev from January 1995 to November 1996 and, after July 1996, delegate to the National Assembly of the Chechen Republic (parliament elected and functioning during Zavgaev's pro-Russian government during the war).

Chimaev, Ruslan: joined the ministry of Foreign Affairs in 1992 and worked in the administration of Vice President Zelimkhan Iandarbiev. Appointed deputy minister of Foreign Affairs in 1994 and minister of Foreign Affairs by acting President Iandarbiev in 1996.

Deniev, Adam: native of the village of Avtury. An outrageous character who titled himself Emir of the Muslims. He started as a Salafist but later moved closer to the Sufis. The authorities accused him of involvement in the killing of Red Cross doctors in Novye Atagi in 1996. In the second military campaign, he tried to take over the leadership of the country, was deputy head of administration in the pro-Russian government of Akhmad-haji Kadyrov, chairman of the movement *Adamalla* (Humanity), and chief editor of the newspaper, *Istina Mira* (World Truth). Killed by militants in 2001 while broadcasting on television.

Dudaev, Dzhokhar: first Chechen to be made general of the Soviet

Army after the formation of the Soviet Union. Veteran of the Afghan War. He commanded the Heavy Bomber Aviation Division and the Nuclear Armed Strategic Bombers of Soviet Long Range Aviation in Tartu (Estonia) from 1987 to 1990. He took the leadership of the All-National Congress of the Chechen People and of the movement for independence in November 1990 and was elected President of Chechnya in October 1991. Killed in a Russian targeted air strike in April 1996. Charismatic and unconventional politician, he gave up a prestigious and rewarding career to lead his people in the troubled years of the USSR's break-up.

El'murzaeva, Ganga: native of the village of Staraia Sunzha. She was chairman of the Committee on Vocational Education of the Chechen-Ingush Republic and member of the executive committee of the movement *Daimokhk* (Fatherland). She was voted deputy of the Supreme Soviet of the Chechen-Ingush Republic in March 1990 and member of the Presidium in October 1990. She chaired the Supreme Soviet's commission on motherhood, childhood, women's work and living conditions, and protection of the family in October. She came out against Chechnya's independence in 1991.

Fatkhi (Sheikh): ethnic Chechen, native of Suveylah in Jordan. Leader of Chechen Salafists and founder of the first Salafi paramilitary unit. Died in Chechnya in 1997.

Gaibov, Idris: native of the village of Kurchaloi. Combatant and social activist. He joined Bislan Gantamirov's squad in 1991 and Turpal-Ali Atgeriev' unit in 1995. He switched to the Russian side at the beginning of the second war.

Gantamirov, Bislan: native of the village of Gekhi. Founded and headed the party, *Islamskii Put'* (Islamic Way) in 1990. Nominated to the executive committee of the All-National Congress of the Chechen People in 1991. President Dudaev appointed him mayor of Grozny in November 1991, and he was chosen chairman of the Grozny City Council in October 1992. He switched to the opposition to Dudaev in April 1993 and, in January 1995, was picked as deputy head of the Territorial Administration of Federal Institutions in the Chechen

Republic, the short-lived (two months) administration set up by Russians after they invaded; in that position, he restored the Grozny City Council and once again acted as its chairman. During the war, he criticized the Russian army for killing civilians. He was arrested in Moscow in 1996 but amnestied on the eve of the second campaign.

Gelaev, Ruslan: native of the village of Komsomol'sk. Prominent commander. Fought in the armed conflict in Abkhazia in 1992–1993 with volunteers of the Confederation of the Mountain People of the Caucasus. After his return from Abkhazia, President Dudaev named him head of Special Forces. During the war, he was field commander on the western front. In March 1996, on Maskhadov's orders, he led his forces into Russian occupied Grozny and held it for three days. In Maskhadov's government he was designated Deputy Prime Minister in April 1997 and Defense Minister in January 1998. After the capture of the village of Komsomol'sk by Russian troops in 2000, he retreated to Georgia, but returned to Chechnya in 2003. He was killed attempting another escape from Chechnya in 2004.

Geliskhanov, Sultan: native of Gudermes. He was chief of police of the Gudermes district in 1992–1993. A supporter of President Dudaev in his struggle with the opposition, he was nominated Minister of Internal Affairs in April 1993 and Head of State Security from September 1993 to March 1995; in this position, he frequently appeared on television making threats against the opposition. He commanded the army special forces in 1995.

Goitemirov, Ramzan: Ph.D. in physics and mathematics and designer of numerous inventions. Taught at the Chechen-Ingush State University. Pacifist by conviction, he was an active participant in the independence movement. He presided over the Green Movement of Chechnya-Ingushetia in 1989 and the All-Caucasian Environmental Council after 1990; and he was a member of the executive committee of the All-National Congress of the Chechen People.

Iamadaev, Sulim: native of Gudermes. Field commander during the war, he was the youngest brigadier general among Chechens; he served as chief of counterintelligence to Khattab, and was later in charge of the Gudermes front. After the war, he took a position against Salafism and chased Arbi Baraev's *Shariah* Regiment out of Gudermes in July 1998. Switched to the Russian side at the beginning of the second conflict, served in the Russian army with the rank of colonel from 2003 to 2008 and led the Russian battalion, *Vostok*, of the 291st Motorized Rifle Regiment of the 42nd Motorized Rifle Division. He was awarded the title "Hero of the Russian Federation" in 2005. Took part with the Russian army in the Five-Day War with Georgia. He was killed in Dubai in March 2010.

Iandarbiev, Zelimkhan: native of the village of Stariye Atagi. Writer, poet, and prominent social activist. He was one of the leaders of the revolution; selected deputy chairman of the executive committee of the All-National Convention of the Chechen People in November 1990; and he led negotiations with the Russian Federation in 1992. A staunch supporter of President Dudaev, he was appointed Vice President in 1993. Served as Acting President after Dudaev's death until Maskhadov took office. He opposed Maskhadov's policies and moved close to the Salafists. Killed by Russian special services in Qatar in February 2004.

Iandarov, Andarbek: native of Urus-Maratan, son of the famous Sufi Sheikh Abdul Khamid Iandarov. Historian and philosopher, he received a Ph.D. in philosophy. He was in charge of the ideology section of the Chechen-Ingush Republican Committee (Obkom) of the Communist Party in 1989 and deputy, later deputy chairman, of the Chechen-Ingush Supreme Soviet from March 1990 to September 1991. Member of the nationalist historical club, *Dosh,* he was appointed Minister of Education in Dudaev's administration in spring 1992. In Kadyrov's pro-Russian administration, he acted as chief specialist and advisor in the "Permanent Mission of the Chechen Republic to the Russian President." He died in a car crash in Moscow in 2012.

Iarikhanov, Khozh-Akhmed: native of Gudermes. Taught at the Grozny Oil Institute. He was named Minister of Higher Education in 1994; he took part in negotiations with Russia in 1995; and was president of the Southern Oil Company from October 1996 to September 1997.

Ibragim, Said-Emin: founder (in 1990) and chairman of the Social Protection Committee, a division of the International Society for Human Rights. Minister in the government of Dudaev, he continued his human rights activities after the war.

Idigov, Akhiad: chief engineer of a subdivision of *Groztruboprovod-stroi* complex (pipelines construction) until 1991. Voted deputy in 1991, he held the office of Speaker of the Parliament from 1991 to 1997. Reelected MP in 1997, he chaired the committee on foreign relations and occupied the post of Minister of Foreign Affairs for six months in 1998. Emigrated during the second war.

Imaev, Usman: native of the village of Zakan-Iurt. Graduate of Moscow State Institute of Foreign Affairs and former adviser to the soviet ambassador in Angola. Occupied the positions of Minister of Justice, Chief Prosecutor, and head of the delegation negotiating with the Russian Federation in 1995. He was dismissed from all his positions in July 1995. Detained by Russian troops and evacuated from Chechnya by helicopter in early 1996, he disappeared without a trace.

Iskhanov, Khusein: native of the village of Zebir-Iurt. Active participant of the independence movement. Acted as Maskhadov's adjutant throughout the war. Voted MP in 1997; sat on the parliament's foreign affairs committee. Continued his political activities after emigration.

Ismailov, Aslanbek: native of Shali. Brigadier-General. Commanded a detachment from Shali during the armed conflict. Led the defense of Argun and took part in the raid on Budennovsk in 1995. At the end of the war, was one of the officers of the joint Russian-Chechen Command in Grozny (August to October 1996). Appointed Maskhadov's Construction Minister after the war and Deputy Commander of the Armed Forces of Ichkeria in July 1998. At the beginning of the second conflict, he was in charge of Grozny's defense and was killed trying to escape its encirclement in February 2000.

Israpilov, Khunkerpasha: native of the village of Alleroi. Took part in the conflict in Abkhazia with a detachment of the Confederation of the Mountain People of the Caucasus. Led a fighting unit during the war; participated in the raid on Kizlar-Pervomaiskoe in January 1996; and commanded the southeastern front in spring and summer 1996. Named director of the Anti-Terrorist Center (headquarters in Gudermes) by Maskhadov in 1997. Joined the opposition in 1998 and together with Basaev and Raduev filed a lawsuit against the President in an effort to remove him. Killed in the second war in Grozny in 2000.

Kadyrov, Akhmad-haji: native of the village of Tsentoroi. Chosen Deputy *Mufti* of Chechnya in 1993 and acting *Mufti* in September 1994; as the new spiritual leader of Ichkeria, he declared *Jihad* on Russia, something the former *Mufti* did not do. He continued as *Mufti* in the interwar period. Joined the opposition to Maskhadov after the beginning of the second war and presided over the new pro-Russian administration. Militants killed him in 2004.

Khadzhiev, Salambek: professor and member of the Russian Academy of Science. Director of the petroleum chemistry research and production company, *Grozneftekhim,* in 1987 and minister of the Petrochemical Industry of the USSR in 1991. Deputy of the Supreme Soviet of the USSR from 1989 to 1991. He came out against Dudaev in 1991. Led the pro-Russian government of National Revival of the Chechen Republic from November 1994 to October 1995

Khalimov, Islam: physician by training. A Salafist, he was a founder of the Islamic Revival Party and of the international group, Islamic Doctors. He had close contacts with the Turkish Salafi association, International Muslim Charity Organization or INN. In the Maskhadov government, he held the positions of Minister and Deputy Prime Minister.

Khambiev, Magomed: native of the village of Benoi. Divisional general, he was Defense Minister and Commander of the National Guard under Maskhadov. Surrendered to the Russians in 2002.

Khambiev, Umar: native of the village of Benoi, brother of Magomed Khambiev. A physician, he was Minister of Health under Maskhadov, who used him as a special envoy to numerous countries. During the second war, he authored numerous reports on crimes perpetrated by the Russian army. Eventually returned to Chechnya.

Khamzatov, Alaudi: native of the village of Guni. Combatant. During the war, he led a detachment into Argun (12 km from Grozny) and captured the regional police building in August 1995. Killed in late 1995, allegedly in a blood feud.

Khasbulatov, Ruslan: professor of economy. Elected deputy for Grozny in the Russian Parliament in 1990 and Speaker of the Russian Parliament in 1991. Engaged in a power struggle with Boris Yeltsin in 1992 and 1993. Returned to Chechnya in March 1994 and joined the opposition to President Dudaev.

Khasimikov, Salman: native of the village of Staraia Sunzha. Acclaimed heavyweight wrestler and honored Master of Sports of the USSR, he was a repeated winner in Russian, European, and world championships. President Dudaev created a National Security Service in March 1992 and appointed Khasimikov to lead it. However, after an unsuccessful attempt to overthrow the President in May 1993, the National Security Service was abolished.

Khattab, Kharbo (Amir Khattab): ethnic Arab, native of Saudi Arabia. Commanded the foreign brigade and founded terrorist training camps after the war. During the second military campaign, was poisoned by a letter sent by Russian secret services in 2002.

Khozhaev, Dolkhan: native of Urus-Martan. He was an historian, author of numerous works on the history of Chechnya, a researcher for the Chechen-Ingush Republican Museum, and head of the republican archives. Killed in the second war in a shootout with Russian Special Forces in the village of Valerik in July 2000.

Khultygov, Lechi: native of the village of Makhkety. Commanded his village's militia in the war. President Maskhadov nominated him head of the National Security Service. Killed by Salman Raduev's men in a raid on the Grozny television center in the spring of 1998.

Labazanov, Ruslan: native of Argun. Martial arts trainer. Arrested for murder in 1990, he organized an uprising in the Grozny jail in November 1991. Later, he led a detachment of former convicts that was part of the Presidential Guard. He came out against Dudaev in May 1994 and took part in combat on the opposition side in the summer and fall of that year. Promoted to colonel in the Russian Army in early 1995, he was killed in 1995.

Madaev, Isa: native of the village of Chiri-Iurt. Commanded a squad in the war and represented the General Staff in negotiations with Russia in 1995. Co-chaired the working group of the Special Supervisory Committee (to further the release of forcibly detained persons). He was nominated Deputy Chief of State Security in 1996.

Makhashev, Kazbek: Director of the jail department of the Ministry of Internal Affairs in 1990, he was appointed Minister of Internal Affairs in October 1994. Took part in negotiations with the Russian Federation. Made Deputy Prime Minister by Maskhadov in September 1997.

Mamodaev, Iaragi: active participant of the revolutionary movement. Selected first Deputy Prime Minister in 1992. Sided with the parliamentary opposition to Dudaev in 1993. Emigrated to Turkey.

Maskhadov, Aslan: native of the village of Zebir-Iurt. Lieutenant colonel in the Soviet army. Returned to Chechnya in 1992 to be of use to his homeland. During the war, was Chief of Staff of the Armed Forces, led negotiations with the Russian Federation, and was the author of the Khasaviurt Accord. He was elected president of Chechnya in 1997. Killed in a Russians special forces operation in the village of Tolstoi-Iurt in 2005.

Mataev, Akhmad (better known as one-legged Akhmad): native of the village of Bachi-Iurt. Active member of the North Caucasian Salafi movement since the 1980s, he was the first spiritual mentor of Chechen Salafists.

Mezhidov, Abdul-Malik: native of the village of Alleroi. He commanded a Salafi unit under Sheikh Fatkhi and the *Shariah* guard of the Supreme *Shariah* Court after the war. He took a position of neutrality in the conflict between Salafists and presidential guards in July 1998 and came out against the overthrow of the President demanded by the Salafists.

Mezhidov, Bek: an active participant of the revolutionary movement, he was member of the executive committee of the All-National Congress of the Chechen People, First Deputy speaker of the parliament from 1991 to 1993, and head of the negotiating delegation with the Russian Federation in January 1993. Switched to the opposition to Dudaev in spring 1993. Worked for the pro-Russian government of Doku Zavgaev during the war. Become a consultant to the Supreme *Shariah* Court after the war.

Movsaev, Abu: was chief of police of Shalidistrict. Field commander during the war, he took part in the raid on Budennovsk. Between March 1995 and July 1997, he occupied the positions of Chief of State Security (renamed National Security Service) and commander of the army special forces. Designated Minister of *Shariah* Security in 1999. Killed during the second war in Shali in spring 2000.

Nukhaev, Khozh-Akhmad: native of the village of Geldygen. Businessman and president of the international holding corporation, *Kavkazskii Obshchii Rynok* (Caucasian Common Market). Leader of the movement, *Nokhchi Latta Islam* (Chechen Islamic Land). He was First Deputy Prime Minister for a few months in 1996. Favored a return to tradition by urging *teip* (clan) representation in power structures. Has not been seen in public since 2004.

Osmaev, Amin: member of the Federation Council (upper chamber of the Russian Parliament) representing the Chechen Republic from 1996 to 1998; chaired the Council's committee on Science, Culture, Education, Health and Environment. Speaker of the Chechen Parliament during the pro-Russian Zavgaev's government, he endeavored to revive that Parliament in the second military campaign.

Raduev, Salman: native of Gudermes. President Dudaev's son-in-law. Held the position of Prefect of Gudermes district in 1992.

Commanded a unit on the eastern front during the war and fought in the battle for Gudermes. Master minded the raid on Kizliar-Pervomaiskoe in 1996. Organized an illegal paramilitary structure after the war. Arrested by Russian troops in 2000 and sentenced to life imprisonment. Died in prison in 2002.

Sadullaev, Abdul-Khalim: native of Argun. He was an active participant of the independence movement and leader of the non-militarized *Jamaat* from Argun. After Maskhadov's death, he assumed the power of the President from March 2005–June 2006. Killed in a gun battle in June 2006.

Saidaev, Mumadi: native of the village of Nesterovskaia. Brigadier general. Field commander during the war, he was a close ally of Maskhadov. Captured in September 2000, he was convicted in Russian court of involvement in illegal armed groups.

Saligov, Lechi: editor of the republican newspaper, *Nezavisimaia Gazeta* (Independent Newspaper). A member of Dudaev's government, he moved to the opposition in 1992.

Shakhabov, Viskhan: A general of aviation. He was Chief of Staff of the armed forces from 1991–1994.

Sheripova, Elza: Adherent of the non-conformist movement. She was an assistant to the Attorney General in the early 1990s, an organizer of the Social Protection Committee (later renamed the Human Rights Committee), delegate to the first All-National Convention of the Chechen People, member of the executive committee of the All-National Congress of the Chechen People, chairman of its legal committee, and Minister of Justice.

Soslambekov, Iusup: born in the village of Zamestitel'. Active participant in the revolutionary movement, he was First Deputy Chairman of the executive committee of the All-National Congress of the Chechen People, chairman of the committee on foreign affairs of the first Parliament, and from 1991 to 1993 Chairman of the Parliament of the Confederation of the Mountain Peoples of the

Caucasus. Stood as candidate in the presidential election in 1997. Murdered in Moscow in 2000.

Suleimenov, Ibragim: native of the village of Pervomaiskoe. Major general in the Russian Army. Selected chairman of the defense committee of the first Chechen Parliament in 1991. Moved to the opposition and organized a National Salvation Committee in 1993, which tried unsuccessfully to overthrow President Dudaev. He was one of the planners of the storming of Grozny on 26 November 1994.

Talkhadov, Il'ias: native of the village of Alleroi. Activist of the movement for independence since the early 1990s, he became chief of Maskhadov's security team in 1994 and commander of the Presidential Guard in 1997. Died in the second war during the retreat from Grozny in February 2000.

Temishev, Musa: native of Gudermes. A founder of the *Vainakh* Democratic Party, he was member of the All-National Congress of the Chechen People, member of the Confederation of the Mountain Peoples of the Caucasus, adviser to President Dudaev on national security, and editor of the government newspaper, *Ichkeria*. Lost his influence after criticizing Dudaev.

Udugov, Movladi: native of Grozny. Supporter of Salafism, he was a founder of the Islamic Revival Party and of the Salafi Congress of the Peoples of Ichkeria and Dagestan. Occupied the following positions: press secretary to President Dudaev, Minister of Information and the Press, First Deputy Prime Minister, Minister of Foreign Affairs, Director of the National Information Service. Candidate in the 1997 presidential elections, he failed to score five per cent.

Umarov, Doku: native of the village of Kharsenoi. Before the war, served in the Special Forces, *Borz*, under Ruslan Gelaev. During the conflict, commanded his own group and ended the war with the rank of colonel. A supporter of Maskhadov, he was appointed Secretary of the Security Council in 1997. Assumed the power of the President in 2006 and proclaimed a Caucasian Emirate, uniting the *Jihadist* forces of the North Caucasus in 2007.

Umarov, Isa: native of the village of Khatun. Brother of Movladi Udugov, he was one of the main Salafi ideologues of the North Caucasus.

Umkhaev, Lecha: active participant of the Chechen revolution,
he was First Deputy Chairman of the executive committee of the
All-National Congress of the Chechen People in 1990–1991. Opposed Dudaev in 1991 but condemned the Russian invasion in 1994.

Usmanov, Lema; native of Urus-Martan. Activist in the early independence movement, he contributed to all its major events. He was
a founder of the scientific society, *Kavkaz* (Caucasus), and of the
anti-Communist committee, *Bart* (Concord) in the late eighties;
was elected Deputy of the Supreme Soviet of the Chechen-Ingush
Republic in 1990; and was a founder of the *Vainakh* Democratic
Party. One of the main leaders of the All-National Congress of the
Chechen People, he chaired its Committee on Foreign Affairs in
1991–1992. Maskhadov appointed him Ichkerian ambassador to the
United States in 1997. He remained in the United States and taught
at the U.S. Department of Defense Languages Institute.

Uvaisaev, Nadzhmutdin: native of the village of Alkhan-Kala. Active
participant of the movement for independence since the early 1990s,
he was president of the National Bank and architect of the national
currency, the *Nahar*, issued in 1994.

Uvaisaev, Shamsutdin: native of the village of Alkhan-Kala.
Worked in the Ministry of Internal Affairs from 1991. Killed in
Shatoi in 1998.

Vatchagaev, Mairbek: native of the village of Avtury. Historian;
received his PhD in 1995. Held the following positions: representative of the Foreign Ministry in Moscow in 1992; head of the propaganda department of the armed forces in 1995; Deputy Chairman
of Maskhadov's election committee in 1996; Deputy Chairman of
the party *Chechenskoe Islamskoe Gosudarstvo* (the Chechen Islamic
State) in 1997; press secretary to the President, First Assistant to the
President, and Head of Analytical Department from 1998– 1999;
and general representative of Chechnya in Russia in the summer of

1999. Arrested in October 1999, detained in *Butyrskaia* prison in Moscow until June 2000. Emigrated in 2000.

Zakaev, Akhmad: native of Urus-Martan. Graduate of Voronezh Institute of Culture, he was a professional actor. Minister of Culture from 1996. Took part in negotiations between Russia and Chechnya in 1995 and 1996. Appointed Vice Premier by Maskhadov just before the second war.

Zavgaev, Doku: native of the village of Beno-Iurt. He was nominated First Secretary of the Chechen-Ingush Republican Committee (Obkom) of the Communist Party in 1989 (the first Chechen in that office) and chairman of the Supreme Soviet of the Chechen-Ingush Republic in March 1991. He was ousted from these positions during the Chechen Revolution in September 1991. He was a People's Deputy in the Russian Parliament from 1990 to 1993. Designated chairman of the pro-Russian Chechen government in October 1995, he was named head of the Chechen Republic in November and "elected" to that post in December in a dubious vote; he occupied that role until November 1996. He was member of the Federation Council of the Russian Federation (upper chamber of the Russian Parliament) until May 1998 and became Russia's ambassador to Tanzania in March 1997. At the beginning of the second campaign, he was appointed Director General of the Russian Ministry of Foreign Affairs and made Russian ambassador to Slovenia in 2009.

Chronology of Events, 1988-1999

Late 1980s

Spring-summer 1988: Members of the non-conformist movement, which included groups such as the green movement, *Dosh*, Prometheus, or Kavkaz, came together to create the Union to Promote Perestroika *(Soiuz Sodeistviia Perestroiki)*, soon reorganized into the People's Front of Chechnya-Ingushetia *(Narodnyi Front Checheno-Ingushetii)* chaired by the engineer Khozh-Akhmed Bisultanov.

Summer 1988–Fall 1989: Mass environmental protests. Scholarly society, Caucasus *(Kavkaz)*, established by members of the nationalist intelligentsia.

1989: Creation of the Chechen-Ingush Social Democratic Party, Chairman Mairbek Vatchagaev and Secretary Timur Muzaev. Emergence of political parties: *Marsho* (Liberty), *Bart* (Concord), and others. In June Doku Zavgaev was named First Secretary of the Chechen-Ingush Communist Party Obkom (highest Party position in the Republic), the first Chechen nominated to this position since the formation of the Soviet Union.

1990

Winter-Spring: Mass protests against government corruption.

November 23–25: The All-National Convention of the Chechen People *(Obshchenatsional'nyi S"ezd Chechenskogo Naroda)* gathered in Grozny uniting moderate nonconformists, liberal members of the Party and state apparatuses, and radical nationalists.

November 27: The Convention raised the issue of a Chechen State *(Nokhchi-cho)* and its secession from the Russian Soviet Federative Socialist Republic (Russian SFSR) and the USSR. The Supreme Soviet of the Chechen-Ingush Republic, newly elected in March, adopted a declaration of sovereignty of the Chechen-Ingush Republic.

1991

Early 1991: Long before the appearance of General Dudaev on the political scene, when the Republic was still led by Doku Zavgaev, the Chechen-Ingush leadership declined to hold Mikhail Gorbachev's referendum on the integrity of the USSR. The rebuff was motivated by North Ossetia's refusal to return the Prigorodny District to the Ingush. This district, settled by Ingush, was transferred to North Ossetia after the deportation of 1944.

May 15: The Chechen-Ingush Supreme Soviet changed the official name of the Republic from Chechen-Ingush Autonomous Soviet Socialist Republic to Chechen-Ingush Republic.

June 8–9: Radical nationalists held a second session of the All-National Convention of the Chechen People and renamed it the All-Nation Congress of the Chechen People *(Obshchenatsional'nyi Kongress Chechenskogo Naroda)*. The session resolved to disband the Chechen-Ingush Supreme Soviet and proclaimed the Chechen Republic *Nokhchi-cho*.

June: Dzokhar Dudaev took over the leadership of the executive committee of the All-National Congress of the Chechen People.

August 16: The Chairman of the committee on Law, Order, and Prevention of Crime of the Supreme Soviet of the Russian SFSR, Aslanbek Aslakhanov, and the Deputy Chairman of the Council of Ministers, Inga Grebeshev, arrived in Grozny.

September 6: Armed coup. Paramilitary units, under the order of the executive committee of the All-National Congress of the Chechen people, dispersed the Chechen-Ingush Supreme Soviet. To justify their action they used the Chechen Party leaders' support for the members of the "State Committee on the State of Emergency" *(Gosudarstvennyi Komitet po Chrezvychainomu Polozheniiu)* in their attempted *coup d'état* against the President of the Soviet Union, Mikhail Gorbachev, on August 18in Moscow.[75]

September 11: The Secretary of State of the Russian SFSR, Gennadi Burbulis, and the Minister of Press and Information, Mikhail Poltoranin, arrived in Chechnya and held four days of negotiations with the warring parties.

September 14: Ruslan Khasbulatov, Deputy of the Supreme Soviet of the Russian SFSR (soon to be its Speaker) and a close ally of Russian President Boris Yeltsin, flew to Grozny.

September 15: Last session of the Chechen-Ingush Supreme Soviet as held under Khasbulatov's guidance. Guardsmen of the All-National Congress of the Chechen People surrounded the Supreme Soviet building. Under Khasbulatov's insistent recommendations, the deputies voted to remove Doku Zavgaev as Chairman of the Supreme Soviet and to disband the Supreme Soviet. New parliamentary elections were scheduled for November 17. In the transitional period, power was transferred to a thirty-two members Provisional Chechen-Supreme Soviet *(Vremennyi Vyshyi Soviet)*, whose members were mainly from the liberal-democratic wing of the former Supreme Soviet.

Less than three weeks after that event, the All-National Congress of the Chechen People disbanded the Provisional Supreme Soviet and assumed full power.

October 1: The Supreme Soviet of the Russian SFSR decided to divide

---

75. "The State Committee on the State of Emergency" was made of eight high-level officials from the Communist Party of the Soviet Union, the Soviet government, and the KGB. The coup failed by August 22. Although the Chechen leadership supported them, the leadership of the Russian Federation did not.

the Chechen-Ingush Republic into two separate entities, a Chechen Republic and an Ingush Republic, without stipulating the boundaries between the two.

October 6: A delegation of the Russian SFSR, headed by Vice President Aleksandr Rutskoi, arrived in Grozny. Rutskoi held several consultations with representatives of various social and political groups, including with members of the All-National Congress of the Chechen People. The Provisional Supreme Soviet met again in Rutskoi's presence, but only for one day.

October 10: The Supreme Soviet of the Russian SFSR adopted a resolution, "On the Situation in the Chechen-Ingush Republic," urging the Vice President and the Council of Ministers to provide the necessary conditions for the restoration of law and order in the area.

October 19: Addressing the leaders of the All-National Congress of the Chechen People, President of the Russian SFSR, Boris Yeltsin, came close to giving them an ultimatum to abandon any notion of independence.

October 24: President Yeltsin appointed the deputy from Chechnya in the Supreme Soviet of the Russian SFSR, Akhmad Arsanov, as his representative in the Chechen Republic.

October 27: Dzhokhar Dudaev elected President of the Chechen Republic by popular vote. Parliamentary elections held simultaneously.

November 1: President-elect Dzhokhar Dudaev unilaterally proclaimed the independence of the Chechen Republic from the Russian SFSR. The Russian authorities did not recognize the independence.

November 2: The Fifth Extraordinary Congress of People's Deputies of the Russian SFSR, after very long deliberation, elected Ruslan Khasbulatov as Chairman of the Russian SFSR Supreme Soviet. Then, the Congress declared the presidential and election held in the Chechen-Ingush Republic on October 27 illegal and decisions adopted by those bodies to be non-binding.

November 2: The first session of the Parliament of the Chechen Republic elected the Deputy Chairman of the executive committee of the All-National Congress of the Chechen People, Khusein Akhmadov, as Speaker. Bek Mezhidov, another member of the same executive committee, also head of the society Kavkaz (Caucasus), was selected Deputy Speaker.

November 7: The President of the Russian SFSR issued a decree introducing a state of emergency in the Chechen Republic. In response, Dudaev proclaimed martial law.

November 9: Dzhokhar Dudaev sworn in as President. He accumulated the positions of President, Chief of the Armed Forces, and Chairman of the Cabinet of Ministers (Prime Minister).

November and December: Basic state organs put into place.

December 25: Mikhail Gorbachev resigned as President of the Union of Soviet Socialist Republics and handed over the presidential functions to Boris Yeltsin. The Soviet Union formally dissolved the following day.

1992

March 3: President Dudaev announced that he would sit down at the negotiating table with Russian authorities only if Moscow recognized Chechnya's independence.

March 12: The Chechen Parliament adopted the Constitution, pronouncing the state independent and secular.

March 14: Chechen and Russian negotiators met in Sochi. Zelimkhan Iandarbiev headed the Chechen delegation and Viktor Zhigulin the Russian one.

March 31: Attempted coup. A group of 150 –armed people seized the television and radio stations, demanding the immediate resignation of President Dudaev and his government, but proceed no further. Forces loyal to the President crushed the rebellion. Members of the coup took refuge in the Nadterechnyi District.

May 2: Russian Defense Minister General Pavel Grachev ordered the transfer of military equipment to Chechnya: 37,795 small arms, 260 Soviet-Czech training planes of the type L-29 and L-39, 42 tanks, 34 infantry fighting vehicles, 14 armored personnel carriers, 942 cars, and more.

May 28: The Russian and Chechen negotiating delegations, previously in Sochi, gathered again in Moscow.

July 7: Withdrawal of Russian troops from Chechnya and disbanding of all structures of the Russian Ministry of Defense. Without encountering much resistance, Chechen authorities seized weapons from the Russian military units.

Spring: Opposition to Dudaev administration gained momentum. The opposition was spearheaded by leaders of the reformist wing of the nationalist movement, Lecha Umkhaev, Salambek Khadzhiev, historian Dzhabrail Gakaev, and retired Foreign Minister Shamil Beno. Members of the intelligentsia, business executives, and entrepreneurs supported the opposition.

Summer: The movement *Daimokhk* (Fatherland) became the heart of the anti-Dudaev movement with Lecha Umkhaev and Ganga El'murzaeva. In August, former USSR Minister Salambek Khadzhiev and historian Dzhabrail Gakaev from the Movement for the Democratic Reform of Chechnya-Ingushetia joined the opposition.

November 2: President Dudaev declared Chechen neutrality in the Ossetian-Ingush conflict. Russian troops, moving through North Ossetia and Ingushetia, took positions on Chechnya's border.

November 10: President Dudaev declared a state of emergency and mobilization.

November 14: President Dudaev declared martial law in the districts bordering on Ingushetia.

November 19: Russian Deputy Prime Minister, Sergei Shakhrai, ordered the Russian troops on Chechnya's border to the highest state of alert.

1993

January 14: In Grozny a Russian delegation met with representatives of the Chechen authorities. The Russian delegation was composed of Deputy Prime Minister and Chairman of the State Committee on Nationalities, Sergei Shakhrai; his Deputy at the State Committee on Nationalities, V. Shuikov; and the Chairman of the Council of Nationalities of the Supreme Soviet, Ramzan Abdulatipov. The Chechen side included the Speaker of the Parliament, Khusein Akhmadov; his Deputy, Bek Mezhidov; the Chairman of the Foreign Affairs committee, Iusup Soslambekov; and the representative of the Chechen Republic in Moscow, Sherip Iusupov.

April 15: The opposition staged an anti-Dudaev rally in Grozny.

April 17: President Dudaev dissolved the Parliament, the Constitutional Court, and the Grozny City Council. He reshuffled the Ministry of Internal Affairs and made unconstitutional appointments (not approved by Parliament) for Vice President and Attorney General. He announced he would rule by decree, and he introduced a curfew. He nominated Zelimkhan Iandarbiev as acting Vice President

May: The Constitutional Court declared the actions of the President unconstitutional.

May 2: Refusing to disband, the Parliament elected Iusup Soslambekov, head of the organization *Bako* (Law), as Speaker. Under Soslambekov's leadership, the Parliament voted to remove Dudaev from the position of Prime Minister and asked Deputy Prime Minister Iaragi Mamodaev to form an opposition "Government of National Trust" *(Pravitel'stvo Narodnogo Doveriia)*. Financed and supported by Russia, the opposition government and parliament survived only until June 1993.

June: Formation of the opposition "Provisional Government of the Chechen Republic" *(Vrenennoe Pravitel'tvo Chechenskoi Respubliki)*. Financed and supported by Russia, it was chaired by Ali Alavdinov in 1994. Alavdinov was a known personality in Chechnya, former minister of President Dudaev. His presence gave this pro-Russian formation some visibility.

June 4: Dudaev's supporters, under the command of Shamil Basaev, seized the Grozny City Council building where the Parliament and the Constitutional Court met and dispersed all three institutions.

June 4: Because of the danger of armed clashes, the opposition rally in Theater Square in Grozny—in progress since April 15—dwindled.

End of June: President Dudaev authorized the Parliament to resume work, but allowed only twenty deputies to reconvene.

July 22: Former Deputy Speaker Akh"iad Idigov became Speaker of the new Parliament, which proceeded to deprive all opposition-leaning deputies of their parliamentary mandate, including former Speakers Akhmadov and Soslambekov.

November 5: Russian Deputy Prime Minister Sergei Shakhrai submitted a proposal to President Yeltsin for a political resolution of the Chechen problem. The plan entailed initiating negotiations with the Chechen government while maintaining strong military pressure in and around Chechnya. The ultimate goal was to compel the Republic to abandon independence.

December 12: The new Constitution of the Russian Federation identified the Chechen Republic as a subject state. President Dudaev added the word *Ichkeria* to the official name of the Republic (Chechen Republic of *Ichkeria*) to differentiate it from the defunct—in his opinion—Chechen Republic of the Russian Constitution.

December 16: President Yeltsin ordered the borders with Chechnya closed and the railroad from and into the Republic monitored. With Moscow's approval the opposition created the so-called "Provisional Council of the Chechen Republic" *(Vremennyi Sovet Chechenskoi Respubliki)*, seemingly according to Shakhrai's plan. Financed and supported by Russia, its Chairman was the mayor of the Nadterechny District, Umar

Avturkhanov, and its Deputy Chairman was the former Head of the executive committee of the Shali District Soviet, Badrudi Dzhamalkhanov. This opposition body remained in existence until March 1995.

December 26: The Provisional Council's mission statement pledged to orient the Chechen Republic toward a union with Russia.

1994

January: Formation of the "Committee of National Salvation" *(Komitet Natsional'nogo Spaseniia)*, one of the many opposition groups financed and supported by Russia; it existed only for a few months. In January its armed units made an unsuccessful attack against government (Dudaev) troops stationed near Grozny.

February 9: State Security arrested Ibragim Suleimenov, one of the leaders of the anti-Dudaev opposition.

Summer: The "Provisional Council of the Chechen Republic" took the lead in the armed opposition to President Dudaev.

June 3–4: A Congress of the People of Chechnya, called by the "Provisional Council of the Chechen Republic," convened in the village of Znamenskoe in the Nadterechny District. This Congress issued a vote of no confidence in President Dudaev's government and designated the Provisional Council as the sole power until new elections could be called.

July 30: The Provisional Council issued a decree dismissing President Dudaev from his functions and assuming full state power.

August 29: The Russian government issued a statement declaring that, were the government of Dzokhar Dudaev to use violence against the opposition, Russian authorities would be forced to intervene to protect the lives and rights of those citizens of the Russian Federation.

July-August: An anti-Dudaev armed group commanded by former Mayor of Grozny, Bislan Gantamirov, took control of the Urus-Martan

District; another group commanded by Dudaev's former Security Chief, Ruslan Labazanov, took control of the town of Argun; and in the village of Tolstoi-Iurt in the Grozny District there appeared a "peacekeeping mission" headed by the former Speaker of the Russian Parliament, Ruslan Khasbulatov. Khasbulatov and his band actually supported the opposition.

September 29: Leaders of the various opposition groups—Avturkhanov, Khasbulatov, Labazanov, and Gantamirov—met in Nadterechny District. They agreed to unite their efforts and act under the auspices of the "Provisional Council of the Chechen Republic." Bislan Gantamirov became commander of the combined armed units of the opposition.

August: President Dudaev decreed the resumption of the Parliament's legislative function.

September 30: The Parliament amended the Constitution. The new amendments granted the President the right to dissolve Parliament and to appoint the Cabinet of Ministers and all the judges without parliamentary approval.

Late August-September: Armed units of the opposition "Provisional Council of the Chechen Republic" began hostilities against the Dudaev government. Those armed units were assisted by Russian security services, their operations supervised by the Chief of the Moscow Section of the FSK, Ievgeni Sevastyanov, and the Deputy Minister for Nationalities, Aleksandr Kotenkov.

September 1: Government troops loyal to Dudaev, commanded by Aslan Maskhadov, defeated Gantemirov's opposition forces and his military base in the village of Ghekhi in the Urus-Martan District.

September: Government troops destroyed the forces controlled by Labazanov in Argun and Grozny and neutralized the units in the village of Tolstoi-Iurt.

November: Formation of the opposition "Government of National Revival" *(Pravitel'stvo Natsional'nogo Vozrozhdeniia)*. Financed and supported by Russia, it was headed by Salambek Khadzhiev.

November 24: Opposition forces of the "Provisional Council of the Chechen Republic," with the help of the Russian military (contract soldiers) specially recruited for the occasion by the FSK, attempted to storm Grozny.

November 30: Secret Russian Presidential Decree, "On measures to restore constitutional legality and the rule of law on the territory of the Chechen Republic." On December 1, by order of the Minister of Defense, military formation—comprised of Army and Interior Ministry troops and Special Forces—were gathering on the border with the Chechen Republic. As early as September, troops of the North Caucasus Military District had been put on high alert.

December 9: Boris Yeltsin signed the Presidential Decree No. 2166, "On measures to curb the activities of illegal armed groups in the Chechen Republic and in the zone of the Ossetian-Ingush conflict." The government of the Russian Federation adopted a resolution stipulating the use of the Armed Forces for an operation in the territory of the Chechen Republic. In Vladikavkaz, negotiations began between the governments of the Russian Federation and the Chechen Republic. First Deputy Minister for Nationalities Vladimir Mikhailov headed the Russian team, and Minister of Justice/Attorney General Usman Imaev, the Chechen team.

December 11: As negotiations in Vladikavkaz proceeded, Russian troops gathered on the Chechen border began moving into Chechnya.

December 14: Suspension of negotiations in Vladikavkaz.

December 17: A Russian Presidential Decree set up the "Territorial Administration of the Federal Executive Authorities in the Chechen Republic" *(Territorial'noe Upravlenie Federal'nykh Ispolnitel'nykh Organov v Chechenskoi Respubliike).*

December 20–21: Russian troops reached the outskirts of Grozny and fighting began.

December 31: Russian troops stormed Grozny. Russian military casualties hampered the success of the attack. About 70 Russian soldiers and officers were captured that day, and dozens of tanks and armored personnel carriers demolished.

1995

January 1: The Russian 131st Motorized Riffle Brigade, known as Maikop Brigade, was completely annihilated near the Grozny railway station. One hundred Chechens surrounded Russian Paratroopers and the 693rd Motorized Rifle Regiment in the Andreevskaia-Domina District of Grozny.

January 3: Russian aviation bombed the settlements of Melkhi-Iurt, Shali, Bamut, and Starye Atagi. It also bombed the village of Arshty in Ingushetia, predominantly inhabited by Chechens. In Shali alone, 55 people were killed and 186 injured.

January 5: Bombing of Chechen-Aul, Tchishki, Bamut, and Tchiri-Iurt.

January 6: With the battle for Grozny in full swing, the Russian Federation Security Council transferred the task of "establishing the rule of law" to Interior Ministry troops. The decision suggested that combat had ended and a police operation was in the process of restoring order in Chechnya.

January 7: Russian command in Grozny re-deployed: "Group North-East" assigned to General Lev Rokhlin and "Group West" to General Ivan Babichev. Artillery, mortars, and multiple rocket launchers were deployed in Grozny.

January 8: Forty-seven soldiers of the 22nd Independent Brigade of the Army Intelligence Special Forces captured near the village of Alkhazurov, south of Grozny. Two-dozen poorly armed Chechens took them prisoners. Russian authorities declared a temporary truce to recover dead soldiers from the streets and exchange prisoners.

January 12: President Dudaev offered to negotiate.

January 13: Marine units from the various fleets of the Russian Federation made their appearance in Grozny.

January 15: Chechen Economic Minister, Taimaz Abubakarov, and Attorney General, Usman Imaev, arrived in Moscow to meet with Russian officials. For two days they tried to negotiate a ceasefire with Sergei Shakhrai.

January 17: Russian Prime Minister, Viktor Chernomyrdin, received Economic Minister T. Abubakarov and Attorney General Imaev.

January 14–17: In Grozny, the battle for the building housing the Council of Ministers, located opposite the Presidential Palace. Russian Marines suffered heavy casualties, including dozens of dead and hundreds of injured.

January 18: Russian "Group North" and "Group West" finally met in the center of Grozny. Russian planners had estimated that the two Groups would link two days after the beginning of hostilities. It took them six weeks. Russian President Boris Yeltsin in a televised address stated that he would not talk to Dzhokhar Dudaev. Chief of Staff Aslan Maskhadov approached Russian General Ivan Babichev about starting negotiations. In response he received an ultimatum to surrender the Presidential Palace and its defenders.

January 19: Chechen forces began retreating from Grozny, across the river Sunzha, towards the South. Russian troops captured the Presidential Palace, previously abandoned by Chechen forces, and hoisted the Russian flag over its ruins. That act allowed Russian officials in Moscow to believe the war was over and that there would be no need to negotiate with Chechens. Boris Yeltsin appeared on television to announce that the military phase of the "restoration of constitutional order" in Chechnya was completed and that peaceful reconstruction was beginning.

January 25: Airstrikes hit settlements throughout the Republic, in particular Bamut and Achkhoi-Martan.

January 26: Exchange of prisoners near Khasaviurt (Chechnya).

Soldiers of the 22nd Brigade of Army Intelligence Special Forces exchanged for Chechen detainees.

January 27: Russian Decree No. 80 appointed Nikolai Semenov Head of the "Territorial Administration of the Federal Executive Authorities in the Chechen Republic," replacing the dismissed Nikolai Iegorov. The same Decree named Umar Avturkhanov and Salambek Khadzhiev First Deputy Heads and Bislan Gantamirov Deputy Head.

Early February: Fighting moved to the mountain districts of Chechnya.

February 1: Dzhokhar Dudaev appeared on the Russian Federation's wanted list. General Anatoli Kulikov appointed Commander of the Joint Group of Federal Forces in Chechnya.

February 4: The pro-Moscow "Provisional Council of the Chechen Republic" requested the Russian government to stop its troops' looting and killing of civilians.

February 8: According to the estimation of Sergei Kovalev—based on visual count—the civilian death toll in Grozny was 25,000; according to Sergei Iushenkov, it was 30,000. Neither set of figures included Chechens killed in Grozny, but whose corpses had been taken away for burial in their family villages.

February 13: For the first time, in the village of Sleptsovskaia, Russian and Chechen forces reached an agreement for a truce. In Grozny, Russians and Chechens exchanged lists of prisoners and removed corpses.

February 17: In Moscow Prime Minister Viktor Chernomyrdin met with the *Mufti* of Chechnya, Khusein Mokhamad Alsambekov. They agreed on a truce until March 5.

February 19: The government of the Russian Federation stated that "The massive attack on Russian troops in the southern part of Grozny violate all peace initiatives…negotiations are canceled."

February 21: The convoy of the Chechen delegation, driving to the village of Sleptsovskaia for negotiations with the Russians, was stopped at 10:00 a.m. by Interior Ministry troops at a post near the village of Samashki. At 12.30 p.m. a squadron of helicopters machine-gunned the stretch of road in front of the Chechen convoy. There was bombing in Gudermes, Argun, and Samashki.

February 25: Twenty-six Russian soldiers and riot police killed while removing mines in the southern outskirts of Grozny.

February 16: In response to the rise in marauding and pillaging by Russian troops, the Commander of the Joint Group of Federal Forces issued a directive, "On urgent measures to strengthen discipline and order among troops of the Joint Group in the territory of the Chechen Republic."

March 6: Federal troops captured the southern District of Grozny, Chernorech'e, nearly three months after the beginning of hostilities.

March 10: Shelling of Chechen positions in Argun, Bamut, and Urus-Martan.

March 20: Heavy shelling and bombing of Argun, Gudermes, Shali, and other settlements throughout Chechnya.

March 23: Russian troops seized Argun. The Russian Presidential Decree No. 309 set up—on the basis of the "Provisional Council of the Chechen Republic"—the "Committee of National Consent" (*Komitet Natsional"nogo Soglasiia*) chaired by Umar Avturkhanov.[76]

---

76. The various pseudo governments and legislative bodies supported and financed by Russia—the Government of National Trust, Provisional Council of the Chechen Republic, Provisional Government of the Chechen Republic, Committee of National Salvation, Government of National Revival, Committee of National Consent—succeeded one another and were generally composed of the same people. Their existence allowed Russia to claim that the deteriorating situation in Chechnya resulted from disputes between various Chechen factions (the Dudaev government versus the opposition), of which Russia was just an arbiter, and not as it really was between the Dudaev government and the Russian Federation.

This Committee was supposed to be the legislative body in the Republic. In October 1995, after the return of Doku Zavgaev, the revived Supreme Soviet of the Chechen Republic replaced it.

End of March: Bodies retrieved from the rubble buried in the central cemetery of Grozny in mass graves 40 feet long to 20 feet wide. None of the bodies could be identified. According to Russian official sources, 70 percent of Grozny's buildings were destroyed during the fighting.

March 28: Chief of Staff Aslan Maskhadov offered to hold peace talks. His initiative was rejected with an ultimatum to surrender and lay down arms.

March 29: Pacific Fleet marines carried out the encirclement of Gudermes and Shali.

March 30: Chechens fighters withdrew from Gudermes avoiding combat.

March 31: Chechen population fled Shali.

April 7–8: Russian Interior Ministry troops carried out an operation in the village of Samashki. House-to-house searches ended in looting, murder, and the burning of homes. Enraged troops hanged and raped the population, killing 103 people, including 20 men over 61 years of age and 13 women. The youngest victim was 15.

April 12: The Russian State Duma, concerned over the troops' behavior in Samashki, prohibited the use of the Armed Forces in the absence of a state of emergency.

April 14: General Mikhail Iegorov took over the command of the Joint Group of Federal Forces, succeeding General Anatoli Kulikov.

April 17: The Organization for Security and Co-operation in Europe (OSCE) Assistance-Group for Chechnya, led by Ambassador Istvan Gyarmati, started work in Grozny. Shelling and bombing of Bamut; Chechen fighters flocked to Bamut to help its defenders.

April 18: Squads *Rusich* and *Vitiaz'* of the Russian Interior Ministry Special Forces were ambushed during the storming of *Lysaia Gora* (Bald Mountain) near Bamut.

April 21: In Gudermes, drunken soldiers started a shoot-out. The remaining Russian troops in town got involved thinking Chechen fighters had attacked the city. Civilians were killed and wounded in the shoot-out.

May 12: After six months of fighting, Russian troops took Bamut, Serzhen-Iurt, Orekhovo, and Chiri-Iurt.

May 17: Prime Minister Chernomyrdin announced the Russian government's readiness to negotiate—with any Chechen in position of authority—a peaceful settlement under the auspices of the OSCE. The statement was an attempt to split the Chechen leadership. Aslan Maskhadov urged the Russian Army to stop the "senseless slaughter" and expressed his willingness to meet with Defense Minister, Pavel Grachev. Grachev responded with an ultimatum to surrender unconditionally.

May 24: Federal forces began a massive attack in the direction of Vedeno and Shatoi.

May 25: Talks mediated by the Head of the OSCE Assistance-Group to Chechnya, Ambassador Sandor Meszaros, began in Grozny.

May 26: Bombing of Shatoi, Vedeno and Itum-Kali Districts continued.

June 1: President Dudaev told the OSCE representatives that negotiations could proceed only after the suspension of hostilities.

June 3: Russian troops occupied Vedeno. Fighting near the villages of Aleroi, Mekhkety and Agishty.

June 4: President Yeltsin signed the decree establishing the 58th Army, to be quartered in Chechnya.

June 13: Russian troops occupied Nozhai-Yurt and Shatoi without fighting.

June 14–20: Shamil Basaev's raid on Budennovsk. Russian forces suffered above 100 dead and hundreds of wounded. More than 1,000 people were taken hostage.

June 15–16: General Anatoli Kulikov (soon to be Russian Interior Minister) and Chief of Staff Aslan Maskhadov met for the first time under the mediation of the OSCE, near the village of Zandak.

June 19–22: Negotiations between Russians and Chechens began under the OSCE auspices. Representing the Russian Federation were Arkadi Volski,[77] Anatoli Kulikov, and Nikolai Semenov (head of the Territorial Administration of the Federal Executive Authorities in the Chechen Republic). Representing the Chechen Republic were Aslan Maskhadov, Usman Imaev, Sultan Geliskhanov, and Shamil Basaev. The parties agreed to a moratorium on fighting, with no time limit.

June 27–30: Second round of negotiations held in Grozny. The parties agreed to an exchange of all prisoners, the disarmament of Chechen combat units, the withdrawal of Federal troops from Chechnya, and free elections.

June 30: As a consequence of the raid on Budennovsk, President Yeltsin dismissed Minister for Nationalities, Nikolai Egorov; Interior Minister, Viktor Yerin; and FSK Director, Sergei Stepashin.

July 7: On the outskirts of Grozny, Russian soldiers brutally murdered the Chechen Chapanov family. The funeral turned into a mass demonstration demanding the withdrawal of Federal forces.

July 15: Air strikes hit a residential block in Gekhi-Chu, destroying dozens of homes and killing and wounding civilians.

July 21: Lieutenant-General Anatoli Romanov (alias A.A. Antonov) appointed Deputy Minister of the Russian Interior Ministry and

---

77. Arkadi Volski: Politician and businessman, served as senior aide to several Russian presidents. Prime Minister Chernomyrdin appointed him to negotiate with the Chechens.

Commander of the Interior Ministry troops in Chechnya.

July 26: The United Nations Commission on Human Rights expressed "deep concern" about the large number of reports of torture, ill-treatment, and arbitrary detention in "filtration camps" set up by Russian troops in Chechnya.

July 30: At 4:15 a.m. Russian and Chechen negotiating parties signed an agreement. Anatoli Romanov and Aslan Maskhadov selected co-Chairmen of the Supervisory Commission set up to oversee the implementation of the agreement.Chechen Commander Abu Movsaev occupied Shali.

August 20: A group of militant Chechens, commanded by Alaudi Khamzatov, captured the district police building in Argun.

August 21: Fighting continued inside the police building in Argun between Khamzatov and Federal forces.

August 24: President Dudaev appointed Abu Movsaev military Commander of Grozny.

August 25: President Dudaev appointed former Head of State Security, Sultan Geliskhanov, Military Commander of Gudermes.

September 6: Mass rallies in Grozny on the anniversary of Chechnya's independence.

September 19: Oleg Lobov, Security Council Secretary and representative of the Russian President, assaulted in Grozny.

October 6: A radio-controlled bomb exploded in the tunnel on Minutka Square in Grozny, destroying General Romanov's car and seriously injuring him. Romanov, who never came out of a coma, was on his way to a meeting with Ruslan Khasbulatov.

October 7: Lieutenant-General Anatoli Shkirko (alias A.A. Shirokov) appointed new Commander of the Joint Group of Federal Forces in Chechnya.

October 8: With the moratorium on fighting still in place, the village of Roshni-Chu bombed in retaliation for the attack on Romanov, killing 28 civilians. The choice of the village was not random; President Dudaevwas presumed to be there.

October 11: The Head of the Chechen negotiating team in Grozny, Khozh-Akhmed Iarikhanov, announced President Dudaev's decision not to resume negotiations until a United Nations security force was deployed in Chechnya.

October 12: Chief of Staff Aslan Maskhadov announced his readiness to negotiate with the Federal forces.

October 20: At a press conference in Moscow—marking the occasion of his return to Chechnya under the protection of Russian troops—Doku Zavgaev stated that the only legitimate power in the Chechen Republic was the Supreme Soviet. Zavgaev was Chairman of the Chechen Supreme Soviet when it was disbanded in September 1991 by Dudaev forces. By his statement, Zavgaev wanted to emphasis the legitimacy of his return. After his return the revived Supreme Soviet of the Chechen Republic superseded the "Committee of National Consent." Zavgaev was sent back to replace the totally incompetent Russian puppets Umar Avturkhanov and Salambek Khadzhiev.

October 25: A Russian military convoy attacked near the village of Tsa-Vedeno, killing 18 soldiers.

October 26: The pro-Moscow government headed by Doku Zavgaev—replacing the "Government of National Revival"—reinstated the former name of Government of the Chechen Republic.

November 20: Doku Zavgaev and some of his employees assaulted in Grozny.

November 14: Operation under the command of Salman Raduev in Gudermes.

December 15: Federal forces fired upon Gudermes with multiple

"Grad" rocket launchers.

December 17: Pseudo elections for the Head of the Republic. The vast majority of the Republic's settlements did not participate. Doku Zavgaev announced that he scored 90 percent of the vote and that 99 percent of the military personnel (Federal Forces) voted for him.

December 21: Fighting in Grozny, Shali, Achkhoi-Martan, Shatoi, Urus-Martan, and Naurskaia.

December 23: Federal Forces captured Gudermes for the second time.

December 29: Russian Presidential Decree No. 1430 appointed Lieutenant-General Viacheslav Tikhomirov Commander of Joint Groups of Federal Forces in the Chechen Republic.

1996

Tim Guldimann named Head of the OSCE mission in Chechnya.

Early January: Open letter, signed by more than 100 prominent intellectuals, called on President Yeltsin to stop the war in Chechnya. Boris Nemtsov (Governor of the Nizhny Novgorod Region) handed the President a letter with a million signatures of his residents demanding a stop to the war.

January 3: Major-General Vladimir Shamanov appointed Commander of the Ministry of Defense forces in Chechnya.

January 9–18: Raid of Salman Raduev on Kizliar-Pervomaiskoe in Dagestan.

January 16: In the Turkish port of Trabzon a group led by M. Tokchan took hostage the ferryboat *Avrasiya* with 191 people on board. Tokchan's demand: a stop to the Russian encirclement of Pervomaiskoe.

February 4–11: Demonstrations in Grozny near the destroyed Presidential Palace and movie theater *Iubilei* (Jubilee), the area decorated with Ichkeria flags and portraits of President Dudaev. The crowd reached 10,000 people.

February 15: The remnants of the Presidential Palace, symbol of Ichkeria, demolished by order of Doku Zavgaev.

February 22: At 5:00 a.m. blow up of the gas pipeline between Chechnya and Dagestan.

March 5-10: Fighters under the command of Ruslan Gelaev entered Grozny, seized two police buildings, and fought bitterly in the district around Minutka Square.

March 14: Federal troops began a second operation to take control of Samashki.

March 17–20: Artillery and air assault against Samashki. On 18 March alone, attack aircrafts hit Samashki 97 times.

March 19: Zavgaev's Supreme Soviet made a strong appeal to the Russian President to stop the killing of the civilian population, pillaging, and looting. Even officials of the pro-Moscow government could not stomach the Russian army behavior toward civilians.

April 1-4: Fierce battle for Goiskoe. Khusein Isabaev, Akhmad Zakaev, and Dolkhan Khozhaev commanded the defense of Goiskoe.

April 16: A Russian armored convoy of the 245th Regiment ambushed in the Shatoi district near the settlement of Iarysh-Mardy. Seventy-six soldiers and officers were killed, 30 of them too burned to identify, 53 soldiers wounded, and 18 armored vehicles destroyed. The convoy, almost out of ammunition and moving without intelligence, was attacked on a narrow path along the cliffs of the Argun River.

April 18: Fighting in the villages of Staryi Achkhoi, Orekhovo, Goiskoe, and Elistanzhi.

April 21: Presdent Dudaev killed by a rocket bomb near Ghekhi-chu.

May 6: Bislan Gantamirov arrested by Russian authorities and charged with embezzling several billion rubles while he was Mayor of Grozny.

May 5: Fifth Russian SU-25 aircraft shot down while on a surveillance flight over Chechnya. More than 40 aircraft were damaged around that time.

May 20: Battle in the vicinity of Bamut involving artillery, aircraft, and tanks. Twenty soldiers killed and 48 wounded.

May 27: A Chechen delegation headed by Acting President Zelimkhan Iandarbiev flew to Moscow via Ingushetia. In the Kremlin, a document agreeing on the cessation of hostilities beginning June 1 was signed.

May 31: FSB Colonel Ruslan Labazanov killed by his security guard.

June 10: Minister for Nationalities Viacheslav Mikhailov and Chief of Staff Aslan Maskhadov, under the mediation of the OSCE representative Tim Guldimann, signed a protocol in Nazran (Ingushetia) calling for the complete withdrawal of the Joint Federal Forces from the territory of the Chechen Republic by the end of August 1996.

July 11: Major General Nikolai Skripnik, Deputy Commander of the North Caucasus Military District's Interior Ministry Forces, killed near the village of Ghekhi.

August 6: Operation *Jihad*. Chechen fighters entered Grozny; 877 Chechen combatants faced 17,000 Russian soldiers and 5,000 Chechen policemen.

August 10: Security Council Secretary, Assistant to the President for National Security, General Aleksandr Lebed, appointed Yeltsin's plenipotentiary in the Chechen Republic.

August 12: President Yeltsin approved Lebed's proposals for a peace settlement in Chechnya.

August 15: Aleksandr Lebed met with Aslan Maskhadov and Zelim-khan Yandarbiev in Novye Atagi.

August 17: Russian General Konstantin Pulikovsky signed Order No. 107 on the cessation of hostilities throughout the territory of Chechnya.

August 19: General Pulikovsky issued an ultimatum to Chechen fighters to leave Grozny within 48 hours or face an all-out attack. Panic gripped the remaining civilian population.

August 22: Aslan Maskhadov and Aleksandr Lebed, in the village of Novye Atagi, signed a document agreeing to the separation of the war-ring parties—Russia agreeing to withdraw all its forces to their bases of Khankala and Severny—and to joint military control of Grozny.

August 31: At 10 a.m. Aleksandr Lebed arrived in Khasaviurt (Dages-tan) to the City Council building and waited for five hours for Aslan Maskhadov to arrive to sign the Khasaviurt Agreement. Lebed ex-claimed, "Let's put an end to this war, enough is enough, we are all fed up with the war."

September 12: A decree signed by Acting President of Ichkeria, Zelimkhan Iandarbiev, ordered the Criminal Code of the Russian Federation—still in force in the Chechen Republic—to be replaced by a new code elaborated on the base of the Sudanese Criminal Code.

October 17: Acting President Iandarbiev named Aslan Maskhadov to the combined functions of Prime Minister and Defense Minister in the interim coalition government. Maskhadov retained his position of Chief of Staff.

November 23: Aslan Maskhadov and Russian Prime Minister Vik-tor Chernomyrdin signed an agreement defining relations between Russia and Chechnya.

December: Russian forces moved out of Chechnya. The last to leave was the 101st Brigade of Interior Ministry Forces.

December 21: The last Federal troops left Khankala.

1997

January 27: Presidential and parliamentary elections. Sixteen candidates run for President; Aslan Maskhadov elected.

February 12: Inauguration day. Aslan Maskhadov sworn in as President of the Chechen Republic of *Ichkeria*.

February 19: Creation of a government commission for negotiations with the Russian Federation, empowered to settle the full range of issues arising in the relationship between two sovereign states. Its members were Akhmad Zakaev, Khozh-Akhmed Iarikhanov, Kazbek Makhashev, and Said-Khasan Abumuslimov. Movladi Udugov headed the commission.

March 10: The pre-war Parliament approved the mandates of the 43 deputies elected on January 27.

March 13: The new Parliament began its functions as the legislative body of the Republic. President Maskhadov established a National Guard, a corps of 2,000 guardsmen commanded by Brigadier General Magomed Khambiev.

March 17: Ruslan Alikhadzhiev, former commander, elected Speaker of the Parliament.

April 10: Presidential Decree modifying the district administrations, replacing the existing Prefectures by District Executive Offices of the President, the heads of the new District Offices to be appointed by the President. Maskhadov replaced 20 of former Prefects (out of 23).

May and June: Elections of village and city councils. In almost all settlements, members or supporters of the armed struggle for independence won.

May 12: In Moscow, Boris Yeltsin and Aslan Maskhadov signed the

Armistice and the Principles of Inter-Relations between the Russian Federation and the Chechen Republic of Ichkeria.

May 15: The new Chief of Staff, Alkhazur Abuev, reorganized the structure of the Armed Forces, eliminating the military staffs of the fronts established during the war.

May 25: President Maskhadov, as the Commander in Chief, abolished the commands of the fronts set up during the wars and reorganized the distribution of the Armed Forces.

May 31: Elections for the Mayor of Grozny. The Election Commission, favoring the incumbent Mayor Lechi Dudaev, disrupted the elections. Field Commander Turpan-Ali Atgeriev won the popular vote, but the Electoral Commission annulled the results.

June 1: Creation of the Security Council. Its Chairman was President Maskhadov and its Secretary, Brigadier General Doku Umarov.

June 2: Creation of the State Commission for the Rehabilitation of War Veterans. Headed by the President, it had thirty members, most of them former field commanders. It included Vice President Arsanov, Speaker of the Parliament Alikhadzhiev, Deputy Prime Ministers Basaev, Gelaev, Zakaev, and Khalimov, Commander of the National Guard Khambiev, Interior Minister Makhashev, and Security Council Secretary Umarov. Deputy Prime Minister Islam Khalimov was put in charge of implementing programs of assistance to war veterans.

June 14: Presidential Decree, "On the Regulation of the Right to Bear Arms," forbade militant groups not belonging to the regular Armed Forces to carry weapons.

June 15: The president ordered field commanders to disband their irregular armed units. They were allowed to keep their bodyguards.

October 28: President Maskhadov announced leadership changes in the government institutions in charge of the economy: the Ministry of the Economy, State Emergency Commission, Tax Department, and also the State Airline. Simultaneously, the state-owned Southern Oil Company was dismantled.

1998

January 10: The President appointed Shamil Basaev Acting Prime Minister. The Russian Federation stipulated that meetings between Russian government officials and Basaev, during the period of Basaev's mandate as head of the Chechen government, would not constitute a violation of the prosecution laws (Basaev was on the Russian wanted list for the raid on Budennovsk).

January 14: A Russian Federation delegation, led by the Security Council Secretary Ivan Rybkin, arrived in Grozny.

January 29: At a press conference, the Russian Security Council Secretary expressed the view that Moscow might accept a sovereign and independent Chechnya, provided it freely joined the Russian Federation. Rybkin played with words. What Russia was offering to Chechnya was the same status as Tatarstan, a "sovereign state," but a member of the Russian Federation, abiding by its laws.

February 3: President Maskhadov stated that the Chechen Republic would never, under any circumstances, agree to remain in the constitutional and legal framework of the Russian Federation.

March: President Maskhadov visited London at the invitation of Lord McAlpine.

March 5: Kidnapping of Valentin Vlasov, representative of the Russian President in Chechnya.

April 20: President Maskhadov appointed his first ambassadors to Turkey, Poland, and Lema Usmanov to the United States.

June 24: State of emergency after rising tensions with the Salafists.

July 14–15: Fundamentalist uprising in Gudermes. Forces loyal to the President clashed with Salafist military formations.

July 23: Attempt on the life of the President, three presidential guards killed and four seriously injured. Maskhadov accused Arbi Baraev, the Akhmadov brothers, and Zelimkhan Iandarbiev of involvement.

July 24: Deputy Commander of the Armed Forces Aslanbek Ismailov ordered the termination of private broadcasting media, in particular the Salafist media functioning with the help of the Russian channel ORT.

August 1: Meeting between Russian Prime Minister, Sergei Kirienko, and President Maskhadov in Nazran (Ingushetia).

August 5: Aslan Maskhadov flew to the United States to participate in the International Islamic Unity Conference held under the auspices of the Islamic Supreme Council of America. Important outcomes for Chechnya ensued from the trip: the allocation of 20 thousand tons of wheat as humanitarian aid from the U.S. Department of Agriculture; an office of the Islamic Development Bank in Grozny; and the hiring (for a short time) of an organization to lobby the U.S. Congress for Chechnya.

September 20: Former commanders Shamil Basaev, Salman Raduev and Khunkerpasha Israpilov appealed to the Parliament and the Supreme *Shariah* Court to impeach the President for violating the Constitution and the oath he took during his inauguration.

September 23: Russian Prime Minister Yevgeny Primakov and President Maskhadov spoke on the phone about the situation in the region and relations between Moscow and Grozny. They agreed to continue to talk.

October 8: President Maskhadov accused Salman Raduev of organizating a coup. Speaking to the Congress of the Chechen People, he said that he would never accept the demands of the extremists and would not sit at the negotiating table with Salman Raduev whom he viewed as a criminal. He thought that the action of Basaev, Raduev, and Israpilov against him exacerbated the situation in the country risking civil war.

October 20: Twelfth day of an anti-Maskhadov rally in the center of Grozny, demanding the President's resignation.

October 21: Presidential Decree gave illegal armed units (not part of the regular Armed Forces) seven days to disband because they were damaging to state power and to national independence.

October 25: Assassination of the Head of the Office for the Suppression of Kidnapping, Shakhid Bargishev, a Maskhadov supporter.

October 26: Attack on the *Mufti* Akhmad Kadyrov. Five people were killed, including three of his relatives. On national television, Kadyrov accused the Salafists and demanded their complete elimination.

October 29: Prime Minister Primakov and President Maskhadov met in Vladikavkaz, North Ossetia.

November 4: The Supreme *Shariah* Court sentenced Salman Raduev to four years imprisonment, finding him guilty of attempting to overthrow the government. Raduev managed to avoid prison for health reasons.

November 17: President Maskhadov ordered a massive police operation to eradicate organized crime.

December 7: Foreign engineers, three Englishmen and one New Zealander, abducted in Grozny on October 3, found beheaded. They were: Peter Kennedy, Darren Hickey, Rudolf Petschi and New Zealander Stanley Shaw. They were in the country to install a mobile telephone system.

December 8: At the military base in Khankala, ceremonial review during which government officials took an oath of allegiance to the President.

December 17: Tens of thousands of people gathered on Liberty Square in Grozny to express their support for President Maskhadov.

December 1998: Chechnya discussed at a session of the Russian Security Council. The topic was information warfare to discredit Chechnya in the opinion of the European and world communities. The outcome was a plan of action consisting in 27 steps with the responsibilities to carry them out clearly assigned to different branches of government. The meeting was top secret; its minutes and ensuing documents were shown exclusively to the top leadership of government. FSB Director, Vladimir Putin, chaired the meeting.

1999

February 3: Presidential Decree introducing full *Shariah* law in the Republic. Maskhadov instructed the Parliament and the Office of the *Mufti* to draft a Constitution based on the *Shariah* within a month.

February 7: Opposition commanders began forming an opposition Council or *Shura,* headed by Shamil Basaev.

February 9: First meeting of the State Council (State *Shura*).

March 5: The Envoy of the Russian Federation in Chechnya, General Gennady Shpigun, kidnapped at the airport in Grozny. President Maskhadov offered a reward of $200,000 U.S. for information leading to his release.

March 16: In the course of a meeting between Prime Minister Primakov and President Yeltsin, the Russian President reiterated his readiness, if necessary, to deal with Maskhadov directly on a one to one basis, as he had done before.

March 22: The Republic security agencies put on high alert because of rising tensions with the Salafists.

March 24: In Moscow Russian Interior Minister Sergei Stepashin met with the Head of the OSCE Assistance Group to Chechnya, Ambassador Odd Gunnar Skagestad.

April 14: Russian Security Council discussed measures to preserve stability in the regions bordering Chechnya. Vladimir Putin, chairing the session, described the situation in Chechnya as critical.

April 26: Russian Interior Minister Stepashin ordered the closure of the border with Chechnya.

May 27: Fighting along the Chechnya-Dagestan border lasting over an hour.

June 2: Chechen authorities proposed to Russian authorities joint patrols along the border.

June 11: In Ingushetia President Maskhadov encountered Russian Prime Minister Sergei Stepashin. Maskhadov raised the issue of the full payment of Russia's economic commitments to Chechnya.

June 22: The Parliament condemned the rise in provocations along the Chechen-Russian border.

June 23: In Moscow Speaker of the Chechen Parliament Ruslan Alikhadzhiev met with the Speaker of the State Duma, Gennady Seleznev, and agreed to an official visit in the fall.

June 25: Prime Minister Stepashin, on a visit to Dagestan, met Vice Premier Turpan-Ali Atgeriev. Atgeriev proposed joint Russian-Chechen operations along the borders to eliminate bandits. Stepashin agreed to provide financial assistance but refused any joint action.

July 14: Turpan-Ali Atgeriev arrested in Moscow for his participation in the Kizliar-Pervomaiskoe raid in 1996.

August 1: Dagestan insurgents crossed from Chechnya into Dagestan and tried to gain a foothold in the mountains. Later, Chechen insurgents joined them.

August 31: Explosion in the heart of Moscow in the mall Okhotnyi Riad on Manezh Square. One person killed and 40 wounded.

September 4: Five-story apartment building blew up in Buinaksk (Dagestan), 64 people killed, including 23 children, and 146 injured.

September 8: Massive explosion at an apartment house on Gurianov Street in Moscow. The terrorist act killed 90 people and wounded 200.

September 13: Massive explosion at an eight-story residential building on Kashira Highway in Moscow. The terrorist act killed more than 120 people.

September 16: Powerful explosion at an apartment building in the center of Volgodonsk, in the Rostov Region, 18 people killed and 310 injured.

September 29: Federal troops crossed the border into Chechnya. The second Chechens war had begun.

DOCUMENTS

Protocol of the Meeting of the Commissions on the Negotiations Regarding a Ceasefire and Cessation of Hostilities and on Measures to Settle the Armed Conflict on the Territory of the Chechen Republic[78]

Nazran, 10 June 1996

For the purpose of implementing the Agreement on a Cease-fire and Cessation of Hostilities and on Measures to Settle the Armed Conflict on the Territory of the Chechen Republic, signed by Mr. V.S. Chernomyrdin and Mr. Z. Yandarbiev on 27 May 1996 in Moscow,

The Negotiations Commission formed by order of the Government of the Russian Federation and under the direction of V. Mikhailov, Minister of the Russian Federation and Federal Relations, and

The Negotiations Commission formed by order of the Cabinet of Ministers of the Chechen Republic of Ichkeriya (CRI)* and under the direction of A. Maskhadov, Chief of Staff of the Armed Forces of the CRI,

Have agreed as follows:

1. The cease-fire and cessation of hostilities completely exclude:

   – The use of any types of armaments for combat purposes, including rocket, artillery and other forms of shelling and aerial bombardment;

   – Any attacks and operations involving troops, including special

---

78. www.peacemaker.un.org/sites/peacemaker.un.org/files/RU_960610_Protocol%20of%20the%20Meeting%20on%20the%20Negotiations%20Regarding%20a%20Ceasefire.pdf

operations (joint working groups shall formulate a definition of the term "special operations"); – The seizure or blockade of inhabited communities, military facilities, and roads; – Any threats to the work of community governments;

– The unlawful bearing of arms (joint working groups shall formulate a definition of "unlawful bearing of arms"); – Acts of terrorism or sabotage;

– Attacks on or mining of roads, railways, lines and pipelines, transport facilities, columns of persons, and military or civilian convoys;

– Abductions, the seizure of hostages, and the pillaging or killing of peaceful inhabitants or military personnel.

In the event of a violation of the provisions of this paragraph, the Parties may take appropriate independent defensive action and joint measures to put an end to the violation in question.

2. Within agreed time-limits:

– Checkpoints on roads leading out of inhabited communities shall be eliminated during the period from 11 June to 7 July 1996.

– For the purpose of protecting formations of the Provisional United Forces, control checkpoints are to be established, which shall be eliminated as those formations are withdrawn.

– The withdrawal of the Provisional United Forces from the territory of the Chechen Republic shall be completed by the end of August 1996. To that end, joint working groups shall draw up a timetable for the stage-by-stage withdrawal and removal of the Provisional United Forces from the territory of the Chechen Republic and for its demilitarization.

3. Joint working groups shall be established to monitor the implementation of paragraphs 1 and 2 of this Protocol.

4. The heads of the working groups – V. Tikhominov, Commander of the Provisional United Forces, and A. Kaskhadov, Chief of Staff

of the Armed Forces of the Chechen Republic of Ichkeriya – shall:

- Carry out an exchange of the data required to monitor the implementation of paragraphs 1 and 2 of the Protocol;

- Delimit the zones of responsibility and designate the persons responsible for the cease-fire and cessation of hostilities in those zones (the joint working groups shall determine the number of zones of responsibility);

- Begin drawing up a timetable for the stage-by-stage withdrawal and removal of the Provisional United Forces from the territory of the Chechen Republic and for its demilitarization, reaching an agreement on this timetable before 15 June 1996 at the level of Negotiations Commission heads.

5. The Negotiations Commissions have agreed that it is necessary to conduct free and democratic elections to the organs of State government of the Chechen Republic at all levels and with the participation of all genuine political forces, with those elections to be subject to public and international monitoring after the withdrawal of the Provisional United Forces from the territory of the Chechen Republic and its demilitarization have been completed.

The question of how the elections to any organ of State government of the Chechen Republic at all levels and with the participation of all genuine political forces are to be conducted is an internal affair of the Chechen Republic.

6. The participants in the negotiations shall refrain from any actions or statements that obstruct or that might obstruct the implementation of the Agreement of 27 May 1996, the Protocol of 28 May 1996, this Protocol, and all subsequent joint decisions by the participants in the negotiations.

This Protocol has been drawn up in three authentic copies.

V. Mikhailov

A. Maskhadov

With the mediation of the representation of the OSCE

T. Guldimann

Members of the Negotiations Commission of the Russian Federation:

V. Zorin. S. Stepashin. N. Bezborodov. B. Jamalkhanov. Kh. Musalatov. A. Piskunov. A. Osmayev. V. Sagayev. N. Semenov. V. Strashko.
V. Tikhomirov. N. Fedosov.

Members of the Negotiations Commission of the Chechen Republic
of Ichkeriya: Kh. Yarikhanov. A. Zakayev. K. Makhashev. M. Udugov.
Ya. Abdulayev. Sh. Basayev. M. Saldayev.

"I CONFIRM"

**Chairman of the Negotiations Commission formed by order of
the Government of the Russian Federation**

V. Mikhailov

"I CONFIRM"

**Chairman of the Negotiations Commission formed by order of
the Cabinet of Ministers of the Chechen Republic of Ichkeriya**

A. Maskhadov

* The Negotiations Commission formed by order of the Government
of the Russian Federation states that the Chechen Republic of Ichkeriya is not recognized under the legislation of the Russian Federation.

Source: Transitional Justice Peace Agreements Database (University
of Ulster, Transitional Justice Institure, Incore)

**Agreement "On Urgent Measures to Stop Fire and Combat Oper-
ations in the City of Grozny and on the Territory of Cheehnya"[79]**

Signed by Alexander Lebed and Aslan Maskhadov on August 22, 1996

1. To stop fire and combat operations as of 1200 on 23 August 1996 and

---

79. www.peacemaker.un.org/sites/peacemaker.un.org/files/RU_960822_Agree-
mentonUrgentMeasurestoStopFireinChechnya.pdf

to begin an exchange, without any preconditions and based on the "all for all" principle, of prisoners, refugees and bodies of the dead.

1.2. In the event of violation of provisions of this point, the sides can take joint measures to cut short such a violation. In other cases, they are obliged to act in conformity with the requirements of the Manual of Garrison and Guard Duties of the Russian Federation Armed Forces.

2. To carry into effect a set of mutually specified and agreed measures on the simultaneous withdrawal of troops to specified areas.

3. The troops shall be withdrawn together with all the arms and ammunition, with the mutual provision of information on the number and strength and arms of formations being withdrawn.

4. To carry out the withdrawal of all warring sides from the city of Groznyand to concurrently set up joint military commandant's offices organized on the basis of the federal troops commandant offices.

7. The sides shall refrain from any actions or statements hampering implementation of this agreement.

8. The control over the observance of all the points in this agreement shall be carried out by an observer commission in correspondence with instructions of the Russian Federation Security Council secretary.

9. The withdrawal of federal troops from the territory of the Chechen Republic and the unblocking of built-up areas shall be implemented in correspondence with the Nazran agreement.

Khasavyourt Joint Declaration and Principles for Mutual Relations[80]

Khasavyourt, Dagestan, 31 August 1996

We, the undersigned,

Taking into account the progress achieved in implementing the agreement on the cessation of military activities,

---

80. www.peacemaker.un.org/russia-khasavyourtdeclaration96

Striving to create mutually acceptable preconditions for a political resolution of the armed conflict,

Recognising the inadmissibility of using armed force or threatening its usage in the resolution of all issues,

Proceeding from the universally recognised right of peoples to self-determination, the principles of equality, voluntary and free expression of will, strengthening interethnic accord and the security of peoples,

Expressing the will to protect unconditionally human rights and freedoms and those of the citizen, irrespective of ethnic origin, religious beliefs, place of residence or any other distinctions, and to prevent acts of violence against political opponents, in doing so proceeding from the 1948 Universal Declaration of Human Rights and the 1966 International Covenant on Civil and Political Rights.

Have jointly developed Principles concerning mutual relations between the Russian Federation and the Chechen Republic, on the basis of which the future negotiation process will be conducted.

(Signed)

A. Lebed A. Maskhadov

B. Khartamov S. Abumuslimov

31 August 1996

In the presence of the Head of the OSCE Assistance Group of the Chechen Republic,

(signed)

T. Guldimann

Principles for Determining the Basis for Mutual Relations between the Russian Federation and the Chechen Republic

An Agreement on the basis for mutual relations between the Russian Federation and the Chechen Republic, to be determined in accordance with universally recognised principles and norms of international law, should be achieved by 31 December 2001.

A Joint Commission shall be established by 1 October 1996, composed of representatives of the organs of state power of the Russian Federation and the Chechen Republic, the tasks of which shall be:

To monitor the implementation of Decree No. 985 of the President of the Russian Federation of 25 June 1995 and to prepare proposals concerning the completion of the withdrawal of troops;

To prepare and monitor the fulfilment of agreed measures against crime, terrorism and manifestations of ethnic and religious enmity;

To prepare proposals for the restoration of currency, financial and budgetary interrelations;

To prepare and submit to the Government of the Russian Federation programmes for the restoration of the socio-economic structure of the Chechen Republic;

To monitor the coordinated interaction of the organs of state power and other interested parties in the provision of food and medicines for the population.

Legislation of the Chechen Republic shall be based on the observance of human and civil rights, the right of peoples to self-determination, the principles of equality among nationalities, the guaranteeing of civil peace, interethnic accord and the security of those residing on the territory of the Chechen Republic, irrespective of their ethnic origin, religious beliefs or other distinctions.

The Joint Commission shall complete its work by mutual agreement.

Source: Transitional Justice Peace Agreements Database (University of Ulster, Transitional Justice Institure, Incore)

Peace Treaty and Principles of Interrelation between Russian Federation and Chechen Republic Ichkeria[81]

The esteemed parties to the agreement, desiring to end their centuries-long antagonism and striving to establish firm, equal and mutually

---

81. www.incore.ulst.ac.uk/services/cds/agreements/pdf/rus2.pdf

beneficial relations, hereby agree:

To reject forever the use of force or threat of force in resolving all matters of dispute.

To develop their relations on generally recognised principles and norms of international law. In doing so, the sides shall interact on the basis of specific concrete agreements.

This treaty shall serve as the basis for concluding further agreements and accords on the full range of relations.

This treaty is written on two copies and both have equal legal power.

This treaty is active from the day of signing.

Moscow, 12 May 1997.

(signed)

B. Yeltsin	A. Maskhadov
President of the	President of the
Russian Federation	Chechen Republic Ichkeria

Source: Transitional Justice Peace Agreements Database (University of Ulster, Transitional Justice Institure, Incore)

CPSIA information can be obtained
at www.ICGtesting.com
Printed in the USA
LVHW030506100223
739116LV00002B/438